Halfdollar

Also by Bil Lepp

Books
Monster Stick
Inept, Impaired, Overwhelmed
Armadillo Recon Unit

CDs
Buck Meets the Monster Stick
Mayhem Dressed Like an Eight Point Buck
Teacher in the Patriotic Bathing Suit
Divine Bovine
Great Rope Swing Misadventure
Punching the Lard
Fire! Fire! Pants on Liar
The King of Little Things

HALFDOLLAR
Bil Lepp

quarrier press

CHARLESTON, WEST VIRGINIA

Quarrier Press
Charleston, WV

© 2008 by Bil Lepp

All rights reserved. No part of this book may be reproduced in any form or in any means, electronic or mechanical, including photocopying, recording, or by any information storage and retrieval system, without permission in writing from the publisher.

First Edition

10 9 8 7 6 5 4 3 2 1

Printed in the United States of America

Library of Congress Control Number: 2008935875
ISBN-13: 978-1891852-60-2
ISBN-10: 1-891852-60-4

Book and cover design: Mark S. Phillips
Front cover photo: Paula Lepp

Distributed by:

West Virginia Book Company
1125 Central Avenue
Charleston, WV 25302
www.wvbookco.com

Author's Note

First off, unlike my other books, cds, and stories, this work is not necessarily suitable for the whole family. My kids have not been allowed to read it. I would suggest, encourage really, that if you are younger than fourteen you take this book to the adult you trust most and ask them to read it first. Say to them, "I trust your sage-like wisdom. I'm not sure that this book is appropriate for someone my age. Will you please read it first and let me know if you think I am ready to handle the topics and situations put forth in this work." Seriously, ask your parent, guardian, uncle, rabbi...whomever you think will give you a straight answer. And then trust that person. Wait a year. Read it then.

I do not believe books should be censored, but I do believe that not every book is suitable for every reader. I once read a book by Peter Straub. I think that was the author. In that book, spiders played a vivid and horrible role. I am quite afraid of spiders. That book was not appropriate for me. Should that book be banned? No. Should it have a huge sticker on it that says, "If you are scared of spiders, don't read this book"? Certainly. I also don't read Stephen King. I just don't like creepy stuff that could happen. No offense to Mr. Straub or Mr. King is intended. Should Mr. Straub or Mr. King be reading this author's note in my book, well, WOW! That is cool. Plus, those two guys write long, long books. I am a slow reader. I don't usually read books much over 400 pages because it might take me a year. I did read *The Green Mile*. That was great. But it was also serialized in six smaller books. I liked that.

Finally, this book could barely be less true. Let me remind you that I am five-time champion of the West Virginia Liars' Contest. I make stuff up all the time. But here is the crazy thing. For a brief period of time I had an agent (thanks Sheila Kay), and that agent read a very early draft of this book. Originally I had written the book in the first person. The character of Edison was never called Edison in the first try. He was called "I" or "me." That agent told me the book read like a memoir. She said it sounded too true, and that I should write it in the third person. I could not believe anyone would think this a true account, but my agent persuaded me. I'm still not sure I agree, but you have no idea how hard it is to go through a book and change every "I" and "me" to "Edison" and "him." I was too stupid to save a copy of the first person account. I'm not going to reverse the process. Anyway, this is a work of fiction. A completely and utterly made up story. Any similarities between characters in this narrative and real persons, living or dead, is entirely coincidental. The same holds for events.

Super finally, I've been working on this book for a long time. One reason it took me so long to finally publish this book is because I am a storyteller. And I don't mean "storyteller" in same sense as we often see it on book covers. "John Sandford is a great storyteller!" I mean "storyteller" in the sense that it is my job to stand up in front of audiences and tell stories. I tell, speak, stories all the time. Sometimes I tell the same story several times a week to a wide variety of audiences. I have the power to change that story anyway I see fit, each time I tell that story. I can drop events, add events, focus on certain characters, hone in on specific ideas, or insert adlib comments. The stories I tell from stage are always and ever changing. I never have to worry about the "final daft" because I'll have, hopefully, a new audience tomorrow, next week, next year. If you hear me tell the same story twice, three times, a dozen times, there will always be something new, or different. But this is a book. This is it. The printed word. I can't change it any more. It would just be awkward if I snuck into your house every night to change things around in the book. And time consuming for me. So, I have to be satisfied with this final draft. Am I? No. There is so much more I would like to do with the stories of Edison, Skeeter, Charolais, Lynn, Sheriff Hasbro, Rev. Janzen… For example, the first time Sheriff Hasbro showed up in one of my stories he was a complete idiot. A real doofus. He was someone Skeeter and I (Edison) were supposed to play with. Hence his name. But now? Now Sheriff Hasbro is one of my favorite characters. I like him, respect him, so much so that I had to send him away in later stories and create a whole different police force for Edison and Skeet to toy with. Sheriff Hasbro started out a dope, but became everything I respect and admire about real police officers.

There is so much more I want to tell you. But, alas, I've got to let this baby go. I've got to seal it. I asked my publisher to quit sending me updated and corrected versions because every time he sends me a "completed version" I change something else. Cut. Add. Rewrite. Retell. Like I do with the stories on stage. So, with great trepidation and worry, I present to you this last written version of Halfdollar. Come see me live sometime soon. You'll learn something new. And, look for sequels. There is a book called "Billy the Kid's Tombstone- A Book about a Bar" sitting finished (except for all the retellings) on my desk. Though it skips a few years, it is the next novel in the Skeet, Edison, Charolais, and Lynn story. Want a copy? And I already know that a novel about the antics of Skeet and Edison's teenage years not included in Halfdollar is on the way. So, there you go. Thanks for reading this novel.

Bil Lepp
Halfdollar, WV
August 1, 2008

For,
and I've thought about this for a long, long time,

Charolais.

If you are she, or she is you,
God bless, good luck, be proud of your name, and break all the arms
you need to.

ONE

1

When Edison Janzen was five years old, he learned the two most important lessons a boy needs to know. The first lesson, and possibly the more influential of the two, he learned from his dog, Deacon. Deacon taught Edison that if you pee on a tree, that tree and all the surrounding area becomes your territory.

Deacon, who was half basset and half German shepherd, was a proficient territory marker. Given the chance, he could pee on every notable tree in Dry County, West Virginia, in a single night. The dog's Teutonic and English ancestors would have been proud of his determined and unending imperial conquest. He was a bad influence and a wonderful educational tool for Edison. A boy needs to learn to drink from puddles with his tongue and pee on trees. Dogs may be man's best friend, but they are also a boy's best teacher.

Watching Deacon pee, Edison asked his father, "Dad, why does Deacon pee on all the trees?"

His father explained, "Son, dogs mark their territory by urinating, peeing, on various landmarks. A dog's urine contains scents that are like your fingerprints. The scents are unique to each dog, and by peeing on a tree Deacon is telling any other dog that happens to be in the area that this is Deacon's land."

"What happens," the boy asked, still holding his dad's hand and watching Deacon, "if another dog pees on a tree that Deacon has peed on?"

"Well," his father answered, "then Deacon has two choices. He can simply give up the territory to the other dog, or he can fight the other dog to see who gets the land."

"What if Deacon loses the fight?"

"Then the other dog gets the land."

Edison was five years-old. He didn't completely understand all of this, but it did give him a brand new respect for real estate agents.

The second important lesson Edison learned also developed during the nightly dog walks. "Edison," his father said, "God is just, and thus all things will eventually, for better or worse, come to a conclusion."

This vague theological position, covering everything from the next day to the Apocalypse, would have appeared predestinarian or lazy in most men. Edison's father, Rev. Janzen, the Methodist preacher, however, was so utterly faithful that even the casual observer soon saw that his optimism and outlook were reflections of the inner peace and satisfaction that he received by doing the Lord's work. Rev. Janzen stood a solid six-foot-three, and was named George, for Edison's grandfather.

"Do you understand what I'm saying? About God being just and in control?" Rev. Janzen asked his son.

Edison shook his head. God knew he'd heard it enough times that he should understand what his father meant, but he just couldn't grasp it. Dogs peeing? Now that he could understand.

"You'll understand, someday." Rev. Janzen squeezed Edison's hand. "When I say things will come out for better or worse," Rev. Janzen continued, "I mean that we, humans, judge things that way. We are the ones who place those labels on outcomes. Where God is involved things cannot come out for the worse, even if it looks that way to us. See what I'm saying?"

"Not really," Edison replied, his mind elsewhere.

"You'll get it someday, just give it time." Rev. Janzen patted his son's head.

"Dad?" Edison continued, still thinking about Deacon. "Aren't we not supposed to fight?"

"Yes. We're pacifists. At least we should be."

"Then how come Deacon gets to fight?"

"Deacon is a dog. Dogs have their own rules and their own religion."

"I want to believe what dogs believe."

"Edison, I'm not sure a child has ever had a more noble aspiration."

2

"Mrs. Crankberry is the single meanest woman I have ever met," Rev. Janzen told Shaney Janzen, Edison's mother.

"That's a bold statement coming from a man who, for the past fifteen years, has served on church committees," she commented dryly.

Mrs. Crankberry lived in the house next door to the Janzens. The old woman hated little kids and had made life miserable for Edison ever since he'd dug up her flower garden with a Tonka truck. Because she was so evil, Mrs. Crankberry, through some twist of universal irony or the great Yin-Yang, had the single greatest backyard ever created. The boy coveted the gentle slope, the flowing waters, and flora of her yard. To her yard he sung his toddler Song of Solomon. But her yard was merely an unattainable dream. Edison would stare at it for hours.

The yard was a four-seasons resort to a five-year-old. For starters, it bordered a tributary to Skitter Creek, the best crawdad, salamander and rope-swinging creek within walking distance of Edison's house. The creek lay on the opposite side of Mrs. Crankberry's yard and so was all but inaccessible to Edison because Mrs. Crankberry wouldn't let anyone cross her domain. Her yard also boasted a winter sledding slope that was second to none in the neighborhood, but the virgin snow that accumulated each year stayed religiously unmolested. And finally, there was an oak tree in her yard that produced bushels and bushels of acorns annually. Acorns are critical to the tactical weapons systems of any five-year-old—pacifists included—but God help the child that tried to access the great Crankberry acorn arsenal. "Get your scrawny butt out of my yard, you pipsqueak!" she screamed if she ever saw Edison in her yard. The child had good reason to be scared. This was, after all, the nineteen-seventies, when it was still legal to hurt children.

But this did not deter him. "I want that yard," Edison whispered to himself again and again.

"Why is she so mean?" he asked his mother.

"She's got nothing in the world. No family, no friends. All she has is her house. As she sees it, nobody gives her anything, so she won't give anything away. Not even the pleasure of her yard, as long she can help it."

"We could be her friends."

"She won't let us."

"Why not?"

"Edison, you're too young to get this, but she had a very hard life. Everybody always took stuff from her. Not just her belongings, but her happiness. So she won't let anybody be her friend now because she's scared they'll take something."

"That's weird."

"It's just the way some people are."

"I bet she'd be less mean if she didn't have a beehive on her head."

Mrs. Janzen laughed. "It's not a beehive. It's just a hairstyle called a beehive."

"Gerry said that Mrs. Crankberry has her hair fixed twice a year." Gerry was Edison's oldest brother. "And that she has a beehive put in her hair, and then she has the whole thing sealed with concrete."

"Gerry was joking."

"Is she related to Mr. McGregor? From Peter Cottontail?"

His mother chuckled. "Best just to stay out of her yard, Edison."

Then one day, Edison got an idea.

He watched, and when he saw Mrs. Crankberry leave her house, get into her car and drive away, he saw his chance. He jumped up and ran into Mrs. Crankberry's yard, got down on his hands and knees, and started sniffing around the base of the great oak tree. Edison didn't know exactly what he was sniffing for, but he knew from watching Deacon that sniffing was an integral element in the acquisition of land. Having sniffed sufficiently, he stood, dropped his pants and peed on the big, old oak tree, thereby making it his.

As he zipped his fly, it occurred to Edison that he had never once seen Mrs. Crankberry pee on that tree so he wasn't even sure that the tree belonged to her in the first place. Edison knew, deep in his young heart, that tree was now his, as was the yard. He had sniffed and peed in proper dog fashion and Edison dared Mrs. Crankberry, or anyone else, to try to take away his land.

The boy vowed that if he ever caught Mrs. Crankberry peeing on his tree, he would convert to Deacon's religion and fight. He did decide, however, that he would practice Christian charity and allow Mrs. Crankberry to stay on his land.

From that day on, Edison snuck into Mrs. Crankberry's yard as often as possible, whizzing on the tree, the birdbath, the garage wall and anything else that proved handy.

And then one day Mrs. Crankberry died. Edison quickly decided that her death and his peeing could not be in any way related. It was pure coincidence. And he wasn't sad. He didn't totally understand death, but he knew Mrs. Crankberry wasn't coming back, and that jibed with his father's idea that through God all things worked out in the end.

With Mrs. Crankberry gone Edison could think of no reason not to expand his domain and claim her entire house as his own. He delivered enough urine onto her old house to float an aircraft carrier. Thus it came as quite a shock when one day he returned from the grocery store with his mother only to discover a moving van in front of Mrs. Crankberry's house. People were hefting furniture into the house—into his house. He had claimed it! To top it off, in the backyard Edison discovered a boy, about his own age, placing toys all over the yard: Edison's duly claimed yard! He felt both concerned and offended. Hadn't these people bothered to sniff?

"Well," Edison resolved, "I know what I gotta do." He walked straight over to the big oak tree, dropped his shorts to his ankles and commenced to take a leak while the new kid wandered about. The new kid stopped and eyed him curiously, then sauntered over to the tree, dropped his pants and let loose.

Well, that was just too much.

"The nerve of him, peeing in my territory," Edison said to himself. He knew what Deacon would do. He slugged the kid in the eye as hard as he could. The kid hit back, and both boys started crying and shouting and throwing punches like tiny madmen. Deacon ran over and started barking. Edison's mother, and then the new boy's mother, soon followed Deacon. The mothers separated the boys—two babies with their pants around their ankles fighting to the death.

"You two apologize to each other!" the mothers yelled.

The boys clung to their respective mothers, bawling their eyes out, and pulling up their pants.

Edison's mother looked at the new kid's mother and said, "My name's Shaney Janzen. I'm so sorry about this."

"Mary Barth," said the kid's mother, offering her hand.

"Well, boys will be boys," they agreed.

Mrs. Janzen and Mrs. Barth made the two boys shake hands and apologize.

Edison mumbled, "I'm sorry."

"Me too," grumbled the kid, not sure what he was sorry about.

"Introduce yourself," Mrs. Janzen commanded her son.

Edison felt like he knew the kid pretty well by this point. You punch a kid, and pee on him, and he does the same to you, what else is there to know? "I'm Edison," he said.

"Skeeter. Skeeter Barth."

The two boys looked into each other's eyes and, though their mothers did not see it, a mischievous, knowing nod was exchanged, as if they were saying to each other, "You and me, pal. You and me." They would be friends. And Halfdollar, West Virginia would never again be the same.

After dinner that night, Edison's mother and father came up to his room. Mrs. Janzen asked, "Why were you boys fighting?" It was the sort of thing, Edison was slowly learning, which interested parents. He was finding his parents' curiosity stranger by the day. The more questionable the acts he committed, the more they were interested in why he had done it. But their response was always the same. It did not seem to matter to them what justification he offered for any given act. His parents always countered by telling him that he was wrong, and that he should not have done whatever he had done. There was no getting out of anything. There was only confession and forced, insincere, penance on Edison's part. Truths, lies, and a five-year-old's sense of ethics meant nothing to his parents.

"Edison," his mother asked, "why were you two fighting?"

"He tried to pee on me."

"No," his dad said absolutely, "we talked to his mother. She was watching and saw you walk over and pee on the tree. First."

"Well?" His mother was looking at him.

"Well," Edison carefully constructed a pointless defense, "Dad told me that the reason Deacon pees on trees is to let other dogs know that it's his tree and his yard. Just before Mrs. Crankberry died I started going next door every day to pee on the tree and yard." The corners of Shaney Janzen's mouth, despite her obvious efforts, lifted just perceptibly toward a smile. The angry look in his father's eyes vanished, replaced by a humorous glint. Edison picked up the shift in his parents' attitude and hastily continued, "I like that yard and I wanted it. I did just what Deacon does. I marked my territory. So those people shouldn't of moved in." Edison's mother's gaze shifted from Edison to his father. There was mirth in his father's eyes. Edison was confused, but rode what seemed to be a good vibe. "So that kid was trying to take over my yard. Dad said that Deacon would fight any dog that came into our yard, so I had to fight Skeeter." It sounded reasonable as far as he was concerned.

Rev. Janzen acted as though he had been struck dumb. "Yes, well, um, that being as it may, don't fight anymore. It's wrong."

Edison watched his folks turn and quickly leave his room, shutting the door behind them.

He heard his mom say, "George, why would you tell the boy that about dogs peeing on trees?"

His dad chuckled. "I didn't want to lie to him, and the biology of the whole thing seemed pretty harmless at the time."

"My goodness, George! You already raised two sons. You should know that there are few biological subjects that are safe in the hands of a growing boy!"

Edison wasn't exactly sure what had just happened, but he knew he wasn't in trouble. He wasn't supposed to fight over yard ownership anymore, but his mom and dad had not said anything about marking territory. He had anticipated much more trouble from the incident, but he wasn't going to beg for it.

3

    Halfdollar was a little town, characteristic of most small West Virginia towns. The town got its name because exactly one half dollar had been bet and lost at the town's first casino before someone got shot. The population in 1975 hovered just over 1,000 people. The town boasted a Methodist Church, a Southern Baptist Church, a Missionary Baptist Church, an Independent Christian Church, a Seventh-Day Adventist Church, an Assembly of God, and a half-dozen run down, dirty, once-white buildings with dilapidated roofs representing various other forms of Christian worship, from snake handlers to heretics. Many of the denominations believed that they were the only real Christians in town and that they were the only folks going to Heaven, provided the Missionary Baptists didn't get there first and bar the gates. There were no Jews. The Catholics lived in the next town, and everybody else was going to hell. There were, among the various denominations, roughly three hundred forty-eight conversions, baptisms, re-baptisms, remembrances of baptisms and Christ-inspired, life-altering moments a year. That wasn't bad for a town of just over 1,000 souls.

    Some folks got saved on a weekly basis. Every Sunday morning they would repent for the backsliding (you wouldn't want to call it sin) they had committed over the past week. They would admit to horrible transgressions, weep openly, get wet all over in a creek, and then make fun of the Catholics for their practice of weekly confession.

    The only useful store within twenty miles was Walker's. It was sort of a late model general store, part grocery, part True Value Hardware, part hunting supply, part Southern States, and part Napa Auto Parts. As far as Edison knew, it was a mall. It even had a food court, if a half dozen hot dogs floating in a greasy crock-pot can be considered a food court. The post office was a tiny, red brick building, the hair salon was in a trailer, and the barbershop was a cinderblock building about twelve feet by twelve feet, and painted white. There was a little diner with a sign in the door, which during business hours read, "Sorry, We're Open."

On one stretch of land, just north of town, were the elementary, junior high, and high school buildings, all constructed from the same peach-colored bricks. And then there was Sullivan's Flea Market. Sullivan's, an old, converted barn, had everything from the rusted out chassis of World War II jeeps to miles of parachute cord on big spools, plus dummy grenades, insignia, old guitars, rifles, shotguns and pistols. On Saturdays Old Man Sullivan held auctions. Sullivan's was likely to be open any day of the year, except during deer season when Sullivan, and most of his customers, were off in the woods looking for bucks.

Halfdollar had a volunteer fire department whose building also housed the town hall, the community center, and the Dry County Sheriff's Office. In 1975 the sheriff of Dry County was a man named Hasbro. Nobody seemed to know his first name, and nobody called him anything but Sheriff. Sheriff Hasbro, a very round, very red faced man, could fight any twelve men at once or take them on one at a time. He was both the nicest and the meanest S.O.B. Edison would ever know. That is to say, he was always an S.O.B.; just sometimes he was a nice one, sometimes a nasty one.

Dry County was so named because back in the 1860s, so much moonshine was cooked in the area that (according to local lore) the heat from the fires dried up all the rain clouds overhead for three solid years, and thus, the creeks ran dry. Ignorant teetotalers moved to Dry County thinking that it was a haven for the sober. In 1975 thirteen places to buy a legal drink existed within ten miles of Halfdollar, along with a hundred places to get drunk.

Whiskey, gambling, and lots of bullets were Halfdollar's legacy. That, and coal mines, labor wars, unemployment, and depression. But in 1975, Skeeter and Edison were five years old. They had worked out pissing rights by the second evening of their friendship and they didn't care about the rest of the world.

4

Ten minutes into their first day of kindergarten, Skeet turned to Edison and asked, "Don't you reckon we oughta make this classroom ours?" The boys jumped up on the nearest table and, back to back, dropped their pants and peed as far across the classroom as they could reach. It was their classroom, and they were prepared to fight anybody that wanted to say different.

In the autumn of 1975, in Halfdollar, West Virginia, kids—boys anyway (a girl was just a girl, as far as Skeet and Edison could tell)—fell into one of three categories: a boy was either a good kid, a wimp, or a troublemaker. There was, arguably, some gray area, some wiggle room, wherein a "good kid," like Edison or Skeet, could in fact cause considerable trouble on a regular basis and yet manage to reside mainly in the "good kid" category. Halfdollar had no school psychiatrists. Any adult with a belt or yardstick could administer counseling and therapy.

After they peed on their classroom, the principal called their parents. Their mothers had apologized. The boys received a stern talking to, and then were released on their own recognizance. The adults agreed that since it was their first day of school, a little slack could be granted.

Unmoved by the stern talking to, the boys set out to consecrate more of their domain. In the library Edison whispered to Skeeter, "Hey, so far we've peed in our classroom. They know about that one. And then you got the lunchroom when nobody was lookin'. I got the playground. Which one of us is gonna get the library?"

"Reckon we'll do this one together," Skeet declared. "You and me, pal."

"Right," Edison agreed.

The boys wandered off behind a bookshelf and before they were halfway done with the job, Mrs. Smathers, the librarian, came into the aisle at a dead run, swinging what most kids called her sawed-off yard stick. She had shortened a standard yardstick so she could swing it with full force between the bookshelves. Even with the modified stick, she had had to develop a specialized swing. Her swing was not the traditional side-armed, tennis-like, paddle swing, but rather more resembled the underhanded swing of a cavalry swordsman. Instead of crossing both buttocks horizontally, the hit generally marked a vertical line running from the top of one buttock down to mid-thigh, or so.

The librarian operated her sawed-off yard stick with an acquired deftness. Skeeter got hit first, and before his scream could reach his friend's ears, Edison had suffered an equally painful blow.

The school nurse was the closest thing in the county school system to psychiatric help. By 1:30 in the afternoon, on the boys' first day of school, Mrs. Barth and Mrs. Janzen had already been called once to discuss their sons' behavior, and now the mothers sat, shamefaced, in the nurse's office discussing the boys' potty training. "It's dirty to wee-wee anywhere but in the toilet," the nurse said to the boys.

Mrs. Janzen had already raised two moderately successful children, eight and ten years older than Edison. Gerry, the oldest, was an Eagle Scout and a great student. Chris, the middle child, was a devoted basketball player and a Star Scout with aspirations. Gerry and Chris both knew that it was dirty to wee-wee anywhere but the toilet—at least when adults were looking.

Skeeter's mother had raised his older sister Erin, who was seven years old and well potty trained, not that girls were nearly as apt to whiz on trees or classrooms.

Both mothers rubbed their hands, not listening to the nurse. They were seething, and Edison and Skeeter could see the trouble brewing, boiling, steeping, and just generally getting stronger by the second. They knew it was going to hit the fan when they got home.

The nurse made the boys stand over the toilet to "wee-wee," just to prove they knew how to do it properly. The only problem was that they had already tapped and used up even their deepest reserves that day. Edison had long been amazed at how Deacon could pee a thousand times in an hour. As a dog, Deacon was the master of the short, controlled burst, and he could stop the flow at any time.

Edison resolved to master that skill, but for now he and Skeet just stood there in the dimly lit, sanitized, nurse's station bathroom, scared to death that their mothers were going to murder them. It simply had not occurred to them that their teachers would be able to communicate with their parents.

All of the sudden, Edison went pale.

"What's the matter buddy?" Skeet asked.

"My brother had a squirt gun," came the whispered explanation. "He squirted somebody with it. They took it away from him. You don't think they're gonna take away our thingies, do you?" His voice held genuine concern.

Skeet thought it through. "My sister had an operation in the hospital once," he finally commented, his voice full of worry. "My mom said she had to have her appendix taken out. I don't know what an appendix is, and I don't remember if she squirted anybody with it, but she must have done something bad if they took it away from her."

Even at age five there was a great, instinctual panic welling up in the boys about losing their thingies. Finally, a trickle of pee issued from Edison. Skeet gave up the attempt. They pulled up their pants, flushed the toilet, and walked out of the bathroom.

The nurse escorted everybody to the principal's office. After a short discussion it was agreed that Skeet and Edison could stay in school, it being their first day and all, but that their parents would have to sit them down and explain proper urination etiquette to them.

The boys were paddled by the principal, and then excused to go sit in the outer office. They heard laughter coming from the office; their mothers and the principal were laughing at something. It was adult laughter, but it was good to hear.

Edison had been holding his thingy in a tight, protective grip, shielding it from being removed. He could see Mrs. Smathers and her sawed-off yard stick doing the job. The laughter calmed his nerves and he loosened his grip. "I reckon they ain't gonna cut our thingies off," he sighed with relief.

That night, Edison's father paddled him, but not too hard. There were loopholes, like spanking, in Rev. Janzen's pacifism that the son did not appreciate. "Only pee in toilets," his parents counseled. Rev. Janzen then made the boy stand in the corner, in the bathroom, for thirty minutes. It was the best punishment his parents could devise. His folks stood outside the bathroom door making jokes and giggling. They had not asked, "Why did you do it?" They knew. It was Deacon again. "That rascal of a dog," laughed Rev. Janzen.

Parents were odd. When Edison had had the fight with Skeeter there was confession, but no real punishment. This time there was no confession, no questions about justification, just punishment—a spanking and a boring half hour in front of the toilet. Though he felt no remorse for his actions, Edison did resolve to keep his thingy in his pants whenever adults were around. It was, as it turned out, a useful resolution.

5

Rev. Janzen's Sunday services were calm and serious, without much pulpit beating or spittle flying, but not without humor. One Easter morning Rev. Janzen began the service by saying, "Well, we have a full house today. Easter, being the day of the Great Miracle, may not be the most popular Christian holiday, but it is certainly the most important, and thus a day of high reverence. In case you're visiting, I'd just like to point out that we are open every Sunday morning, not just Easter and Christmas."

Rev. Janzen liked to preach about grace whenever he could fit it in. "The Church Fathers," he would intone, "speak of justifying grace and sanctifying grace. Or, justification and sanctification. Justifying grace is the grace that allows us to come into God's presence, and achieve salvation. Sanctifying grace is the grace God provides so that we can maintain holy and virtuous lives. John Wesley adds to this the idea of prevenient grace. Wesley contends that this is the first grace we encounter. Prevenient grace is the grace that comes to us when we are in total sin, and calls us to take the first steps toward God, towards justification.

"I preach to the justified. This is not a beginner's church. You are not beginner Christians. Most of you reside in justified grace, with occasional side trips in and out. How do I know how to preach to you, the justified? How do I know how to bring you to sanctification? I watch the children, and the very old. The Church is a circle. Salvation is a circle.

"But what if I were to disagree with Wesley? What if I was to say that prevenient grace is not the first grace we experience? What if we are born in sanctification and then, as we grow older, as we experience the world, we slip downward into justifying grace? What if this slide continues as we mature until we leave grace altogether, somewhere in our teens? Maybe prevenient grace then surfaces, not to call us in the first place, but to remind us of the grace we once had, to remind us that we were once, whether we knew it or not, sanctified. That would mean that only the very young and the very old would be sanctified. I grant that this goes against Original Sin, but hear me out.

"Jesus says in Matthew 18:3, 'Unless you change and become like little children, you will not enter Heaven.' In Mark 10:14-15 we read, 'Suffer the little children to come unto me and forbid them not, for of such is the kingdom of God. I tell you the truth, anyone who will not receive the kingdom of God as a little child, will never enter it.' Only two groups of people have the faith of a child. Children, and the very old, who have reverted to childhood. Watch these people and you will be watching the sanctified, the innocent. Sanctification is one of those things in life which, if you think you have achieved, you are probably too self-involved to be capable of receiving."

The theme of peace was also often present in Rev. Janzen's sermons. In those days, 1975, there was still a lot of talk about the War—the Vietnam War—and general relief that the war had ended. As a pastor, and the child of Mennonites, Rev. Janzen leaned heavily toward pacifism, but Halfdollar was no place to openly deride soldiers. Edison would listen to his father say things like, "War is wrong. Killing is wrong. All the peaceful solutions need to be exhausted before armed conflicts are started," but the boy never, ever, heard his dad say that soldiers were sinners. Or at least that soldiers were any more sinful than everyone else. Most of the men in 1975 Halfdollar had either fought or served in the military during World War II or Korea, and a large number of them had sons in Vietnam.

Halfdollar was a town of coal miners and loggers. Folks were poor, and only a small percentage of the population had college degrees. When war came to America or, more properly, when America went to a war, Uncle Sam tapped on Halfdollar's shoulder, and the shoulders of towns like her all across the country, and said, "Come on." And the young men went.

Edison was five years old in 1975 and so he didn't know much, or care much, about any war. He knew, vaguely, that his uncle had been fighting The War and that had been a cause for great concern. But the uncle was back now and the war was over. The boy once heard his dad tell all the old men in the church, "Now I can get back to doing funerals for old folks instead of boys." Even though the old men seemed to agree that what Rev. Janzen said was a good thing, it still seemed odd to tell all those old guys that they were going to die. And for them to be happy about it. And there was always somebody mentioning how the city of Saigon had fallen. Edison knew that couldn't be good. A whole city falling? He tried to imagine Halfdollar falling. It was wedged so tightly into the mountains that Edison figured Halfdollar really had no place to fall. That was comforting.

But, church was church. Mrs. Janzen would give Edison a scrub down on Saturday night, and then he and Skeeter would meet Sunday morning in the backyard and try to stay clean until their families were ready to walk over to Halfdollar United Methodist Church. Rev. Janzen would have long since been in his office, sitting at his desk, rehearsing his sermon.

The Barths were Methodists, too, which was good for the two friends, but not so nice for the little blue haired ladies in the church. There were two teachers for the Kindergarten Sunday school class, Mrs. Milly and Mrs. Gwinn. Both were needed. Skeeter and Edison were hard enough to sit on for forty-five minutes, but the rest of the kids in the class were no angels either. Both of these ladies were retired schoolteachers, having retired from one-room schoolhouses to which they had had to walk in the mornings, over mountain paths, in wind and rain. Both Mrs. Milly and Mrs. Gwinn firmly believed that a carefully selected birch stick was, at times, the greatest educational tool at their disposal. Both ladies secretly scoffed at Mrs. Smather's sawed-off yard stick. "It might work nice in the library aisles," Mrs. Milly would say, "but those extra inches she sawed off take away a lot of leverage!"

Just before Skeet and Edison walked into their Sunday school classroom, Mrs. Barth said to them, "Now look here you two, I shouldn't have to say this, but this is Sunday school. This church belongs to God. All the rooms belong to God. Do not, under any circumstances, pee in or on anything but the toilet. God is not happy when little boys pee in His classrooms to mark their territory."

Mrs. Barth stared down hard at them. "You understand?"

The boys nodded. "Yes, ma'am," Skeet said.

They stepped into the classroom and Mrs. Milly looked down at them. "Either of you boys pulls your penis out in this classroom and I'll whack it clean off. You understand?"

News traveled fast in Halfdollar.

"Yes Mrs. Milly," they said.

Edison's father stepped into the classroom and walked over to the boys. He reached down and picked up both of them and then turned them over so that he was holding each boy by an ankle. Rev. Janzen shook them until they giggled. "No peeing in here!" he said, smiling. The boys laughed out loud.

"Preacher George," Mrs. Gwinn said sharply, "that sort of behavior will not be tolerated in this classroom."

Rev. Janzen quit shaking the boys; the smile left his face. Edison and Skeeter were suspended two feet off the floor. "Oh, of course not. I'm sorry Mrs. Gwinn, Mrs. Milly." The preacher put the boys gently on the floor, tucked his shirt back in, tugged on his jacket, and walked out of the room. Skeet and Edison lay still on the floor. "Get up boys, and come sit down at the table," Mrs. Milly commanded. They obeyed.

God, to a five-year-old, is a remarkably impressive figure. God, in Halfdollar, will always be the unrivaled ruler of the universe, and God's gender will always be determined by the fact the author of Genesis could come up with no better way to describe Adam except to say that he was made in God's image. Adam was a male. Therefore God is a male. Adam's body would forever determine God's physical being. Tough break for God. Had the author of Genesis known that largely unimaginative readers would take that statement and run with it well into the future, surely God would have used other language. But even way back in Biblical times there must have been a hope that way down deep the human race might be good, and that they might understand the limited use of the personal pronoun, figurative language, and be able to grasp metaphor.

Anyway, to a five-year-old, it's probably just as well that God was a male. Since Mrs. Milly and Mrs. Gwinn were faced with the task of teaching kindergartners who God was, they had to start somewhere. There was just no sense bringing up the limited ability of pronouns to describe God to a group of children who had trouble understanding the concept of "too much glitter." Not that Mrs. Milly and Mrs. Gwinn had any trouble, or doubt, concerning God's identity as a male. It was fine with them. It was easy to see why the world was so screwed up, why there was evil, why good things went undone- a being like Rev. Janzen, a male, was in charge of the Universe.

So the kids in Edison's Sunday school class learned about God, and to them He was an old man with a long flowing beard and white clothes. God commanded the Universe, loved everybody, sent flooding waters and snakes among His people when they acted-up, and otherwise played the role of a parent. God had a son named Jesus. Jesus loved all the people of the world, was born in a manger, died on a cross, and rose from the dead three days later. Somehow, the other deity that controlled Edison's destiny, Santa Claus, was wrapped up in the events of Jesus being born in a manger. Edison slept easy at night in the warm but firm hands of that theology. No reason to doubt existed, no reason to worry, and every reason to behave. Heaven might be a long way off, but Christmas was never more than twelve months away.

6

The thing is, no matter how near or far away Christmas was, there seemed always just enough time to make amends with God, Santa and parents. That said, Skeeter and Edison were six years old when they discovered fire. Obviously, they had been introduced to fire in the past as a way to heat the house or cook a hotdog. They already knew fire had value as a tool. Now they discovered that fire could be a toy.

"No wonder they told us not to play with it! Look what it can do!" Skeet's eyes reflected the leaping flames that consumed a book of matches on the dirt patch behind his garage. The flames roared and sprung into the air, bright yellow and alive. A single flame leapt above the others, full of grace and wonder. Edison thought the flame was the most beautiful thing he had ever seen. Leaves thrown atop the matchbook exploded in color, smoke, and ashes. Handfuls of dry grass smoked and then flared.

Edison had managed to take a whole box of matchbooks from his brother Gerry's bedroom. Gerry had had them in the pocket of his Boy Scout backpack. Fifty books of matches. Edison and Skeeter were down to about twenty books. Quickly bored by lighting a single match at a time, they had graduated to igniting full packs all at once, then two or three packs at a time. Now they were getting bored of that.

"Know what my dad said?" Skeet asked. "He said 'That sumbitch Jimmy Carter is going to get elected President.'"

"Uh-oh." Edison answered. "That's bad. My dad said that if Carter gets elected, the whole country is going to go to Hell."

"Crap. You're dad's a minister. If anyone knows who is going to Hell, your dad does."

"I know. What are we going to do?"

In early June, 1976, the country was gearing up to celebrate its 200th birthday. Ford, Carter and Anderson were running for President. Little of that, except the promise of a huge fireworks show, and the prospect of going to Hell, meant much to Skeeter and Edison.

Skeeter looked at the box of matchbooks. He held it up, weighed it in his hands as if trying to discern its value. "Look here," he announced, "we'll just stop Carter from getting elected."

"How?"

"You know that sign across the street, in Mrs. Miller's yard? The one that says 'Vote Jimmy Carter for President'?"

"Yeah."

"Well, if we crossed the street and burned that sign, then nobody would know to vote for him. Right?"

"Yeah. I guess if there wasn't a sign, nobody would know."

The plan was crystal clear. Skeet and Edison were about to save the world from going to Hell. There was just one problem.

"I'm not allowed to cross the street without my mom," Edison said.

"Crap. Me either."

"We are trying to save the world. Maybe your mom would go with us."

"Maybe."

"But," Edison added, "I'm not allowed to play with matches, either. Even if she let us cross the street, there is no way she'd let us burn Mrs. Miller's sign."

"And she'd probably wonder where we got the matches."

They stood quietly, watching the blackened matchbooks smolder in the sun. They were on the very brink of saving the world—real salvation. Salvation from Hell. Jesus salvation. They held the power and means to keep the whole world from going to Hell, but they weren't allowed out of the yard to do it. Edison pushed some dust with his toe, put his hands in the rough back pockets of his Toughskin jeans, and looked straight at the sun, a giant ball of fire hanging in the sky.

Halfdollar was traditionally a Republican town. West Virginia, as a rule, votes Democrat. A whole town with Republican voting tendencies is about as odd as it gets.

Perhaps a better way to describe the situation is to say that Democrats hold the power in the state, but not the same sort of Democrats you'd find in Chapel Hill, North Carolina, or Berkeley,

California. A West Virginia liberal is not the same bird (or Byrd) as West Coast liberal. Your average West Virginia Democrat has an NRA sticker in the back window of his, or her, pickup truck. They are the sort of Democrats that become Navy SEALS and CIA operatives. In short, your average Democrat in West Virginia is a person who votes the Democratic ticket but has strong Republican tendencies.

But Halfdollar actually voted Republican, all the time. Edison's and Skeeter's dads were Republicans and didn't care who knew. Skeeter and Edison, however, understood the electoral process about as well as they understood Trinitarian theology. All they knew for sure was that there was at least one real Democrat in town, that that sumbitch Carter might win, and that if he did, they were all going to go to Hell. Conundrums come quick and hard when you are six.

"Look," Edison exclaimed, "we just have to be brave. We'll just run across the street, burn the sign, and run back. We have to. To save the world."

"You and me, pal." Skeeter agreed.

They came around the corner of the garage trying to look innocent. They walked straight beneath the kitchen window, past the side porch and into the front yard. This was dangerous ground in itself. Usually, they needed adult supervision to be in the front yard, but that rule had been relaxed somewhat over the past few months. Edison swallowed hard and wiped his hand across his wet brow. He clasped a matchbook in the palm of his hand. He had never crossed the street, any street, on his own before. Skeeter was visibly upset. They crept to the edge of the lawn, drawing ever nearer the shoulder of the road. Edison felt like he had swallowed a cat, and that it was about to have kittens.

A car came into view down the road. The boys froze. Two figures beneath the blazing sun in a shelterless lawn, their intentions printed on their faces. The car slowed to a stop in front of them. Sheriff Hasbro, his huge, red head drenched in sweat, leaned out of the car window. He had a Pall Mall clenched in the corner of his lips. "Now lookie 'ere." He spoke almost exclusively through his nose. "You boys wasn't about ta try and cross this 'ere street, was ya?"

He didn't wait for an answer. "'Cause I hap'n ta know fer a fact that you boys ain't 'llowed ta cross the street 'lone. In fact, yer mamas both told me that if ever I saw y'all 'bout ta cross the street I should A-rest ya on the spot, handcuff ya, take ya ta jail and lock ya up. Ferever. Yes, Sir, both your mamas told me that. Ya hear?" The boys nodded. "I said, DO YOU HEAR?!"

"Yes, Sir!" they chimed.

"Sheriff?" It was Edison's mother's voice, from behind them. "Sheriff, is everything OK? Are these boys in trouble?" Her voice held a hint of concern. "Were they playing in the street?"

"No, ma'am. Nooo, not a'tall." He laughed a little, dismissing the notion. "I seen 'em in the backyard and called out to 'em ta come 'ere a sec. Thought they might'a seen a lost dog I was a'lookin fer." Hasbro smiled at her, spit out his cigarette and winked at the boys. The sheriff's car started to pull away. "You boys be careful now, ya hear?" he called back.

"Edison, Skeeter," Mrs. Janzen began, "you boys go back and play in the backyard. It makes me nervous with you out here." They obeyed, silently turning and marching back, faces to the ground.

"That," Skeeter said, exhaling sharply as they rounded the corner of the garage, "was close!"

"If he could put us in jail for being in the street, think what he would have done to us if he'd caught us burning that sign! He'd probably call the FBI."

"But we still have to stop Jimmy Carter from getting elected!"

Edison opened the matchbook in his hand and struck a match. He watched it burn between his fingers, and then dropped it in the hot dust. He lit another. He thought about how Mrs. Gwinn and Mrs. Milly had taught them that God sometimes spoke to people, like Moses and Abraham and Noah and told them what to do. "Skeet," he asked, "Why do you figure that God told Noah to build that boat?"

"I guess so Noah could save the world, like Mrs. Milly said."

"Same thing you figure with Moses? And Abraham? You reckon God talked to them so they could save the world?"

"I guess so. I can't figure any other reason." Skeet stared at Edison, squinting in the sunlight, his left foot on top of his right foot, a book of matches in each hand, his lips curled up in thought.

"God wanted all those people to live right, so God picked out some of them to tell the others how to live right."

Edison stared back. He shielded his eyes from the sun with his hand. A fly nibbled at the mustard on his T-shirt. He swallowed hard, looked at the pile of blackened matchbooks at his feet, and watched an ant carrying a breadcrumb twice his size. "You reckon," he asked Skeet, his throat dry, "that God talked to us? That it was God told us burn that Carter sign?"

Skeet looked way off into the distance, then up toward the sun, then at the matchbook in his hand. "Reckon?" He shrugged.

"Remember how Mrs. Gwinn said that Moses got picked to be the spokesman for his people even though he couldn't talk good? Maybe God picked us 'cause we can't cross the street." Edison watched the ant again. "Maybe if we pray, God will show us what to do?"

"Okay."

"You do it."

"No," Skeet shook his head, "your dad's the preacher. You pray."

Edison bowed his head, embarrassed to pray out loud in front of his friend. It felt weird. Finally, he uttered, "Dear God, help us keep Carter from getting elected so the world won't go to Hell. Amen."

The boys raised their heads and opened their eyes. Nothing. No answer.

And then Skeet yelled, "Bottle rockets!" He snapped his fingers and took off running. He ran through the backdoor into his house. A minute later he ran back out, his hand under his shirt. He walked quickly over to Edison, and then lifted his shirt. He had a handful of bottle rockets. "My dad had these in the closet in his room. He got them when we went down to Myrtle Beach for the Fourth of July."

"So?"

"So? So we can burn that sign by hitting it with these rockets. And the best part is that we won't get in trouble 'cause we can do it without crossing the street! I think we can even do it from the backyard. We have to," he said confidently. "God talked to us."

"I don't know," Edison argued. "We could burn down the whole town."

"God told us to!"

"I never heard God say 'bottle rockets.'"

"Look," Skeet pleaded, "you prayed, and then I thought of bottle rockets right after. That's how God talks."

"And the Devil. Devil'd be more likely to say 'bottle rockets' than God would."

Skeet shrugged, sure he was right. "It's God. I know it is. I'm sure."

Edison said, "Well, if you're sure you're sure. But how come he talked to you and not me?"

"I reckon God figured we're such good friends that I'd tell you what he said. 'Sides, I knew where the bottle rockets were. If God said 'bottle rockets' to you, you wouldn't know where to go look."

"Well, that's true," Edison agreed. "But if we save the world and they put us in the Bible for keepin' that sumbitch Carter from gettin' elected, I want my name in there, too."

"Fair enough. You and me, pal. Now, let's find a bottle."

When they'd found a bottle, Skeeter laid it in the grass, the neck of the bottle pointed across the street like a rifle barrel. Then the boys took their time aiming the bottle straight at the Carter sign in Mrs. Miller's yard. They had as clear a line of sight as they could manage by taking turns peering, with one eye open, over an empty bottle. Skeet took one bottle rocket and stuck it in the bottle. Edison pulled a match out of the book in his hand. He drug the matchhead across the strike pad and watched the yellow flame jump into existence, then grow an inch tall. Kneeling on one knee, he slowly lowered the flame to the wick of the bottle rocket.

It was a hot, windless day in the middle of June in Dry County, West Virginia. It was seldom so windless in Dry County that a six-year-old boy could light a match while standing up, kneel down with the match still in his young, uncoordinated fingers, lower his hand to the ground, and touch the match to the wick of a bottle rocket without the match going out. And yet it happened. The wick began to burn, a small cloud of sparks dancing around it like gnats around a skinned knee.

One lesson life teaches over and over again is that things only go right at the most inopportune times. The conditions were perfect to launch a bottle rocket across the street exactly the way Skeet and Edison had planned, and God knows the skies should have opened in a torrent of rain and hail, complemented by gale force winds. Instead, the rocket leapt to life in the mouth of the bottle and then shot forward. The boys stood, awestruck. It was beautiful! The rocket flew straight as an arrow and hit the Carter sign right between the first r and the t. Skeeter and Edison were in the initial stages of a high-five when they saw the rocket bounce off the sign. The hard cardboard of the sign, rather than bursting into flame, deflected the burning projectile. The bottle rocket ricocheted, pointed itself straight down, and dove into the ground. With a lackluster crack! it exploded in a burst of red flame and tiny shards of green tissue paper.

Mr. Miller was not the kind of guy who bothered to rake his yard after mowing it and thus loose piles of dried grass clippings commonly lay scattered around the yard. Add to that the fact that it had not rained in Halfdollar since just after Easter and suddenly the harmless report of a bottle rocket became a veritable spark in a powder keg.

"Oh crap," Skeeter whispered.

"Told you so," muttered Edison.

"No you didn't."

"I said it could be the devil talkin' to you."

"No you didn't."

"Did so. Guess that's why I didn't hear anybody say 'bottle rockets.' Cause I'm too good to hear the devil."

"You were right here with me, pal."

As the yard burst into flame, Edison's mother, having heard the report of the bottle rocket, came out the front door of the house. Mrs. Miller came around the corner of her house twenty seconds later, flushed, and brandishing a pot of water and a fire extinguisher.

There just wasn't any chance that Skeet and Edison were going to get out of this predicament without bodily harm. The saddest fact of life is that the true error of your ways never shines quite so brightly as it does just after you have screwed up irrecoverably.

As the Millers' lawn burst into short flames, it occurred to Edison how dumb it was to shoot bottle rockets across the street at signs that read "Vote Jimmy Carter for President." He'd readily grant now that it was a bad idea, but what really hit him the hardest was the notion that he and Skeet should have waited until after dark. Edison was consumed with misery, not because he was going to get into trouble, but because with better planning they could have pulled the whole operation off without a hitch or a drop of suspicion. Instead, because they had acted hastily, Mrs. Miller was ankle deep in flame, and they would soon be up the creek.

Edison's mother raced across the street and tried to help her neighbor stamp out the flames. The fire was not a big one. The flames never even blackened the pine shaft holding the Carter sign. With the two women jumping frantically on the burning grass, aided by Mrs. Miller's liberal use of the fire extinguisher, the blaze was soon squashed.

Both women stared across the street, their eyes boring tiny holes right through Edison and Skeeter. The boys stood, dumbstruck, knowing that flight and lies would only prolong the spiritual desolation and physical misery they were about to endure. Edison's mother stormed over and grabbed each boy by the upper arm. She lifted them off the ground and beelined to Skeeter's back porch. Mrs. Barth, her maternal senses on full power, was already on her stoop with a scowl and a wooden spoon. The scowl broke the boys' spirits, and the spoon soon found its way across their bottoms.

Only after they had been paddled, screamed at by their mothers, sent to their rooms and forced to wait until their respective fathers arrived home, were they allowed to defend their actions. Edison knew enough to do two things. First, he confessed to every aspect of the crime in utter honesty, full disclosure. Secondly, he shifted blame and guilt to his parents.

He could not be sure what Skeeter was going to say, but he knew that both sets of parents would talk about the incident. Edison felt it best to go with the truth from the get-go because that way, even if the boys had different stories, well, at least his version would be the truth. However, he was fairly certain that Skeeter would opt for full confession as well. The truth involved was so good, so innocent, and so complex, that Edison's folks would have to buy it. There was just no way they would think he had made up the events and motive.

And that was where the shift of blame came in. It was, after all, the boys' parents' fault. Edison's dad had clearly said, "If Carter gets elected President, we will all go to Hell."

Edison's gut said, "Tell the truth; it'll work out." After all, his father often told him, "God is just and thus all things will eventually, for better or worse, come to a conclusion."

When his parents had finally come into his room and started to ask, "Why did you do…," and Edison immediately began to cry. "I'm sorry! I had to burn that sign! I had to save the World! You said it was going to Hell! I hate that sumbitch Carter!"

The "Hell" and "Sumbitch" caused his parents to jolt as though stung by wasps, his mother's hand going to her chest. His dad said, "What? What in the world are you talking about?"

And just like that, the discussion left the dangerous realm of "Why in the world did you do that?!" and entered the far less threatening realm of "What in the world are you talking about?"

7

In January of 1977, Jimmy Carter took office. If they all went to Hell, well, Edison couldn't tell Hell from Halfdollar. Many days lay ahead when he would be hard pressed to tell the two apart.

Skeet turned seven years old in the spring. Edison had his seventh birthday in the fall.

That winter Skeeter realized that Charolais Fester was a girl. Perhaps it would be better to say Skeeter realized girls were in some ways far more interesting than boys, and that if a fella was going to associate with a girl, it might as well be Charolais. After that, Skeeter lost all interest in both politics and salvation.

Charolais was the daughter of Angus Fester, a dairy farmer who was so possessed by his desire to have cows around him that his children all bore the names of bovine species. There were the boys — Angus Jr., Malvi, Guernsey, Jersey, Beefalo and Hereford — and then his daughter, Charolais. Fortunately, Charolais' mother had intervened on her behalf and demanded that if the poor girl had to be named after a cow, at least the name should sound feminine. It was a small victory.

But Charolais was a better girl than most. She didn't mind getting hit in the head with a snowball, and she could throw a savage punch. Skeeter and Charolais passed notes back and forth in class and promised to love each other forever. Edison thought it was the most dehumanizing thing he had ever seen happen to his best pal. Fortunately, the relationship was only carried on at school which freed up Skeet to play in the afternoons as usual.

The biggest problem with the whole affair was that it had to be kept strictly secret. Angus Fester was a bitter drunk who, on a regular basis, could be seen downtown kicking in someone's teeth, getting his own teeth kicked in, or sitting in the back of Sheriff Hasbro's cruiser. How he ever managed a farm was beyond Edison. Much later Edison learned that had it not been for Helen Fester, Charolais' mother, the whole farm would have collapsed into dust and cow patties long ago. The story was that Angus was such a bad farmer Helen actually encouraged him to drink. Since he never drank at home, and his drinking binges lasted for weeks, followed by months of hospitalization, jail sentences, or some combination of the two, she could go about the business of farming while he was away.

All of Angus' sons were stupid, mean, and protective of their little sister, but only as an excuse to be brutal. Thus, in order to keep himself alive, Skeeter's relationship with Charolais had to be kept very quiet. But Halfdollar was a small town, and Charolais was pretty enough that the other boys in class were willing to rat Skeet out for a chance of their own to write notes to pretty, young Ms. Fester.

Angus Jr. had achieved the status of ninth grader not because he was a good student, but because he had passed the maximum age allowed by law for an eighth grader. Malvi had generously stayed in the seventh grade two years in a row to wait for Guernsey and Jersey, who were identical twins, identical in every way except that Jersey had, at the last minute, been held back and thus occupied a seat in the sixth grade with Beefalo. Hereford was in the fifth grade and showing signs of passing. Charolais was the only Fester anyone expected to pass through all twelve grades without being lapped by the next generation. For that matter, she was the only Fester anyone expected to even see the twelfth grade.

The elementary, junior high, and high school all had lunch at the same hour and, following lunch, no matter the season, the students from all three schools spent half an hour outdoors. The elementary school playground was frozen solid, a thick veneer of dirty ice pocked with footprints covering it from end to end. It looked to Edison like the surface of the moon with a merry-go-round and a sliding board.

He watched curiously as Angus Jr. jumped the fence that divided the junior high school recess area from the elementary school play area. Angus Jr. wore only a denim jacket and a knit cap against the twenty-degree weather. The cap was handmade of brown and white yarn. It had a puffy ball sewn to the top and sizable holes torn into it. Edison had seen better hats on the side of the road.

Angus Jr. wasn't wearing gloves. Huge, blue veins clearly visible under the dry skin emphasized his cold hands. Edison unconsciously looked down at his own hands clad in thick, insulated gloves. The hat he wore was a hand-me-down from his brother, but it was still in good shape. His folks weren't rich, but he had new gloves, a very warm coat, and a good hat.

Angus headed straight toward Skeet and Edison. The boys glanced at each other. Guys didnt't jump the fence unless they meant trouble.

Charolais started over from the wall she had leaned against while talking to her friends. All the kids stopped playing and stared at Angus Jr. as he headed toward Skeeter and Edison like mustard gas drifting toward the English trenches. When all of the kids on the elementary side of the fence hushed up, the kids on the junior high side slowly turned their way. Angus Jr., at seventeen, towered over all the little kids. It was obvious where he was headed, and why. His brothers on the elementary school side of the fence filed in behind him; his brothers on the junior-high side jumped the fence and jogged to catch up. Skeeter pushed his shoulder against Edison's and said to him, "You and me, pal."

"Yeah, you and me, but you got us into this one on your own." They balled their small fists.

Angus Jr. had twenty-four inches, and at least a hundred and fifty pounds on Skeet and Edison. The rest of the Fester herd, except Charolais, circled the two boys. "Where are the teachers?" Edison wondered. Angus Jr. looked down at Skeet and ordered, "You leave my sister the hell alone or I'll bust yer ass." And then he swung his dry, blue fist, and caught Skeet full force on the end of his jaw. Skeet came off his feet and flew backwards. He hit the ice on his back and slid to a stop three feet away. Edison did the only thing he thought might be useful. He plunged his fist as hard as he could into Angus Jr.'s groin. Edison was a little runt, but a blast in the balls is a blast in the balls. Angus Jr. curled up like a pillbug and dropped to the ice.

The Fester herd jumped Edison full force, and those among them that could not find room on Edison to plant a fist, started in on Skeet. Angus Jr. soon joined in on Edison. He'd hit him a couple of licks and then vomit, all the while protecting his groin. Charolais slugged away on her brothers' backs, trying to hurt them and pull them off. Edison saw Skeet's sister, Erin, running toward the junior high fence. She spotted his brother, Chris, and yelled, "They're beatin' up Edison and Skeet. Really poundin' them!"

Chris waved his arm and yelled to his friends, "Someone go tell Gerry, the rest of you come with me."

One kid hurried off to get Edison's oldest brother from the high school while Chris, and five others, jumped the fence. They started laying into Festers, punching and throwing bodies around. One good thing about the Festers was that they were such bastards they had absolutely no playground allies outside of their immediate clan.

By the time Gerry arrived, a number of teachers were finally on the scene. Edison was bleeding from his nose, lips and cheeks. His eyes were already swelling shut and he could just make out Skeeter turning black and blue three feet away. Chris stood over Edison, his face flushed, tears in his eyes, rage flaring in his nostrils. Gerry was hunched over Skeeter, cradling his head. Charolais knelt by Skeeter's side, holding his hand.

Chris smiled at his younger brother and asked, "You all right kid?" Edison heard Gerry yell, "Get an ambulance and call the dern'd sheriff!" Edison worried about Skeet for about a second, and then drifted into another world.

He woke up in the hospital, confused and sore. He quickly scanned the room. Skeet was in the bed next to him. Mrs. Janzen stood at Edison's bedside. She told him gently that she loved him, and that he a broken rib. He burst into tears and his mother held him until he fell back to sleep.

The next time he awoke, the sun had left the window and a hard wind rattled the loose panes, managing to billow the curtains. Of the two, Edison was relieved that only the sun could pass through the glass with much effect.

His mom had gone somewhere. The wind reminded him of the cold outside, and the thought of the icy air made him think of how cold Angus Jr.'s hands must be. Edison wondered if Angus Jr.'s breath was as cold as the wind, if he blew icy air into his cupped hands when he held them in front of his mouth. Edison had thought as Angus Jr. punched him that the bully must have sandpaper knuckles. Now, he wondered if it wasn't frost, the sort of frost that builds up in the freezer, inches thick and as sharp as a serrated blade. Edison thought it was funny how he remembered the texture of Angus Jr.'s fist against his cheek, his temple, more clearly than the thudding blows.

Skeeter cleared his throat, coughed, groaned, "Oooh," and sucked a breath in between his teeth. "What in the world happened to us? I was standing there talking to you and thinking about the Pop-Tart in my lunch bag when that big jerk came over and clocked me. Next thing I knew, I was sliding across the ice on my butt watching blood pour out of my nose and onto the ice. And then the Fester herd was on top of me."

"Only half the herd. The other half jumped me. But I nailed Angus Jr. square in his sack. I racked him good!"

Skeet laughed. "My arm's in a cast," he said, holding up a white forearm.

"I got a busted rib," Edison responded.

"Broke arm's better than a broke rib."

"Is not."

"Is too. People can see my cast. And I can hit people with it. A broken rib is nothin'. People will just think yer a wuss. Besides, you don't get a cast. Can't knock someone out with a broken rib."

Edison knew Skeet was right. There he lay, his butt kicked on Skeet's behalf, and Skeet making fun of his wounds. Skeet was right. What a bunch of crap. And for a girl. Skeet's girl! Bunch of crap right there in a cast in the bed next to him.

"Know what though?" Skeet asked.

"What?"

"While they were putting me in the ambulance, she ran over and kissed me."

Bunch of crap. At least he had racked Angus Jr. At least he had that.

The door opened and Mrs. Barth stuck her head in. She saw that the boys were awake and turned to say something to someone in the hall. Skeet's folks and sister came in, followed by Edison's folks and brothers. Chris sported a shiner growing deep blue on his left eye, and Gerry's knuckles were scabbing over. He had a bruise on his cheek.

"You all right kid?" Chris asked, smiling.

"Thanks to you."

"You two ought not pick fights with the Festers," Mr. Barth chided, winking at Edison and tousling Skeet's hair.

"Not a bad showing for a bunch of boys raised pacifists," Rev. Janzen chuckled. "But what in the name of God were those Festers thinking?"

"I don't know," Edison said. And then he asked, "Why are they so mean?"

"Same reason you boys are nice, I reckon," declared Rev. Janzen.

"But you brought me up to be nice. I just can't help it."

"Yep," his Dad nodded.

8

Nothing much came of it. Edison's rib healed, and Skeet got his cast off before he could ever knock anyone out with it. He did almost get kicked out of Cub Scouts, though. The boys had joined the Cub pack at the church while they were healing. Miss Milly was the den leader. They knew better than to pee on anything, but Skeet had taken a swipe at a kid with his cast. Hit him pretty good, too, but not hard enough to knock him out. Miss Milly explained that that sort of behavior was not encouraged by the Boy Scout code.

Following the fight, Angus Jr. got permanently expelled from school, cold hands and all. His brothers were suspended to various degrees. Even Edison's brother, Chris, got to stay home from school for three days, suspended for fighting.

Edison lamented to Skeeter, "We got our butts kicked, had bones broken, and the rest of those guys got to stay home from school in perfect health. It don't seem fair to me."

"We got to eat all that ice cream in the hospital though."

"That don't make it right," Edison complained.

Skeeter and Edison had been the innocent victims in the whole process—Edison even more so than Skeet since Edison hadn't had anything to do with Charolais—and yet they were the ones who suffered the most. Except that Skeet got kissed by the best-looking girl in class. It burned Edison up that the sinners received vacation while he struggled for breath. What kind of justice was that? What sort of penance did that amount to? "God is just, and thus all things will eventually, for better or worse, come to a conclusion," his father had said. Just what sort of crap was God up to?

To add insult to injury, the Cub Scout den that Skeet and Edison joined was studying the United States government. The Cubs learned about the three branches of the government, and then Miss Milly informed them, "You are each going to write the President a letter. I've been doing this since Eisenhower was in office. We always get such a nice response."

Each Cub wrote essentially the same letter:

Dear President Carter,
 Thank you for being President. I think you are doing a great job. What is it like living in the White House? What is your favorite sport?
  Sincerely,
  Edison

Edison wanted to ask President Carter when he planned on making everybody go to Hell, but he refrained. Best not to draw attention to that old matter.

The weeks went by. "I don't reckon that President is gonna write us back," Edison announced at the dinner table.

"Maybe he heard about what you did to his sign," Rev. Janzen laughed.

"Now, now. Let's just be patient. The President is a busy man," his mother ended the conversation.

By all indications the President was too busy to respond to a dozen letters from loyal Cub Scouts. "What could he possibly have to do all day long?" Edison asked Skeet.

"Maybe he's gotta pee on stuff and fight other guys who want to be President," Skeet suggested.

"Could be."

For two straight weeks after he sent the letter, Edison rushed to the mailbox as soon as he got home from school. There was never anything there for him. As the weeks passed, he went less quickly to the mailbox. He couldn't really remember Ford being in office, but he was sure that Ford would have at least written back.

God had let Edison get his butt kicked for nothing, and the President of the United States wouldn't even write him back. What a miserable world.

Edison's brother, Gerry, had written much the same note when he was a Cub Scout and had received a bronze medallion from President Johnson. Chris had gotten a model of Apollo 11 for his efforts.

Then one day Skeet got a package. "It's official mail from the

White House," he told Edison as they stood beside their mailboxes. "It ain't even got a stamp on it!" He tore open the package as Edison stared. The box contained an American flag with a certificate verifying that it had flown over the U.S. Capital, a Presidential coloring book and a box of eight big crayons, all compliments of President Jimmy Carter. "Whoa, that is cool!" Skeet yelled as he rushed in to show his mother.

Three days later, Edison got a flat envelope from the White House containing an 8x10 photograph of Jimmy Carter, with an index card on which was printed:

Thank you for your support.
Jimmy Carter.

A clear, present and absolute unfairness existed in the world. Edison didn't know much about politics, but he knew he was going to be a Republican when he grew up.

9

Hunting in Halfdollar was not just a hobby, but a practice derived from the frontier, agrarian and economically depressed heritage that made seeking game for sustenance necessary for survival. Most every male, and many females, in Halfdollar hunted. Some guys hunted all year with whatever creature was in season in their sights. Some families hunted because they needed the food. A few men hunted for trophies. A very few hunted out of season and by illegal methods. But most of the hunters from Halfdollar hunted because it was what people from Halfdollar did, like sending their kids to school, or going to church on Sunday. It was a cultural and communal event that had nothing to do with cruelty, or the wanton destruction of animals.

Edison couldn't remember the first time he'd seen a skinned deer hanging behind the garage because he'd seen them there every November since before his memory solidified. The sight of skinned deer in November was as natural as snow in December. Trying to describe the first time he'd seen a skinned deer would have been like trying to describe the first time he'd seen a tree. They were just there. He could remember the first time he'd met Skeeter, and maybe he could remember Christmas when he was three, but back beyond that, there was nothing. His mother, his father, Halfdollar, the sun, the moon, and skinned deer in November were just part of the natural order.

Edison had always wanted to go hunting. Especially deer hunting. Every November his dad packed up the car for his annual buck hunt. And every year Edison and his brothers would ask to go along. It was decided in the Janzen household that a boy had to be in the fourth grade to go on his first deer hunting trip. This was Edison's year.

His father woke him a 3:00 in the morning. His mother had cooked a big breakfast of eggs and bacon.

"Now listen," his dad said. "We are going to be cold and

miserable out there. We're going to be out in the woods all day long, and you are going to have to sit still and not make any noise. You got that?"

"Sure. I can do that. Do I get to carry rifle?"

"No. We've been through that. I'll carry the rifle. If we see a deer, I might let you shoot at it. Maybe, okay?"

"Okay," Edison agreed.

"Do you have your mittens?"

"Yes."

"Boots?"

"On my feet."

"Thermal underwear?"

"Under my clothes."

"Hand warmer?"

"George," his mother broke in, "let the boy be. He's got all that stuff. You dressed him yourself."

"I just don't want him complaining all day," George said to his wife.

"Well, you are going to give him reasons he's never dreamt of to complain about if you keep pestering him."

"Dad, I won't complain. Honest."

"Right. I know. You'll be great. You're a tough kid. You'll do fine."

"George," his mother said, "it's the first day of the season. You have two more weeks to go out and hunt on your own. Just be patient with the boy." She smiled, kissed Edison, and then her husband.

Edison and his dad walked out of the kitchen door and into the cold. It was 3:30 a.m., and eight inches of ice-crusted snow covered the ground. The wind blew hard, and the temperature was well below freezing.

Edison had been outside for no more than a minute and he was chilled to the bone. His lips were chapped, his eyes watered, and his nose ran. The cold wind snaked through his scarf and down his neck. The fabric of his clothes did nothing to stop the frigid air. All Edison wanted to do was go back in the house and curl up under a blanket in his mother's lap. Had he really always wanted to go hunting?

"If this wind quits it'll be a great day," his dad exclaimed.

Edison made it to the car and crawled into the backseat as if it were the first shelter he'd had in days. He curled himself into a tight ball and sat shivering. His dad opened the front door of the car, reached in, and started the engine. "I'll be right back. I'm gonna go tell Frank and Skeeter that we're ready."

Moments later Skeeter jumped into the backseat and huddled close to Edison. Their fathers climbed into the front seats.

"Gonna be a great day," Frank assured them, slapping his hands together. "Boys, you're in for a real treat. Your first deer hunt! By tonight, you boys will be men!"

"If the wind quits," George added.

"Yeah, great," Skeeter whispered. "And if we don't freeze to death on the way there."

It was a long drive. George and Frank liked to be in the woods by sun-up, and so they left at 4:00 to make sure they were in the parking area of the National Forest by 5:30. By 4:15 the engine was hot enough to warm the car and both boys were sound asleep in the backseat.

Edison was aware of a sudden and horrible change in climate as he slowly awoke. They had arrived. His dad and Skeeter's dad had left the car doors open while they got their gear out of the trunk. It was cold again. And now he'd have to get out of the car and go sit in the woods all day long.

"When does it get fun?" Edison whispered to Skeeter.

"Alright boys," Frank declared, "time to go get some deer!"

Edison and Skeeter climbed from the car.

"Hey," Edison said, "I think it has warmed up some."

"Yep," his dad agreed, "it was eighteen degrees when we left the house. It's gotta be at least twenty-three by now."

"At least," Frank agreed. "I may have to loosen my scarf."

Frank gave each of the boys a backpack. "Put these on. They have all our food and gear in them. Don't take them off and then forget them someplace in the woods."

Edison was too cold to talk. He just nodded and pulled the pack over his shoulders.

Frank set the pace. It was a long walk back to their chosen

hunting spot. And the first part was uphill. Edison and Skeeter soon lagged behind.

"Tell them to slow down," Skeet told Edison.

"No. I'm not allowed to complain."

"Me either."

"These bags are heavy."

"My feet are freezing."

"I think my fingers are going to break off."

"My nose hurts."

"You and me, pal."

"How long is this hill?"

"How you boys doing back there?" asked Edison's dad.

Edison waved. "Just fine. Just a little slow."

"Well, your legs are shorter. We'll take a breather."

The sky lightened just a little. It would be full light soon. "Now listen," Frank told the boys, "the wind has pretty much stopped. That's good 'cause the deer don't like to move in the wind because their primary sense to detect trouble is their sense of smell." Frank was getting into the subject. "And if the wind is blowing all around, they can't get a good reading on what's around them, so they bed down. But the wind stopped, so they'll be up and moving. And it's the first day of buck season, so there'll be a lot of guys in the woods and that'll stir the deer up, too. Make them do things they wouldn't normally do. Gives us a better chance." In his excitement Frank spoke rapidly. "And in the morning the thermals in the air begin to rise, and the deer rise with them, climbing higher up the mountains. That's why we are hiking up this mountain. In the afternoon, if we don't get anything this morning, we'll go down into the drainages…"

"Frank," George laughed, "calm down. We'll tell them all this as the day goes on. We don't gotta give it all to them now. Even if they both listen as hard as they can, they'll never retain everything you're saying."

Frank looked at Edison and Skeeter. Both boys were wide-eyed and shivering. "Right. Sorry. I get excited. George, you've had your boys hunt with you before. This is the first time I've had my kid with me. I'm excited. Let's head out."

Before long, Frank and George were ahead of the boys again. Edison asked Skeeter, "What was your dad talking about?"

"I don't know. He told me the same thing last night, and I didn't understand it then either.

Fifteen minutes later the sky had turned light grey, and the four hunters stopped at the top of a hill. Before them was a huge field of tall grass. The bowl-shaped field formed a natural amphitheater around the hunters. They would have a clear view of the whole field once the sun came up. To the right stood a long row of pine trees that bent around the field.

Edison's dad announced, "This is the place. We'll nestle into these trees and watch that big field there. We've taken a lot of deer out of that field."

Frank had three small folding stools with him. He handed one to each of the boys. "Find a place to sit where you can see the field. There's a big apple tree in the middle of it. We'll keep a sharp eye on that tree."

Frank found a spot, set up his stool, and kicked all the snow, leaves and sticks away from his general area. "You boys do the same. Save you from making noise or tripping when you stand up to shoot."

Edison and Skeeter followed suit.

"I have to pee," Edison groaned, hoping it wasn't a complaint.

"Me too," Skeet echoed.

"Me too," Edison's dad added. "Let's go over here."

"Hope it don't freeze off," Skeet said.

"These woods are mine now," Edison giggled.

When they were finished, George set up his own seat, and the four hunters sat.

They were facing east and could see the sky growing lighter and lighter, but the mountain in front of them kept the sun hidden until after eight. Edison hoped the rising sun would warm him up. He was freezing. He'd been sitting on the hard stool for over an hour. Needles shot through his sore feet if he moved them even a little, making him sure he was frostbitten. He was positive his nose would fall off if he touched it. He hunched farther over and shivered. He looked over at Skeeter. His friend suffered in the same condition. Skeet's scarf was pulled up over his mouth and nose, and a sheen of ice covered the scarf.

"Holy cow!" Edison thought. "His face is frozen! He's gonna die! Or at least lose his face. Should I say something? Would that be complaining?"

Edison steeled his nerves and whispered, "Dad. Skeet's face is frozen."

His dad looked at Skeeter, then at his son. He smiled and said, "So is yours. It's just frozen condensation."

Edison went back to his silent musings. "I wish a deer would come soon. I'll go nuts sitting here all day. This is worse than school. Worse than church. I'm freezing."

Just when he was sure he couldn't stand another moment Frank announced, "Time for a treat." He reached into the pack Skeeter was wearing and pulled out four Snickers bars. "They might be frozen, but they'll give your body plenty of energy to burn. That'll keep you warm."

Skeet sounded impressed. "You mean I get to eat a whole candy bar before nine o'clock?"

"Yep."

"Cool."

The candy bars were frozen solid. To eat them, the boys had to suck on them, and then gnaw off little chunks. It took Skeet half an hour to eat the candy bar. He was warm the whole time.

From then on Frank and George brought out some little thing or another to distract the boys whenever the time seemed right.

Just after 10:00 Frank stood up. "I think me and Skeet will walk into those pines, see if we can drive a deer out toward you. Come on, son."

About forty-five minutes later, Edison's dad suddenly pointed at the field. A buck leisurely crossed the field. Edison watched as his father raised his binoculars. The deer stopped and lifted its head.

Edison's heart pumped. His breath came hard. The buck stood in the field, broadside. His dad motioned Edison to stand and then handed him the Winchester lever action .30-.30 rifle. Edison sighted through the scope just as he'd been taught. With both eyes open he took a deep breath, let out half, and pulled the trigger. The .30-.30 usually kicked his shoulder pretty hard, but today he never felt a thing. The buck took four or five steps and dropped to the ground.

Edison's dad grabbed his shoulder and shook him in a way which let Edison know his father was proud. "Congratulations!"

"What do we do now?" Edison asked.

"We wait about twenty minutes. You want to make sure it's dead before you approach it. I'd say you hit it right in the boilermaker. Right in the heart and lungs."

Frank and Skeeter came up through the pines a few minutes later. They knew by the smile on Edison's face that he'd gotten a deer. "I thought I heard you guys shoot," Frank said. "You get him Edison? Or did your dad shoot?"

"I got him. All by myself."

Skeet grumbled sourly, "Big deal. People kill deer all the time. It doesn't make you special or anything."

"Skeet," Frank chided, "now be nice. Your friend got a deer. Let's celebrate each other's victories."

"Congratulations," Skeet said grudgingly.

After waiting the twenty minutes, all four hunters walked out across the snow to where the deer lay. "Wow," Edison exclaimed, "a four point."

"He's giant!" George's voice expressed appropriate awe.

Gutting the deer nearly made Edison sick. His father did the cutting, but insisted his son help roll the gut sac out of the deer. The inside of the deer smelled like hot, wet grass clippings and old, wet paper. Blood pooled inside the thorax and Frank had to tip the deer over to get all of it to flow out. It turned the snow a sickly, sticky red.

George reached into the deer's chest and pulled out the heart and lungs. He pointed at the heart. "See, look at that. You shot him clean through the heart."

Edison grinned.

"Lucky shot," Skeet mumbled.

"Edison," Rev. Janzen said while lashing the deer's front legs to its antlers, "you did good. Now we just gotta haul this thing out of here." Having secured the rope, he started dragging the deer back toward the car.

Edison watched his dad haul the carcass across the snow. It slid easily. Strapping the .30-.30 over his shoulder to wear back to the car, Edison realized he hadn't been cold since he pulled the trigger, but his feet were starting to ache again. Soon his toes were so cold he thought they might break off.

Skeet wore his dad's gun as well, but he held way back and wouldn't talk to his friend. Frank alternated between dragging the deer and keeping Skeeter moving fast enough.

Edison didn't care about Skeet being mad or jealous. He was too worried about his toe. He was pretty sure a toe had fallen off into his sock. A frozen, toe-sized object definitely floated around in his sock. But he'd just killed his first deer. He couldn't complain now, he'd just have to tough it out. He just hoped no more toes broke free. Edison had pretty much decided he could live with nine toes, if they could just get back to the car. "Heck," he thought. "It's frozen. Maybe the doctors could sew it back on." He considered stopping to take off his boot and look, but it would be too much to bear if the toe really had frozen off. Besides, his dad was working so hard, dragging that deer. Can't stop now, even for a toe, he decided resolutely.

Every few steps the frozen toe in his sock worked its way under his foot and he stepped on it, painfully. "What if I smashed it? What if I smashed my frozen toe?" He was just about to stop when a rifle sounded. Edison whirled around and there was Skeeter, rifle lowered at his shoulder, standing beside his dad and looking off into the woods. Edison sucked up his pain and headed back toward them. His dad stopped and called back, "You get one?"

"Yep," Skeet answered. "A nice one!"

Edison praised him. "Good job Skeet." He tried not to be jealous. He'd wanted to be the kid who got a deer. Be special. But now Skeet had gotten one, too.

They had twenty minutes to wait, so Edison finally spoke up. "Dad," he started sobbing, "I'm not complaining. But I think my toe broke off in my sock."

His father laughed a disbelieving but loving laugh. He wrapped his arm around Edison. "I doubt your toe fell off, but let's have a look."

Edison started to his pull off his boot. He remembered how the blood had poured out of the deer and just knew the blood would come out of his boot the same way—but it didn't. His father grabbed the end of the sock, ready to pull it off Edison's foot.

"Oh," his father chuckled, "I see." He pulled the sock off and handed it to Edison. The tip of his sock had bunched up in the front of his boot and frozen into a little ball. "It looks like a toe, and I bet it felt like a toe flopping around in your boot, but it's just a hunk of frozen sock."

Edison sighed, relieved. He put his sock and boot back on and waited to go see Skeet's deer. His friend stood beside him now, and the two of them talked about how they'd shot their deer.

Frank lit a cigarette and looked off into the woods. His son had shot a deer. Heck of thing. "Fellas," he said aloud, "someday all four of us will go do some real hunting. Some Out West hunting. Maybe we'll hunt bighorns in Colorado or black bear in Montana. Someday we'll all go do and that."

Finally, it was time to go check on Skeet's deer.

Skeet got there first. When Edison walked up behind him, Skeet said, "It's a six point. Yours is just a four point."

"So? Mine has a bigger body."

"Does not."

"Does too. Go look."

"I don't gotta look. I know. I can't wait to tell Charolais."

"I can't wait to tell her I got my deer first."

"I can't wait to tell her…"

"Boys!" George snapped. "Knock it off. They're both nice deer."

10

The four seasons didn't seem the same three months long. Summer was so slippery, so elusive. It came and went in a single breath. And so Edison and Skeeter never breathed during the summer. They sucked in a deep breath of air on the last day of school and held it until they passed out on Labor Day.

As far as Skeeter and Edison were concerned church during summer was just wrong, a colossal mistake. How could a good God want boys to be inside, listening to a sermon and singing, when they could be outside doing permanent damage to Creation by fishing, bothering wildlife, and peeing in creeks? It just didn't make sense.

Skeeter became a little more resigned to the whole idea of church when, one Sunday, Mrs. Fester and Charolais walked in the door. Mrs. Fester wore an old but well kept dress with dark and sturdy shoes, her hair done up in a bun. It looked to Edison as though she had a bruise on her cheek, under her make up. Mrs. Fester smiled and chatted with the other ladies while Charolais wandered over toward Skeeter.

"Hi Skeeter," she whispered, blushing.

"Hi Charolais. I ain't seen you since school let out."

"I ain't seen you neither," she rejoined.

"That sure is a pretty dress you got on."

"Thanks," she whispered to the floor.

Skeeter commenting on the girl's dress? This was just too much for Edison. He looked around for the rest of the Fester herd. He didn't reckon they were above pounding Skeet and Edison again, even if they were in a church. The extended Fester clan didn't seem to be coming and, since Skeet was so obviously preoccupied, Edison walked away.

Rev. Janzen was in his office going over his sermon. Edison climbed up on his dad's lap and the minister hugged him with one arm. "What's up buddy?" he asked, still reading his sermon.

"Nuthin'. Skeeter is talking to a girl. What are you doing?"

"Going over my sermon, making sure I have it down, like always."

"I thought God was just supposed to put the words into your mouth, like you could just get up there and WHAM! you knew what to say. That's how the Baptist preacher does it, a kid at school told me. He said that God must not be talking to you since you have to make your sermon up."

"That's what a kid at school told you, huh?"

"Yep. Is it true?"

"Nope. I guess I'm just lucky, or God knows I'm dumb. God tells me what to write down long before Sunday morning so I can make sure I say it right."

"Can't God just make you say it right?"

"I guess God could, and sometimes it does happen that way, but mostly I practice before hand."

"Because God might trick you?"

"No," Rev. Janzen laughed. "Because humans—people—just aren't perfect. God might tell me to say one thing, and I might get it all wrong when I open my mouth. If I write it down beforehand, then I can reread it a couple of times, to make sure I have it right."

"So if it's so important for you to get it right, how come you wait 'til Saturday night to start writing it down?"

His father laughed. "Okay pal, go find your mom, I gotta get this show on the road." Rev. Janzen kissed the top of his son's head and lifted him off his lap. Edison walked out of the office.

He found his mother sitting next to Skeeter's mom. Usually Skeet and Edison sat together in one of the front two pews. It was a Methodist church, so the adults occupied the pews in the back. The younger the parishioner, the closer to the front pew he or she sat. But today Skeet was sitting next to Charolais in the eighth pew back, the two of them holding hands between an old woman and Mrs. Fester. So Edison sat with his mother and brothers.

When church was over and Charolais finally left, Skeeter returned his attentions to Edison. Skeet returning to Edison was like a dog that, having been left at home alone by his people, scouted out a worn toy to keep him company until his family returned.

"Have fun with your new best pal?" Edison spat, as they stepped outside.

"Actually," Skeet said, squinting at the sun, "it was kind of boring. I think she actually listened to the sermon. She wasn't interested in passing notes, talking about fishing, or even throwing things. I don't know how long I can put up with that."

"You and me both, pal. At least I got to enjoy the company of our mothers. Let's change clothes and go fishing."

They jogged home, changed into shorts and T-shirts, met in Skeet's backyard, and then gathered their fishing gear. "It's been so hot and dry," Skeet remarked, "that I bet Skitter Creek is near dried up."

"Maybe, but there will still be water in our hole, and the way I figure it, the less water there is in the creek, the fewer places there are for the fish to hide."

"That's a good point."

When Skeet and Edison got to the creek, they laid down their rods and started scouting for worms and grubs. The day was hot and dry. The water shimmered like gasoline on concrete, and the ground was dust six inches down. The leaves blanketing the forest floor were as rough and unwelcoming as cheap, dirty carpet. The sandstone rocks glittered like disco balls and were warm to the touch. It seemed that all of nature had been accidentally left atop a burning woodstove. The whole place smelled like an attic in July, and a body would be hard pressed to find an earthworm in an attic in July. So the boys dug deep into the summer ground and the sandy soil came up in great wormless shovelfuls.

"Where do they go?" Skeet asked.

"Don't know, I guess the worms just keep going down and down," Edison answered.

"Reckon the whole center of the earth is just crawling with them?"

"That'd be kind of nasty, wouldn't it? All of the sudden you dig into a huge ball of worms, eighty feet down?"

They dug a little deeper.

Skeet asked, "How do you figure fish learned to eat worms? I mean, how did the first fish get the first worm? Fish live underwater and worms live underground. How do fish know that worms are good?"

"Gosh," Edison exclaimed, "I don't know. I mean, if the first time a fish saw a worm was on the end of a fishing line, why did he bite it? And if it was good, how could he have told anyone else?"

"Maybe," Skeet mused, "it's the same way with boys and girls. After the first two got together, well maybe everyone else was just curious about what the fuss was all about."

"Humph." Edison muttered. "You'd know."

"Shut up. I don't know nothin'."

"You know something about Charolais. She's a girl."

"I guess so. It's weird. I like her fine, but not like I like you."

They fell silent and continued digging for worms, three great mysteries hovering over their heads in the summer smell. Where do the worms go? Why do fish like worms? And why do boys like girls?

The boys found out that worms go deep. As to the other two questions, well, Skeet and Edison never did get a credible answer as to why fish like worms.

TWO

11

One day in early April 1981, Edison's mother sat him down and opened a book she had taken out of the library. It was full of illustrations and words describing the penis, the womb, menstruation, sperm, birth, and the works. Mrs. Janzen explained the birds and the bees. Edison was ten and bored. The pictures were neat though, if confusing. Mrs. Janzen ended the conversation by stating, "You were conceived," as if Edison might understand what she was talking about, "by a lake in upper Ohio on July 4, 1969."

When Mrs. Janzen said that, Edison about fell out of his chair. He was old enough to understand that pregnant women carried babies in their bellies and thus he understood that he was alive in July of 1969. That was a total, life altering, boon. It meant that he had, in fact, been present for what he considered history's most important moment.

"Mom," he began, looking at her earnestly from across the kitchen table. "Can I ask you a question?"

She smiled, "Yes honey. Anything you like." She gripped the library book, with the color illustrations of wombs and penises, placing a finger randomly inside the pages, eagerly awaiting the opportunity to turn to the proper page and answer her son's question.

"Did you watch the moon landing, the one with Neil Armstrong?" he asked.

She twitched as if a fly had flown down her throat. The book in her hands wilted to the table. She shook her head, squinted like she had a headache. "What?" she asked. "What does that have to do with reproduction?"

"I don't know," Edison answered. "But did you? Did you watch the moon landing?"

"Well, yes, everyone did," she stammered, confused.

She eyed Edison suspiciously. He was counting on his fingers. "Mom, can a baby see out of the womb?"

"No," she answered, still flustered. "Why?"

"How 'bout feel?" he pressed.

"I guess, maybe." She turned some pages in the book, looking for something, anything, to tie in with his line of questioning. "I suppose," she said, "that a baby experiences some of the emotions the mother feels. Like great stress—or joy."

"So," Edison continued, having just finished counting his fingers a second time, to make sure, "I was sixteen days old when the Eagle landed on the moon? On July 20, 1969?"

Edison's mother looked around the kitchen, hoping to find a string of evidence to connect his questions with her thorough explanation of reproduction. "Well," she finally said, "yes, I guess you had been conceived for sixteen days by then, why?"

"So, were you excited? About the moon landing?"

"Very," she said with a smile. "In fact, your father and I bought a color TV just so we could watch it. It was the first color TV we ever owned. We got it at Sears. We had been saving money for one ever since we got married and sort of waiting for a special occasion to get one. We decided that there was hardly a better reason than the moon landing to get a new TV.

"I remember," she continued, "that I was working at a hospital, at the arrivals desk, at the time. I was scheduled to work that day. Now, Edison, I try not to lie. But when I saw that schedule, and that I had to work, well, I knew I just couldn't work that day. We'd bought that TV, and me and your father and your brothers, we were going to pop popcorn and sit there and watch the moon landing, come heck or high water. I called in sick, told my boss I had the flu and couldn't make it in. Of course he didn't believe me, but what could he do? Anyway, it worked out pretty well because a few days later I found out that I was pregnant with you, so he figured I really had been sick. Your father, brothers, and I, and I guess you, sat on the couch in front of our new TV and watched those men walk on the moon. It was fantastic. I was so excited that I am sure you felt it."

"Cool," Edison said, sealing a plan away in his mind. He had already known the outline, now he had both the infrastructure and a way to shift blame to his mom if his plot was uncovered. He swore himself to secrecy. He wasn't even going to be able to tell this to Skeet.

12

On the morning of April 12, 1981, Edison stayed in bed even after his mom threatened to hurt him. It was a school day; just a week or so after the day Mrs. Janzen had tried to explain conception to him. He had to play this just right. His mother came into his room. "Honey," she said sharply, "it's time to get up for school." Edison lay still, clutching his stomach under the sheets.

"I don't feel good," he whined. "My stomach hurts."

She looked him over, felt his forehead, glared. Edison couldn't read her, didn't know if she would put it together. She smiled her Mom's smile. "Well, honey, just get up and go on to school. If you still feel bad later, have the nurse call me, and you can come home."

Edison suppressed a triumphant smile. She wasn't catching on. He had watched the first mission to the moon from his mother's womb, even before she knew she was with child. Today, they were launching the very first space shuttle. The Columbia would rocket into space. It was his generation's moon landing and he wasn't going to miss it.

Edison knew that his class at school was going to watch the launch. The whole school would assemble in the gym and watch the events unfold on the biggest TV the teachers could find. But this, he felt, was something to be seen in the comfort of your own home. His mother had said as much herself about the moon landing. She had called in sick so she could stay home. Was Edison doing any worse?

Edison got out of bed, dressed and made his way to the kitchen. He passed on breakfast, clutching his stomach. As he was leaving for school, his mother put her hand on his forehead. "Still no fever. You might feel better after you walk to school though." She kissed his cheek and he walked out the door.

Skeet was on his back porch waiting for Edison.

"Hey," Skeet shouted, "this is the big day! The Space Shuttle!"

Edison nodded, looked to see if his mom had heard. She hadn't.

"What's wrong?" Skeet asked.

"My stomach hurts. I don't feel good."

"Why you going to school then?"

"My mom said I had to, said if I started feeling bad I could come home."

Skeet was buying it, too.

"Well," Skeet said, "this is no day to feel bad. The Space Shuttle!"

The boys walked in silence. The April morning broke into a beautiful spring day. Halfdollar smelled like turned earth and wet leaves. Charolais joined them about halfway. She and Skeet sort of hugged awkwardly and then clasped hands. No kiss. "Good morning," she said to Edison. The three of them walked on.

"Edison doesn't feel good," Skeet said for Charolais' benefit.

"Oh. That's too bad. I know you boys are excited about the launch."

Edison nodded, then stole a glance at Skeet. Nothing to show he'd put it together.

As soon as he got to class, Edison told his teacher, Mrs. Lazonno, he wasn't feeling well. She touched his forehead, an expression of disbelief on her face. "You don't feel hot," she commented, as if fever were the only symptom of illness adults could accept.

"It's my stomach. My mom said that if I felt bad later, to call her at work, and maybe I could go home," Edison explained.

"We'll see. You don't want to miss the launch though," she answered, already shifting gears to get the class settled.

Edison slouched in his desk trying to look uncomfortable. Once he even rushed to the bathroom, holding his gut. He had to play it just right. He had to get sick enough quick enough so that he could get home in time to see the lift-off. At ten o'clock the teacher called him to her desk. She felt his forehead. No expression. She put her hand on his belly and he groaned a little. Couldn't over play it. She said, "OK, let's walk down to the office and call your mother. I hate that you are going to miss the launch. This is really an historic event."

Edison smiled inwardly, and then noticed that Skeet was watching him. In an instant Edison knew that Skeet had figured it out, and was jealous, but also that Skeet would never rat him out. Charolais winked at Edison. Nice to know who your friends are. He and the teacher walked slowly down the silent, cinderblock halls painted elementary school green, to the office. She asked the secretary for Mrs. Janzen's work number.

"Mrs. Janzen? This is Mrs. Lazonno. Edison is feeling under the weather."

A pause while she listened to the voice on the other end.

"OK, he said you had told him that he could walk home if it persisted. I just wanted to check with you, first."

Another pause.

"Yes, you too. Bye now."

Edison and his teacher walked back to class. He felt so good that he thought he might float. He struggled to keep the glee out of his eyes. He couldn't blow it now.

Back in class, Edison gathered his jacket and books and headed for the door. He stole a quick look at Skeeter who gave him a thumbs-up sign under his desk. Edison felt even better knowing that Skeet understood why he had had to do it this way.

Edison walked out of the school feeling like a flower opening to the sun. In fact, he had seldom felt better. He forced himself to walk slowly until he was out sight of the school. After all, he had about half an hour to get home. Plenty of time. He stared up at the sky as he walked.

The moon still hung pale white in the corner of the sky. Edison figured that the moon wanted to watch the lift-off, too. He figured the moon was lonely. All those years up there in the sky and so few visitors. Just a few men. And the moon, Edison thought, loved her visitors so much that she never sent a storm to wash away their footprints. The moon was a sentimental rock who always wanted to remember when her friends came to visit, a sad but resigned aunt who could only watch as her sister, so near, so beautiful, had child after child. And so few ever cared to visit, but those who came were so excited to be there with her, that she would never forget, never erase the signs of their visits. The moon left her nephews' toys out in the yard for the Universe to see they had come and played.

Earth, Edison figured, told the moon that she was crazy, that having people wasn't all it was cracked up to be.

The moon would be so excited to see the shuttle blast off, so disappointed when the shuttle turned short of her, remaining near Mother Earth, circling, so far away.

Edison got his house key from under the rock by the back door and let himself in. He took off his jacket and shoes and went straight to the refrigerator. He was starving. He considered making popcorn but only had a few minutes to spare and besides, his mom didn't like him using the stove when she wasn't home. Instead, he pulled the peanut butter and jelly out of the fridge and put together a sandwich worthy of a space launch. He carried it into the living room, turned on the TV, and sat down on the couch.

There it was, the huge Columbia shining in the sun, fastened to those three giant white tanks, like a moth strapped to bottle rockets. Thin streams of pure white smoke curled up from underneath the rockets, some trailing away into the blue sky, others wrapping themselves around the orange super structure Columbia was leaning against. Four minutes until launch. The reporters were talking about how historic this moment was for humankind, saying that the viewers were witnesses to the future, and that nobody should miss this monumental event.

Edison bit his sandwich, felt the cold jelly fill his mouth, the comfort of the couch, the coolness of the air in the room. And then he thought of Skeet and the rest of his class sitting on the hard floor of the gym. The gym floor was always gritty, and the room smelled like sweat, always with the hint of vomit. Edison knew that those kids were hot and uncomfortable. The worst part for his class was that since they were sixth graders they were the biggest kids, and thus would be seated behind everyone else, farthest away from the TV set, pushed back behind all those little kids who didn't care or understand what they were causing others to see from a distance.

T-minus one minute. The shuttle jumped on the orange housing as it started to come to life, great plumes of smoke billowing from beneath it like steam from a boiling pot. At thirty seconds to go, everything was sound and power. Ten seconds and the whole world shook. Florida quaked under the power. Flames. Beautiful, bright flames cascaded across the hot, dry ground. Suddenly, fire and smoke shrouded the shuttle. And then it rose from the cloud, pure and white, straight up and rolling slightly, pushing, pushing its way into the clear sky. As it rose it grew smaller, and the reporter on the TV explained that the fuel tanks were going to come off any second now.

"God, but it's beautiful," Edison muttered under his breath.

The two missile-shaped tanks dipped away from the shuttle, trailed smoke, lost momentum, and dropped. Their departure did not faze the shuttle; it just kept climbing, upside down, but ever upward. It grew smaller and smaller until only a dot and a trail of smoke remained shaking in the sky, far out in front of the chaser aircraft.

Edison leaned back into the couch and realized that his mouth was wide open, his eyes dry from not having dared to blink, and jelly was running down his arm from the sandwich crushed in his hand. He had heard and seen it up close, a few feet from the TV! Skeet was probably straining to hear what the reporter said. Edison would have to fill him in later.

"Sometimes," Edison thought, "it is good and right to lie."

13

In the seventh grade, Skeeter's and Edison's English teacher started talking about literature. Most of the students were, quite naturally, suspicious. The teacher passed out worn, paperback copies of a book called Whitefang, by a guy named Jack London, to each student. The students had one week to read the book.

"Well," Skeet said after class, "at least there is a picture of a big, mean looking dog on the cover."

"Yep," Edison agreed, "it can't be all that bad. And it looks like this guy wrote a story called To Build a Fire. Fire is always good."

"Reading though? Seems like a waste of time."

"Couldn't agree more."

On the way to school the next morning Skeet asked, "You read any of that book?"

Edison nodded, "A bit. You?"

"As much as I hate to admit it, I read the whole thing."

"Me too. Not bad. I wonder if that guy wrote anything else, beside that Fire thing?"

Skeet groaned. "It was a tricky play by the teacher, passing out a book that was so good. We'll have to watch her or she'll turn us into scholars."

That February, with deer season long since closed, and being sick of winter and looking hard for something to do until spring, Skeet and Edison walked into the Public Library.

"Holy cow! All these books! How will we know where to begin?" Skeet exclaimed.

"Shhhh!" replied the librarian. "What are you two looking for?"

"Mrs. Smathers? You quit at the elementary school?" Edison asked the librarian.

"Nope. I work here part time. Have for years. And I have my sawed off yard stick right beside me. Don't pee on anything. Now, what do you want?"

Edison said, "Something to read until the weather gets nice."

"You didn't bring those tiny fishing poles with you, did you?" asked Mrs. Smathers. This was a reference to an embarrassing, if understandable, incident that had occurred after the boys had heard there were microfiche at the library.

"No. No we didn't," Edison answered quietly.

"Hmm. Fiction or non-fiction?" she asked.

"Fiction," Skeet said, "we get enough non-fiction at school."

The librarian pointed the boys to the fiction stacks and said, "Why not start with the letter A and search till you find something."

Edison didn't get far. He found a book called The Monkey Wrench Gang, by Edward Abbey. It was thick, critics had said that it was funny, and Edison figured it would take a while to read it. Maybe he could stretch it out until April. Skeet made it to Tolkien before he settled on a book.

When they got to the checkout desk, they found Sheriff Hasbro talking to the librarian. "Good Lord!" Hasbro said. "I figured it was jist a rumor, but here you two are, in the lieberry. Lemme see what ya got."

Skeet and Edison handed him their books. Sheriff Hasbro looked at the covers and then said, "Holy God. Edison, this *Monkey Wrench Gang* is a dang'ris book fer you ta be readin'. I find out you try and do anything in this book, I'll come lookin'. You unner'stand."

"Yes, Sir," Edison whispered. "I didn't know it was dangerous."

"In the hands of the likes ah you two, this here book is a right out threat ta decent folk," the sheriff said, shaking his head. "But it's funny as hell."

Now that was a resoundingly positive critique. Edison could see that Skeet was jealous. Sheriff Hasbro was one mean son of a cuss, but both boys looked up to the guy.

Skeet asked, "What about my book?"

Hasbro said, "Not nearly so dangerous, but jist as good, maybe better."

Edison and Skeeter left the library, proud to have their reading materials endorsed by such a person as Sheriff Hasbro. Edison smiled and said, "Hasbro sorta suggested that we are threat to decent folks."

"Nice to know who you are," Skeet said.

"You know what my dad says about Hasbro?" Edison asked Skeet.

"I've heard yer dad say a lot things about Hasbro," Skeet answered.

"Well, just the other day Dad said, 'Say what you want to about Hasbro, but he's the sort of fella that don't mind if your dog pisses on his tomato plants.'"

Skeet laughed. "You know Charolais reads all the time?"

"I guess it makes sense, she's pretty smart."

"I kissed her, I mean for real."

"About time."

"You kissed anybody yet?"

"I ain't sayin."

"Why?"

"You'd laugh."

"Won't."

"Promise?"

"Yep."

"The other day, in a fit of madness, on both sides, I kissed Alicia Snitch."

Skeeter broke his promise. "Why her?"

"Well, she is pretty. We were talking, and she'd never kissed anybody, and neither had I, so we did," Edison defended himself. "But we aren't going out or anything."

"Good," Skeet said. And then, seeing the hurt in Edison's eyes, he added, "She is pretty."

"But there's no flame, you know what I mean?"

"Yep. I sure do."

14

One day Angus Jr., Charolais' oldest brother, went missing. People tended not to go missing from Halfdollar, so it was quite an exciting time. People left Halfdollar, but they seldom just up and went missing. The events leading up to Angus Jr.'s disappearance were the highest rated gossip item on the chatter circuit.

It seems that Angus Jr. had been making eyes at Easter Boggins. Easter was seventeen and came from the other side of the ridge, where the folks were generally regarded as lazy. Most folks who lived in town were poor but the town's folk worked hard and came by their poverty honestly, to hear the men at the diner tell. The folks on the other side of the ridge were "on the check." That is to say, they got a payment from the government every month. The men in the diner found that to be particularly unacceptable.

Long before Angus Jr. had disappeared, Edison had asked his dad why the town's people hated the people from the other side of the ridge and why folks didn't want the people from the ridge to get welfare.

Rev. Janzen had taken a deep breath before he answered. "The folks who live on the other side of the ridge are a racially mixed group. They are white, black and American Indian. Like in any society there are a few bad eggs, but most of them are nice enough. They've always been poor and marginalized by the white folks in town. They were brought to Halfdollar for labor, to work in the mines and coalfields. There were no schools for them before integration and no decent jobs offered, so there was really no way for them to get out of the circle of poverty created for them by the early settlers of Halfdollar. With the mechanization of coal mining and timber, well, the townsfolk totally discarded the folks on the ridge. About the only time the prominent white men of Halfdollar go over the ridge now is when they want a, well, a discrete mistress."

Easter Boggins was the illegitimate daughter of one of the rich guys in the diner. And she was stacked to high heaven, like the girls in the magazines Edison's brother kept under his mattress. Angus Jr. fell for her, and Easter fell back.

"I reckon," Charolais was now telling Skeet and Edison, "that Easter was looking for a better life than she had over the ridge. Had to be pretty bad if she was dating my brother. Angus Jr. treated her like Dad treats Mom.

"Anyway, what I heard was that one night Easter and Angus Jr. were parked in the alley off Main Street. I guess they were, you know," she blushed, "screwing around. I guess Easter told Hasbro that she was on top of Angus and then there was a knock on the car window. Easter was buck-naked, in the back seat of his car. Angus Jr. had his pants pulled down around his ankles. Easter said that Angus Jr. rolled down the window of the car and struck up a conversation with the two men who had knocked on the car window. Easter was frantically trying to dress but she couldn't find her clothes. Angus Jr. was striking up a deal with the two fellows at the car window for Easter. Easter figured she was in a real jam so she leapt out the car wearing only tennis shoes and a bra, and ran down the alley to Main Street.

"Sheriff Hasbro found Easter running along, wrapped her in a blanket, listened to the story, and then shot out after Angus Jr. He didn't catch him. And even if he had, he wouldn't have been able to do much. The two men were unidentifiable and so it was Easter's word against Angus Jr.'s. So nothing happened." Charolais shrugged, as if to say, "See what I live with? This crap doesn't happen at your houses."

"And then Angus Jr. came up missing," Charolais eventually continued. "He was seen leaving town after having told my brothers that he had some business to take care of over the ridge. His car was found down by the waterfalls on the river. Easter's panties were in the back seat, but then they would have been since she left them there the night Angus Jr. tried to pimp her."

Later—weeks late—the naked body of a young man was found in the coal on a barge headed down the Ohio River. The body was determined to be that of Angus Fester, Jr. He had a deep knife wound on the shaft of his penis, but he had apparently died from injuries sustained in a fall.

The cops figured out that the coal on the barge had come to the Ohio River from mines in Faybour County, West Virginia, and they further surmised that Angus Jr. had come with the coal. The working theory was that Angus Jr. had fallen onto the train from a height of about thirty feet, and had broken his back. The train had dumped its coal by the river, burying Angus' body. When the coal was shoveled onto the barge, the body surfaced.

Trains from the coalmines in Faybour County ran through Halfdollar, and then down by the falls on the Tygart River, near where Angus Jr.'s car was found. Not far from the falls there is a cliff, maybe thirty feet tall, below which the trains pass. A person could easily fall from the cliff and land on the coal cars as they passed beneath.

In the leaves above the cliff's edge the police found a hunting knife with Angus Jr.'s blood on it. There were no fingerprints on the knife, but it was common knowledge that the knife belonged to Angus Jr., and that he kept it in his car.

Sheriff Hasbro stopped by the Boggins' house every day for a week after the body was found, but he got the same answer each time. Easter had gone to live with her brother in Charleston and probably wouldn't be back.

"Nope," Sheriff Hasbro told Mrs. Boggins, "I don't reckon she'll be back. Glad to hear she's done got out'a this town. Rough place fer a pretty girl, the likes ah her."

"Yes, Sir. I do agree," said Mrs. Boggins.

On his last visit, as the sheriff was getting himself into his car, Mrs. Boggins said, "Sheriff? You reckon that was the craziest suicide you ever heard of? That boy cuttin' his pecker like that, an' then jumpin' onta that train?"

"Mrs. Boggins," Sheriff Hasbro said as he settled into the seat and started the engine, "I reckon if I cut my pecker with a huntin' knife like 'at, I'd jist as soon leap onto a train as try an' explain what the hell I was doin' with that knife on my pecker." And then he added, "You tell Easter, best if she stays with her brother awhile, ya hear?"

Mrs. Boggins smiled and nodded. "Sheriff?" she called.

He looked her way.

"Thank-you. You always been good, fair, to us folks on the Ridge. Ever'body here knows that when you dole out an ass whoopin', well, an ass whoopin' was called fer."

15

Helen Fester asked Rev. Janzen to do Angus Jr.'s funeral. Edison didn't go. Skeet asked his folks if he could go, but they told him he had better not. Rev. Janzen told the boys there had been nothing but a graveside service. "Mrs. Fester cried silent tears and shook her head throughout the service," Rev. Janzen said. "And," he told Skeet, "Mrs. Fester held Charolais in front of her, and Charolais merely kept her head down."

According to Edison's dad, Angus Sr. showed up late, lit a cigarette halfway through the service, and opened a beer directly following. He had a cooler in the back of his truck.

"You want one?" he had asked Rev. Janzen.

Rev. Janzen declined, invited Angus Sr. to church, and then walked Helen and Charolais to their car.

Charolais showed up at Skeeter's about dusk. Skeet, Charolais, and Edison sat on Skeet's back porch, silent for a long time. Charolais sat next to Skeeter in the swing, and Edison sat on the top step, leaning on the railing and facing them.

Charolais finally said, in a quiet voice, "I don't know what to feel. I was pretty glad when I thought he had just run away, but when I found out he was dead, well, I felt—feel—pretty guilty."

"It ain't yer fault," Skeet assured her.

"I know, but, still, he was my brother. Funny thing is, all I feel is guilt. Not loss, not sadness, certainly not happiness." She threw her hands in the air and then nestled into Skeet's shoulder. Muffled by Skeet's shoulder, Edison heard her say, "My poor mom. She feels bad, real bad. He was her first born. Even if he was a peckerweed, she loved him. I guess if I feel sad at all, it is for her."

Edison wanted to say, and he bet Skeet wanted to say, "Angus Jr. was a pile of crap six feet high. He broke my bones and my face. He treated you, your mother, and everyone else, especially Easter Boggins, like crap." Neither of the boys could find the voice to say it though.

Skeet did ask, "You think Easter did it?"

Charolais shrugged in the cool night air, brushed away a bug by her ear, and said, "I don't know. I don't guess I care if it was her. I seriously doubt he did it to himself. If he did what folks say he did to her, well, I guess, brother or not, he sort'a had somethin' comin.' See that though? I just don't feel nothin' for him."

"I reckon," Skeet said, "that maybe you'll figure out what you feel someday, sooner or later. Till then, I wouldn't worry about it."

"You don't have to worry about it," she said, a little less softly. "I don't mean nothin' against you and Edison, but you two live different than me and my cow-named brothers, and my mom and my drunk dad. You got, both of you got, two parents that love you to death, that hold down jobs, that work together, that don't scream all the time at each other. My dad hits my mom in the face, in the stomach, in front of us kids. He screws other women. Mom does all the work. Dad spends all our money and tells the boys 'Don't worry about doin' nothin'. Let the women take care of it. Whatever it is.' My poor mom has to live with all that everyday. Your brothers and sister and parents, they love each other, maybe they fight now and then, but they don't punch. All you two worry about is gettin' out of school, when you can go fishin', and if you'll have to eat salad at dinner."

"I do hate salad," Edison remarked. Then he stood up, flapped his hands at his sides, took a step toward Charolais, stopped, drew a breath, and walked to her. He leaned over and hugged her. He caught Skeet with the hug, too. The three of them held tight for a few seconds.

"Piss," Skeet said, "I wish there was something I could do. Anything."

"I know," Charolais answered. "I know either of you would do whatever I asked. I love you, Edison, like a brother." She pulled him tight to her, then let go.

"What about me?" Skeet asked.

"I've kissed you on the lips, hard. If I loved you like a brother, well, that would just be wrong."

Mrs. Barth came out the back door and said, "Charolais, why don't you come inside for a sec?"

Charolais kissed Skeet on the cheek, stood, put her arm around Mrs. Barth, and then the two of them went in the door.

"She's right," Skeet nodded his head. "We got it good. Just think about how many people we know whose folks don't get along or are divorced."

"Yep. You and me, pal," Edison agreed.

"Unfortunately," Skeet sighed, "you're all the brother I've got."

16

As the two boys grew into true adolescence, Charolais became a more and more permanent figure in Skeeter's, and thus in Edison's, life. Skeet and Charolais graduated from trading love notes in the hallway at school to trading kisses. They started holding hands all the time, and hugging, and saying long good-byes when they parted for any length of time. And Edison could see genuine warmth in their glances toward each other. Charolais hugged Edison too, often enough, and pecked his cheek like a close friend would, but Edison tried hard to keep his distance.

Charolais out ran both boys in the race to physical and emotional maturity, hands down. Her breasts were forming nicely and her hips slid out from her waist and down to her thighs almost overnight. Her face was reshaping itself into that of a woman's. Skeet and Edison had some body hair, and they were filling out here and there, but that was about it.

One night, in the midst of Charolais' beautiful transformation, Skeeter called Edison to inform him that he thought he had some chest hair sprouting, and that he had just bought the latest G.I. Joe action figure.

"Great!" Edison congratulated him, and then asked, "Your collection complete again, then?"

"Yep," Skeet said excitedly, "we'll have to take them out back and have a proper battle."

"How 'bout Saturday?"

"As long we're done by noon," was Skeet's answer. "My mom is going to take Charolais and me into Beckley to see a movie."

"What movie?" Edison asked.

"I don't know, maybe the new Harrison Ford flick, unless Charolais wants to see something with love and tears."

"Can I go?"

"No, man. It's a date."

"How 'bout if I ask Stephanie Ford to come, then it'll be a

double date? I've been looking for a reason to ask her out."

"Look," Skeet answer softly, "it's just gonna be me and her. Sorry."

"Oh," Edison said, and the added angrily, "Well, piss off then!" He slammed the phone down and whispered, "You and me pal," to himself. After sulking in his room for a few minutes, he went downstairs to find his brother Gerry. Home for a visit from college, Gerry was in the basement working on a fly rod. When Edison walked into the room the older brother asked, "What's up?"

"I think," Gerry smiled after Edison had filled him in on the Charolais/Skeeter situation, "that you are a little jealous."

"I am not. There are a lot of girls in this world besides Charolais. A lot of girls who aren't named for cows, I might add," Edison answered hotly.

"You're not jealous that Skeeter has her," Gerry explained. "You're jealous that she has Skeet."

Edison couldn't answer that so he shrugged and asked Gerry a question about fishing. He didn't care about the answer, but it diverted his thoughts from his own pettiness. A guy can't go around knowing that his big brother sees through him.

The next day, Edison caught Charolais alone in the hall at school as she was walking toward the auditorium, and asked, "What's it like not having an older sister?"

She stopped and looked up at Edison with her soft brown eyes, squinted, twisted her lips, and finally said, "I don't know. I mean, I don't know what it's like having a big sister, so I can't hardly say what it's like not having one."

"Well, do you care what your brothers think about you?"

They started off toward the auditorium.

Charolais frowned. "My brothers? The ones that beat you and Skeeter up because I talked to him in elementary school? You remember what Angus Jr. did, or they say he did, to Easter Boggin? Right?"

"I know them, but still? Would you go to them in pinch?"

She laughed sarcastically. "If I needed someone killed, maybe. The only person in my family I would ever go to is my mother."

"Okay. So she's like a big sister?"

"I guess, except that she's my mom. Why are you asking?" Charolais stopped at the auditorium door and turned to face Edison, her eyes warm.

"Well," Edison stammered, caught off guard, "I was talking to my brother about… Well, something important in my life, and he, Gerry, saw right through me." Edison looked away, blushing a little.

"What were you talking to him about?" She put her hand on Edison's shoulder.

He was stuck. "Nothing. A friend. A girl."

Charolais took his chin in her hand and gently made their eyes meet. She smiled and said softly, "I don't have much in my life, Edison. I'm named for a breed of cows. My dad is a pile of werewolf dung. My brothers are peckerweeds. I have my mother; I have you as a friend, and Skeeter as a boyfriend. I can see through you, too, just like Gerry. It's not hard; in fact it's been obvious since we were little kids. Then we were just pals, all three of us really, but we aren't little kids anymore. Now I have these perky little boobs, of which I am quite proud. These boobs," she paused, shook his chin. "Quit looking at them. These boobs, and everything that goes with them, want something different out of Skeeter now. We ain't done much, yet," here she blushed and paused. "Let me say this right. I'm not giving Skeeter anything you would be giving him, anyway. And I'm not taking anything from him that he would otherwise be giving you. You know I'm not trying to take him from you. I've had little enough my whole life to know better than to take something from someone else, if it means everybody gets hurt. And, he wouldn't be him if it wasn't for you. And I wouldn't be me if it wasn't for you. Look, we three grew up together. We're kind of like a tricycle. And I ain't saying you're a third wheel, either. What I mean to say is that each of us is what makes us who we are. You can't just take a wheel off a trike and call it a bike. You know what I mean? He's hurt, by the way, that you hung-up on him and haven't spoken to him since."

Edison smiled and coughed, covering up. "Can you see through Skeeter, too?"

Charolais returned the smile. "Like through a window."

"What's in there?" Edison asked, trying to make the whole thing a joke.

"Less than you'd think, but what's there is great guns."

They both laughed out loud; short, happy bursts of laughter which animated the emotions that had risen between them like gold from the silt in a forty-niner's pan.

"Yeah," Edison said, "that's what I always thought, too."

"Edison," she said seriously, "someday—soon I imagine—you'll meet a girl, a real girl. And not that Stephanie girl. She's kind of icky. You could do a lot better."

"I've found that I can't be all that choosey."

"You'll meet a girl—a good, non-icky girl—and she'll understand you and Skeet just like I do. If she doesn't, don't bother with her. I hope I get to meet her. It would be fun if there were four of us."

"What's that do to the tricycle analogy?"

"We'll rebuild the frame. But not for nothin' icky." She stood on her toes and kissed his cheek.

Edison nodded in agreement. Charolais turned to go into the auditorium. As the door was closing on her, he turned to walk away. Abruptly, he stopped in his tracks and spun around toward the swinging door. "You hope to get to meet her? Where are you going?"

But Charolais was gone.

17

That Friday Edison called Skeet. "Sorry about hanging up on you the other day. I was just pissed. Come over and the spend the night."

"Can't, got somethin' to do."

Edison stifled his irritation. This was, after all, an attempted apology. Skeet should come over and then they'd hangout and everything would be cool between them again. Edison asked, "What?"

"Um, some stuff with my family," lied Skeet.

Edison could tell Skeet was lying. It was a Friday. Skeeter had been too vague about what he had to do, and that made it even more pissy. If he really had something to do, he would have said something about it earlier in the day. Not that Edison had spoken to him during the day, but still. Skeet was obviously up to something, but it was something Skeet didn't want Edison to know about. It had to be Charolais. Maybe Skeet and Charolais had a secret plan. Except for the space shuttle incident back in the sixth grade, Skeet and Edison had always shared their plans. Had to be Charolais.

"Well, all right then. Don't come over." Edison was hot, but he didn't want to hang up again. "Have fun at your movie tomorrow."

"Thanks," Skeet said guiltily.

"Bye."

"Bye."

"Peckerweed," Edison muttered after he'd put the phone down. He went to his room to sulk. He knew that it had to have something to do with Charolais, but Skeeter wouldn't just come out and it say it, that was the real trouble.

Edison sat down at his desk and stared at a few books that were lying there. He wasn't just mad at Skeet, he knew. Stephanie Ford had turned him down when he'd finally gathered the courage to ask her out. The fact that Skeet was probably going to spend the evening with Charolais just made the Stephanie thing worse—even if she was sort of icky.

Edison looked at the books a little closer. MacDonald or Stark? He had to be careful with the John D. MacDonald stuff because his mother didn't like the covers. There was always a scantily clad girl on the cover, but that was generally about the most graphic thing in the book. And MacDonald's Travis McGee had a conscience. Edison didn't want innuendo and moral rationalization. He selected a well-read Richard Stark novel. Stark's Parker had no moral code and didn't mind shootin' as many folks as it took. Edison needed a little raw violence.

Around midnight he heard a girl's giggle. It had to be real. People don't giggle in Parker novels. Edison walked over and looked out his window. Through the hedges he could see Charolais' silhouette framed by the light coming out of Skeeter's window. He saw Skeet unhitch the screen, pull it through his window, and then help Charolais into his room. Skeet shut the window. Edison switched off his bedroom light and sunk into his chair.

How long had that window been his and Skeeter's escape? Their secret passage into the night. "Peckerweed," Edison muttered to himself. He had gotten his butt kicked for that girl, and he had gotten nothing for it but grief. She'd said she wasn't taking anything from him, but wasn't that window his and Skeeter's portal? She had no right. But he really did like her. Try as he might, he couldn't raise much bile.

And then he started thinking about what they might be doing in there.

Travis McGee would likely reason that it was none of his business. Parker wouldn't mind taking a look if he wasn't too into the job.

"Good thing I'm reading Parker tonight," Edison said to the walls.

He pulled the screen out his window, let himself fall softly to the ground, and crept over to Skeet's window. Peeking in, he could see Skeeter sitting on his bed, his shirt off. Charolais stepped into view. She sat down on the bed and they started kissing, hands fumbling over each others' bodies. Edison figured that Skeet had felt Charolais' boobs, through her shirt, at sometime in their long relationship, but he didn't know how far the two had gone. Not very far, to hear Charolais tell it. Skeet put a hand up the back of Charolais' T-shirt and she pulled away from him. Edison had, on a very few occasions, experienced the same reaction from a girl.

Charolais whispered something to Skeeter, and Skeeter shrugged, apparently at a loss for anything to say. Edison thought they looked like they were talking about something pretty serious, but he couldn't figure out what. They were making out. What serious subject could possibly come up? Then, Skeet and Charolais leaned toward each other, rested their foreheads together, smiled, and talked quietly. And then she sat up, grabbed the bottom of her shirt with both hands, and pulled it up over her head. She wasn't wearing a bra. Her breasts just stood there, her whole torso blushing. Skeet's mouth dropped open, his eyes bulged. Edison almost yelped.

Skeeter's hands rose from his waist and drifted in the air just inches from Charolais' tits. Skeet, Charolais and Edison were all staring at Charolais' breasts as if they might explode like a can of Pillsbury biscuits or turn into birds and fly away. She sat back down on the bed. Skeet's hands followed her down, but never made contact. Charolais' neck was bent, her chin almost resting on her sternum. Her eyes darted from her tits to Skeet's hands, suspended three inches out like orbiting satellites. Skeet was focused on the tits, his hands no longer under his control. He didn't know what to do. None of them did. Skeet kept looking slightly left, then slightly right. Edison was far enough away that he didn't need to shift his eyes. He could see everything perfectly. Had he died right then, he would have been happy.

And then Edison realized this was none of his business, no matter how cool it was. He took two steps away from the window. Then, overcome, he looked back just one more time at those tits. They were the first tits he'd ever seen outside of a magazine. Satisfied that he would never, ever, forget what they looked like, he turned and went back through the hedge.

Edison crawled back through his own window, put the screen back in place, then lay down on the bed, smiling. It turned out to be a happy night. Charolais hadn't been misleading him, he just hadn't understood. He'd known Charolais so long, been around her so much that, even when he saw Skeet and Charolais kissing, it hadn't occurred to Edison until tonight that she was a girl in the real sense of the word. It made her different in ways that he was only starting to understand. She wasn't just another friend of Skeeter's who Skeet sometimes kissed. They were really boyfriend and girlfriend. And if they didn't want him around all the time, well, that made some sense now. Someday, Edison sincerely hoped, he wouldn't want them around, either.

18

Edison and Skeeter were in their world history class. The teacher, Mr. Martini, looked suspicious when Skeet, an accomplished teacher baiter, raised his hand.

"Yes, Mr. Barth?"

"So," Skeet began, "You're saying that Albert Einstein never actually graduated from high school?"

"That's right," nodded Martini.

"And Thomas Edison went to a formal, regular school, for not more than a year?" Skeet asked.

"Yep."

"And the Wright brothers, they never graduated?"

"None of those guys did."

Skeet looked around the classroom, examining it as though appraising the value of the room. He said, "Hum, ain't that something."

Edison smiled at the idea.

"The thing is, Skeet," Mr. Martini said, "and you too, Edison, is that those guys all had a plan. They weren't lazy, and they were dedicated to seeing their ideas through."

"I have an idea I'd like to follow through," Edison said.

"Keep it to yourself," Martini warned, pointing.

After class Skeet said to Edison, "You remember in the sixth grade when they wanted to teach us about sex education and most of the parents went nuts?"

"Yeah," Edison said, moving toward his locker. He smiled, thinking about the space shuttle.

"You remember when half the town wanted the science books thrown out 'cause they taught evolution?"

"Yep," Edison kept moving toward his locker.

"Well, don't you think that it's funny that parents don't want us to hear about evolution because they think we will all go to Hell?"

Skeet was getting excited. "And some parents don't want us to hear the word vagina, or the girls to hear penis, because they reckon the next thing we'll do is try to get some, and so parents don't want us to hear about sexually transmitted diseases or birth control because the teachers have to say vagina and penis to describe those things, and so, we'd try to get some? And yet today, right out in the open, in front of God and everyone, Mr. Martini stands there and tells us that four of the most successful people in the world ever, all dropped out of school. Parents don't mind that sort of inflammatory, even explosive, information being thrown around the classroom, but try to tell us how to not get a disease that will rot our peckers off or how to not get a girl pregnant and watch out. It's unbelievable."

Edison couldn't help but agree. He nodded as he got his books out of his locker. "So, let's drop out. Invent something. Make a million."

"Nah," Skeet groaned, "Martini's right. We got no ideas, and we're sort of lazy. Plus, I guess it would be pretty obvious if we dropped out of school. I mean, we'd be home everyday. Our folks are sharp. They'd catch on. On the other hand, if a guy does it right, he can keep his folks from findin' out what he does with his girlfriend, whether teachers say vagina or not. Speakin' of such, who are you interested in these days?"

"There's so many," Edison said, "and so few who are interested back. You're lucky to have Charolais, not just because she's Charolais, but because you don't have to be worried about not having her, or wanting to approach her. I was thinking of asking Tiffany Marsh out, but I'd probably have a better chance of dropping out of school and discovering relativity."

"Relativity has already been discovered, and by a much more gifted guy than you," Skeet explained.

"So has Tiffany Marsh. I think she's seein' the quarterback from Middle Creek."

"Oh, that sucks. Guys should keep to their own schools, or at least counties."

"I feel the same. I did meet that girl at the mall the other day. We saw a movie, kissed a bit in the back of the theater, but I don't see that developing into anything. Besides, as we just stated, each to his or her own county."

"Ali Martini is hot, and nice."

"She's also Mr. Martini's daughter. I'm not sure I want to be in class with him if I'm involved with his daughter. Remember what he did to Gus Deever when he caught Deever with his hand on Claudia Martini's butt? Besides, he's sort of pro-jock and anti-dork. I'm pretty squarely in the dork division."

"Yeah. Good points."

"Small towns sort of limit the possibilities."

"There's always Alicia Snitch," Skeet offered.

"No, she's nice and I did kiss her that once, but we just don't get along well. She's always been sort of a goodie-goodie, ya know?"

Skeet nodded in agreement. "Well, look on the bright side. If we went to a bigger school, there'd be lots more girls who would be willing to reject you."

"Maybe I will drop out of school and reinvent myself. I'll discover a better, more handsome, irresistible me."

"See, now there's a plan. I'll drop out with you. Be your aid."

"First, we gotta go to English. I heard Hundfoos is substituting in the class today. No sense dropping out before that. Maybe he'll do us a favor and expel us. It'd be handy to get expelled through deer season."

Principal Hundfoos had started his career as an English teacher. He liked to sub a few times a year to "Stay in touch with the kids," as he was well known to say. He never followed a lesson plan. He just taught what he wanted, or could remember.

"Synonyms," Hundfoos was saying, "are words that share the same or similar meanings, like tizzy and tantrum. Antonyms are words with opposite meanings, like purify and taint."

Skeet raised his hand and said smugly, "And tizzy is an antonym of taint."

Charolais, who was sitting beside Skeet, whispered, "Don't!"

Mr. Hundfoos looked at Skeet awkwardly. "What in the world are you talking about, Mr. Barth?"

"Well," said Skeet, winking at Charolais, "I'll use them in a sentence. Let's say one guy is asking a second guy if a third guy is insane. The first guy might say, "'Tis he crazy?' And the second guy would answer, "No, he t'aint." Skeet smiled triumphantly as the class broke out in laughter.

Mr. Hundfoos balled up his fists as his face turned pink. "All right, Mr. Barth," he said quietly, "that'll be enough of that!" He cleared his throat. "Now then, a homonym is when two words are spelled or pronounced the same, but have different meanings."

Without raising his hand, Edison asked, "So are synonyms antonyms of homonyms?"

Mr. Hundfoos momentarily lost control of his cheek muscles. "Well," he said slowly, giving the matter some thought, "I guess so. I guess you could say that. Why do ask?"

"Um," Edison said, "I was just wondering."

"I don't get it," Mr. Hundfoss said, taking a step backward. "Where's the joke?"

"Honest," Edison said, "I was just asking. Trying to learn."

Hundfoos straightened his belt, tugged on his sweater, "I'm watching you, Janzen. There's something in that question that is supposed to foul me up, but I'm on to you."

The class began giggling.

"See!" he shouted. "I don't get it, but I bet it's dirty." Hundfoos was pointing at Edison, glaring.

Skeet asked, "What are some other synonyms?"

Caught off guard, Mr. Hundfoos jerked his head toward Skeeter. "Well," he said, pulling at his sweater, "I suppose but and yet are synonymous."

"I don't think so," replied Skeet.

"What?" asked Hundfoos. "Do you have a degree in English?"

"No," answered Skeet, "but I think yet suggests something positive, while but implies a negative."

"I think the two words are interchangeable, but if you're so sure, give me an example," said Hundfoos smugly.

Skeet leaned back in his chair while Hundfoos walked around the teacher's desk, opened the center drawer, found a bottle of antacids, and swallowed two. "Well?" he asked Skeet, "have you come up with an example where but and yet are not synonymous?"

Skeet said, "Not but, yet I'm thinking."

THREE

19

On the morning of Skeeter's sixteenth birthday there was a beat-up, green, Ford pickup truck parked in his drive way. Under the windshield wiper was a birthday card and a key. Just like that, Skeet and Edison were mobile. Their world had just expanded exponentially.

"Is that a vanity plate?" Edison asked, looking at the license plate.

"Nope. Dad said if I wanted one, I'd have to pay the $20 myself. Why?" Skeet looked at the plate, squinted. He read it aloud, "M zero R zero N. M zero R zero N. Oh, piss! It says M0R0N."

"More like a humility plate, if you ask me," Edison laughed.

Rev. Janzen wandered over, looked at the truck, and just shook his head. "That truck isn't a good idea. You boys get in that truck, you're going to be leaving Justifying grace standing by the side of the road."

Skeeter laughed. "It can ride in the back."

"Either way, you boys can kiss it good-bye."

"Why Justifying grace, Dad?" Edison asked. "What happened to Sanctifying grace?"

"I would suspect you boys," Rev. Janzen said, "ain't been sanctified since Charolais hit puberty. Mind you, it's not her fault. She may, despite your efforts young Mr. Barth, still be sanctified."

Skeet blushed.

"What's that got to do with me?" Edison asked.

"Don't pretend you haven't looked and thought, son." Rev. Janzen nodded his head slowly. "Well, had to happen sometime or another. It ain't the truck's fault."

Later that fall, Skeeter showed up at Edison's house at 3:30 in the morning wearing a grin so diabolical that Edison thought he ought better plead illness and stay in bed rather than hear his friend out, but he gave Skeeter a cup of coffee and listened to his plan instead. It was the day before buck season opened. Skeeter reached into a paper bag he had at his feet and said to Edison, "I've been up all night. Sewing." Edison wasn't used to Skeeter sewing, and did not know what to make of it.

"Aren't we going to go up the hunting camp today?"

"This is better than that." Skeeter pulled something long, brown, and furry out of the bag. He flipped the thing open and pulled it on his head. "By gosh," thought Edison, "that boy can sew." Skeet had sewn, and was now wearing, a mask, a perfect replica of an eight point buck's head.

"Don't worry," Skeet mumbled from inside the mask. "I made one for you, too."

Edison knew that there had to be more to the plan, so he put the mask on and waited. Finally, Skeet said, "I also took a mannequin I bought at Sullivan's, dressed him in hunter's orange, and tied him to the front of my truck. What I want to do is drive around town like it's people season! And we got one! We'll drive up to the checking station and check our human. Everybody will think it's funny."

It was funny, but not the sort of funny Edison wanted his dad to find out about. And it was the day before buck season, not actually buck season, so the chance of getting shot was slim. Furthermore, Skeeter promised that they would not go anywhere near the woods, nor would they, under any circumstances, get out of the truck.

To keep their fathers from finding out, the boys left the house before dawn. Edison didn't want to worry his mother or lie to her, so he left her a note explaining his whereabouts. The note read, "Out with the deer and the dummy." That way, she would know he was doing something pertaining to deer season and that he was with Skeeter.

"We have to wait until first light if we want anyone to see us," Skeet said. They drove up to the service road at the city park, the masks at their feet, and tried to sleep for a few hours. Usually the park was a safe place to hide. It did not open until sunrise, and, generally speaking, the police did not bother about the park much, especially if a fella parked way up the service road.

The pre-dawn air was bitter cold. Because the boys were low on cash, they hadn't put much gas in the truck and thus they couldn't run the engine and the heater. The wind was blowing, which normally wouldn't have mattered except that the passenger side window was frozen in the down position. Before long, there was frost on the windshield, frost on the dummy tied to the hood, and frost in their veins. "You've led us into some sick Robert Service ballad," Edison groaned. The only way to stay warm was to put on the deer masks.

Edison woke up to the sound of a car horn. Someone sat in a car facing the boys. The driver of the car had his bright lights on. In the early morning gray, Edison could just barely make out the silhouette of a police car. "Of all the days in the year," he muttered, "this would be the day the cops decided to check out the service road." The driver's side door of the car opened slowly and Sheriff Hasbro cautiously advanced toward Skeeter's truck, his flashlight drawn. Hasbro had as bewildered a look on his face as Edison had ever seen. He had good cause to look so confused. It is not everyday that he came across a pickup truck stopped in the park with a man tied to the hood and two figures staring out from the cab; two figures who looked remarkably like a couple of deer caught in headlights. Edison stuck his head out of the window and grunted like a full-fledged buck. Sheriff Hasbro jumped sky high.

Skeeter started the truck and pulled quickly around the police car and down the service road. Sheriff Hasbro had not asked a single question nor suggested, in any manner that the two could understand, that they were in trouble. He had not read them their rights, said "Freeze," or arrested them. Thus, the boys did not feel like they were "fleeing arrest." But, as they found out later that morning, Sheriff Hasbro saw things in a different light.

Edison turned the CB to the police channel. Sheriff Hasbro was saying, "Well Tom, I don't care if ya do think I'm crazy! There was two deer drivin' Skeeter Barth's pickup truck down the service road an', by God, I b'lieve they got Skeeter tied ta the hood!"

"We can only hope so," was the reply. The comment was not lost on the two deer impersonators.

"Well," continued the sheriff, "whoever it is, they're headed straight for Main Street. They won't get away."

Edison turned the CB off.

"The smartest thing to do when you are obviously caught,"

said Skeeter, "is to give up, count your loses, and head home. Unfortunately, doing the smartest thing is not our strong suit. And as long as we are driving down Main Street in deer costumes with a man tied to the hood, it is a pretty safe bet that this is not going to be the day we turn over new leaves."

Small towns have many quaint traits that make them special and endear them to folks, little traditions that can be counted on to make one feel at home, and one thing that be could counted on in Halfdollar, West Virginia, was that folks would be up and listening to their police scanners while drinking their morning coffee. As Skeeter and Edison came into town they saw throngs of people—most still in their robes and slippers—lining the street. Having heard the sheriff's conversation about the two deer driving the stolen pickup, the townsfolk turned out in droves to see the show. Edison commented drily, "You'd think H. G. Wells was landing a space ship at city hall."   Skeeter turned the CB back on.

Sheriff Hasbro was still on the radio trying to figure out the best way to stop the renegade deer. He was none too eager to pull over two heavily armed and obviously dangerous deer. Opting for the better part of valor, Sheriff Hasbro was not following the boys with lights flashing, but was rather discretely developing a plan. In fact, if they hadn't picked up his transmissions on the radio, Skeet and Edison wouldn't have known that he cared about them at all. Unprovoked and unimpeded, they drove through town at a safe speed with no thought of surrender, waving all the while.

And then over the CB they heard, "…better call Skeeter's dad, Animal Control, and the FBI…" The words sent a shudder through their bones. It had to mean one of two things. Either Edison's dog was an international terrorist and the sheriff was calling Mr. Barth to let him know that Animal Control had been authorized by the Feds to have the mutt "taken out," or Skeet and Edison were in a lot of trouble, and Deputy Tom was about to start calling their parents. "Our dads scare me a lot more than the FBI," Edison said. Skeet decided that it would be best to pull over and wait for the sheriff.

After he and Skeeter had received tickets for the crime of mayhem dressed as an eight point buck, causing a public spectacle, and creating a public nuisance, Edison remarked, "They say that true forgiveness only comes after absolute repentance, and that the sinner must promise to change his ways and never take any glory from the sinful action."

"Well," answered Skeeter, "then I say, from the bottom of my heart, that we may never be forgiven for our actions today."

They laughed all the way home.

20

According to Rev. Janzen, Skeet's truck not only hastened the boys away from Grace, but also redefined the means by which, and the geographic scope in which, they could cause mischief. "But it's more than that, too," Skeet explained to Edison one afternoon. "Charolais loves that truck, like nothing else. Man, she just likes to sit beside me up in the cab and ride and ride. We find dirt roads and just drive with the windows down. I know it sounds like a Springsteen song, but it's the truth. She gets something from it. And we're not out there just foolin' around, either."

Edison had seen it, the look on Charolais' face when she instructed Skeeter, "Find me a dirt road down by a river, and drive me into the sun." And away they went. Occasionally, Edison rode along on the long, long rides. Skeet would drive, Charolais would nestle in beside Skeet, and Edison would sometimes sit in the bed, but more often he would sit in the cab, over by the right-side door. Sometimes he'd rest his forearms on the windowsill, then his chin on his wrist. Edison could be on one side of the truck, looking out the window, drifting through his thoughts, and Skeet and Charolais could be six hundred miles away over by the steering wheel.

This trip though, Edison leaned back in the seat with his feet on the dashboard. None of them knew exactly where they were, except that they had headed north about noon, turned off all the major roads and were now bouncing slowly down a dirt road running alongside a river headed mostly west now. Skeet had a knack for finding roads that ran along waterways. Of course, it isn't all that hard in West Virginia to a find a road beside a waterway. The only places in the state flat enough to build roads are in the valleys, and there is flowing waters in most valleys. Edison figured they were somewhere in Webster, or maybe Pocahontas County. He was pretty sure they were in the Monongahela National Forest. Again though, on that side of the state, it was difficult not to be in a national forest. Maybe the river was the Williams, or the Elk, or the Gauley. It didn't matter. He knew Skeet would get them home.

Edison could see Charolais' reflection in the rearview mirror. Charolais was gone someplace down the road. She didn't know he was looking. Edison still didn't have a steady girl. But that's not why he was looking at her so intently. He was, despite his inhibitions, waxing philosophical. He was considering Charolais' beauty, not ogling. In fact, he was looking at her in the mirror because, that way, all he could see was her face and shoulders. And that way he wouldn't notice as much that her bikini top had slipped a little. Not much, but too much for Edison to feel good about looking, and too much for him to point it out without embarrassment to all parties concerned. He stuck with the mirror.

Charolais was beautiful. Everybody said so. And it was a raw, natural beauty of which only the most inimical could be jealous. She was pretty like a field of wild black-eyed Susans and Queen Anne's lace. She was like a splendid rock formation, or a stately oak. She could be viewed from any angle and never fail to impress the viewer. Charolais was even more beautiful because, like a tree, or a field, or a rock, there was nothing pretentious about her. She was radiant, and couldn't do any more about it than a sandstone formation can help but sparkle in the sun. "Funny," Edison thought as they drove down the dirt road, "that I think rock formation, or oak tree. But she's tiny. Everybody forgets that, if they ever knew in the first place."

He saw something else besides her beauty there, though. It was in her eyes, or at least at the corners of her eyes. Edison rarely saw it, but it was present right then. It crept in like some visible glaucoma, and then Charolais could only see what was in front of her. Only ahead. Edison wasn't sure if the look was the result of something that made her happy or sad. It was just some sort of elemental emotion; she could build whatever feeling she wanted out of it.

Charolais had her head on Skeet's shoulder; her bangs were fluttering in the wind from the open window, her hands on Skeet's leg. Golden dust filled the cab and danced around as they drove into the sun. Charolais suddenly looked into Edison's eyes in the mirror. Something had called her back. She smiled at him, "You tryin' to see my perky tits, Edison?"

"Actually, I'm looking in the mirror because I'm trying not to see them."

Charolais looked down, noticed that she was slightly more exposed than modesty allowed, blushed, fixed her top, and asked, "Why'nt you tell me?"

"'Cause I would have had to see it to mention it, and I didn't want you to think I was lookin."

She turned to Skeet. "Why didn't you say anything?"

"Me?" Skeet asked. "Oh, well, I was lookin'."

She punched him.

A little further down the road Charolais reached over and patted Edison's leg. She said to him, "Sometimes, when my mom is watching TV, or doing the dishes, she'll touch the bottom of her ring finger with the tip of her thumb, just to make sure her mother's diamond ring is still on her finger." She smiled at Edison across the cab of the truck and said, "That ring ain't worth much, but it does mean something special to her to have it nearby."

"Oh, sappy bullsh…," Skeeter started to say, laughing. Charolais punched him again.

21

After they dropped Charolais off, Skeeter and Edison drove a few more back roads. The night was clear and mild; the moon so bright that it cast shadows and made Edison squint when he looked right at it. "That is the brightest moon I've ever seen," he commented.

Skeet didn't answer. He seemed lost in thought and so Edison just sat watching the night move by the open window. Ten minutes later, Skeet asked, "You ever drink any beer?"

"Skeet, you've known me since I was five," Edison answered.

"Well, I mean ever? Once my dad gave me a sip from the can he was drinking. When I was about eight. It was awful." He screwed up his face in remembrance.

"I guess I've had a few sips that way, but I've never drank a whole can. I recall the stuff is a little bitter," Edison said.

"Yeah, that's what I recall, too. So why do folks drink it?" Skeet asked, mostly to himself.

"To get drunk, I guess."

"My dad says getting drunk is the best way he knows to feel like crap in the morning."

"That's what I hear."

"Angus sure likes it," Skeet said. "Not that that is much of an endorsement."

"Lot's of folks seem to like it."

Skeet took his eyes off the road and looked at Edison. He asked, "You talked yourself into it yet?"

Edison laughed. "Yep. But we can't tell Charolais. The way her dad is, I don't think she'd want us drinkin'. And where do we get any? I reckon either of our dads would miss it if we took it from them."

"I heard my dad telling my mom about some guy named Page Rex who lives up Lockbridge Holler. Dad told Mom that the guy is a bootlegger, a hijacker, a poacher, a pirate, and, if I recall correctly, an incorrigible rascal with a deep, dry sense of humor."

"Gosh, sounds like our kind of guy. A role model. Why hasn't anybody told us about him before?"

"Edison," Skeet reasoned, "if you knew there was a bootlegging, hijacking, poaching pirate living near here, would you tell us?"

"I see your point. But what does this Rex have to do with us and beer?"

"Dad says the guy will sell it to anyone with money."

"Hum," Edison mused. "That sounds interesting."

"If you want, we'll try and find his place."

"Why," Edison asked, "does it have to be if I want?"

"So I can blame you later—tell folks it was your idea."

"That's what I thought. You're driving. You decide."

"Okay, we'll do it."

Skeet turned up Lockbridge holler, his hands tight on the steering wheel. The two pals had left good sense back on the main road. Their two controlling emotions now were false bravado and trepidation. From the way Skeet drove, Edison figured trepidation was his prime motivator.

"This fella, Page Rex, sounds like he might be, I don't know, unhappy to see us pull up in the middle of night," Skeet finally said.

"Do you even know where his place is?"

"Dad said it was just beyond that new pottery place. On the left. He said that this Rex guy has a big, green, five-ton truck that he leaves at the end of his drive. I think he sells farm equipment—hay bailers—as a legitimate job." Skeet was scanning the road as he talked.

"A pottery place?" Edison asked, rhetorically, "Is it a studio? Does the guy make the pottery right there?"

"I guess so," Skeet answered. "Dad says the guy's name is Deal, but spells it crazy, like D-i-e-h-l, or something like that. Makes bowls and coffee cups and saucers."

"You can make a living doing that?"

"I can't imagine you can. That guy must have some serious gumption. But I guess somebody's gotta make pottery. Keep your eyes open for the big, green truck."

"There," Edison said, pointing to a big green moving van pulled up into the trees on the shoulder. "Still, you'd think," he continued, "that if an honest-to-God pirate lived up here, we would have heard about him by now. I'm a little disappointed you didn't tell me about this sooner. And you'd think that he would have something cooler than a moving van parked out front of his place."

"It just slipped my mind," Skeet said. "Sorry. Let's focus though. How are we going to do this? Just pull up the road and wait for this guy to come out? We don't even know how far up the road he lives. Could be a hundred yards, could be three miles."

"Could be ten miles, for all we know. Stop stalling and get going. Let's start by driving up, but be ready to drive back down this road in reverse. And fast!"

"Right."

"How much gas do we have?"

Skeeter looked between the steering wheel struts, grimaced, and said, "Let's just say it would be better if the place was a hundred yards up the road."

He drove slowly. Rex's road was long, rutted, and washed out. Skeet put the truck in four-wheel drive, maneuvering around exposed boulders and root systems. The woods closed in around them and the track sank deeper beneath the forest floor until Skeet was driving down a shoestring trace sunk three feet beneath the surrounding forest. The road continued deeper and deeper into the woods and inclined steadily. It curved and dipped in wild seizures as though the builder had consciously flaunted the contour of the land. The road zigzagged in the flat, open spaces, but shot straight up rises without thought of a cutback. The dips, Edison suspected, had been made by explosives employed to remove troublesome stumps and rocks, and to divert the course of waterways.

"This road," Skeet commented, his eyes focused on the track, "was clearly built with nothing but dynamite and erosion."

Edison stared straight down the roadway, too. "It's almost as if the road was built somewhere else and then brought here second hand. It just doesn't fit. Maybe he adopted it."

"Crap," Skeet muttered, "I sure hope we don't have to back down here fast, or slow even. There is no place to turn around. You know what Charolais would say if she knew we were doing this?"

"It is almost as if God is letting us know ahead of time what the wages for this particular sin are going to be. It is a narrow, hard road that we are embarking on, I'm guessing."

"Shut up, preacher boy."

The drive crested the mountain and opened into a small clearing. There was a wide, unkempt lawn. A trailer sat backed against the trees thirty yards from the mouth of the drive. The lights were on in the trailer. There were a number of sheds and a few rusting pieces of machinery strewn about the place. The headlights exposed an old fence built of rotting posts and sagging wires.

"What now?" Edison asked.

Skeet was already working on that. He drove through the lawn in a short half circle, pointing the front of the truck back down the drive.

"Good thinking," his pal complimented him.

"Every now and then, I do think good. The problem is that I only seem to do it when I am already knee deep and sinking in my own poor thinking."

"You and me, pal."

As Skeet completed his sentence, and as though it were a punctuation mark, a shotgun barrel slid into the driver's side window and pointed almost straight toward the metal roof of the cab. If it went off the blast would tear a gaping hole in the sheet metal of the cab, blind and deafen Skeeter and Edison, but otherwise do no harm. The pair sat back in their seats and watched the gun.

"Well?" came an old man's voice, sanded by years of tobacco use. The "Well" seemed to carry no malice. It was just a form of greeting. The shotgun, apparently, was intended to convey emotion. "Well?" the voice asked again, this time with impatience. The barrel of the gun danced around the cab of the truck.

"Um," Skeet started, his hands drifting upwards as though he were being robbed.

"'Um' don't cut it stranger!" The voice barked.

"Beer," Edison stammered. It was the best he could manage.

The shotgun barrel seemed to relax a little.

"What about it?" came the voice at the other end of the gun. The guy was tucked in behind Skeet's door, somehow out of view in the side mirror. The guy reminded Edison of a vampire crossed with a cautious cop.

"We'd like some," Skeet said.

"Who the hell wouldn't?" the voice barked.

"We understand," Skeet continued, leaning toward the driver's side door and looking out into the bright night, "that you might be in the business of selling beer."

"You understand wrong," came the voice, the gun barrel jerking.

"Look," Skeet said, "we obviously don't know how this works, but what if I just dropped, say, ten dollars out the window."

"Reckon I'd pick it up," said the voice.

"What if I dropped twenty?"

"Reckon I'd pick it up and walk away. Then you'd drive away. And when you were far from here you'd look in the back of your truck and the good Lord might jist have performed some sort of six-pack miracle in your cargo bed," the man said, flatly.

"A six-pack? For twenty dollars?" Skeet asked, incredulous.

"God ain't cheap when it comes to beer miracles," the voice assured them.

Skeet, to Edison's amazement, released the brake and the truck started forward, just rolling.

"Wait," said the shotgun, not distraught, "maybe it would be a twelve pack if you prayed real hard."

Skeet stopped the truck.

Edison asked out the window and into the night, "You any kin to Sullivan down to the flea market?"

The voice behind the gun chuckled and the gun slid out of the window. "Local boys, I see. Ol' Sullivan, now he drives a righteous bargain."

Skeet stuck a twenty out of the window. A hand clutched it. The boys heard footsteps moving away from the truck, a door open, then nothing for a minute or two. They heard the door open again, the footsteps drawing near, and then something heavy thumped into the bed of the truck. Without turning around to look Skeet put the truck in gear and headed carefully back down the trace.

Before they had gone more than twenty yards down the road

Skeet hit the brakes, threw the truck into reverse, and headed back into the shotgun's yard.

"What are you doing?" Edison almost shouted.

"Cigarettes. I figure we might as well go all the way. I bet that guy has a spare pack or two."

This time there was no shotgun, just an impatient voice drifting from the darkness. A deal was struck, money fell out of the truck window, and a pack of Pall Malls arced up through the window. And again, Skeeter and Edison started down the peculiar road.

"That guy," Edison said, "is sort of creepy."

"How do you know? We never saw him."

Edison was tearing the cellophane wrapper off of the smokes. "That's what was so creepy," he answered, fiddling with the package of cigarettes until he had torn most of the foil off of the top of the pack, dropped three cigarettes on the floor, and crushed another. "Do you know how to smoke?"

"I don't know if there is a 'know how' about it. I've watched my dad do it all my life. You put the cigarette in you mouth, light it, and breathe," Skeet instructed.

Edison put a cigarette into his mouth. "Do we have any sort of light?"

"Are we Edison and Skeeter?" Skeet answered, reaching over and flipping open the glove box. Inside the box were layers upon layers of matches, fire starters, lighters, and fire works.

"It's nice to know who you are."

"You and me, brother."

Edison struck a match and held it to the tip of the cigarette. Nothing much happened, except that the match burned down to his finger. "Ouch," he said, tossing the match out the window.

"What?" Skeet asked.

"Well, nothin' happened, except that I burnt my finger."

"Is it lit?"

"My finger? No, it's just burnt."

"Peckerweed. The cigarette."

"I don't have any idea," Edison answered, taking the cigarette from his mouth and turning it so that he could see the tip.

"Is it smoking?"

"No."

"Well, then it ain't lit."

"Hum," Edison said.

"I think," Skeet said, "that you have to suck on it as you light it, to get it burning."

Edison tried it again, this time inhaling hard. Smoke stormed into his lungs, searing his throat as it went. He gagged and dropped the cigarette on the floorboard as his head filled up like a balloon and he floated there in the passenger compartment for a moment before drifting back down to the seat. He coughed violently and his head still wasn't on as tight as it had been, but he was regaining his composure. He heard Skeet yelling, "Pick up the cigarette off the floor!" Edison cast his eyes down to the floor. He saw a red ember burning between his shoes. "There must be three packs of fireworks down there!" Skeet yelled. Edison reached frantically for the cigarette, coughing all the way, and waiting for the firecrackers to start blowing his toes off. His eyes wouldn't focus. He grabbed the wayward cigarette at last, looked at it carefully, and then took another drag.

"Pretty good," he croaked to Skeet, "but maybe you shouldn't smoke while you are driving."

"From where I'm sittin'," Skeet commented, "it didn't look good."

"It is both debilitating and wonderful all at the same time." Edison paused to take another drag, "but the second hit, though less violent, was not as remarkable the first, and the third even less exciting.

"So," he asked, "where do we go to drink it?"

Skeet thought, and then said, "It's late, and not too cold. We'll go behind your garage. That way we won't have to drive and if any of our folks happen to wake up and wonder where we are, well, they'll see my truck in the drive and figure we're at the other guy's house."

"Good enough," Edison agreed.

They drove through the quiet streets of Halfdollar. Edison had decided to wait before he smoked anymore. The sheriff knew Skeet's truck, and both boys thought it would be risky to drive through town with the glowing tips of cigarettes burning in the cab. "Be sort of a dead give away," Edison commented, "if he saw us with burning cigs in our hands."

"Let's not call them cigs. Let's stick with cigarettes. 'Cigs' just sounds goofy."

Skeeter pulled into his driveway as quietly as possible. There were no lights on in either house. As Edison got out of the truck he grabbed a box of wooden matches from the glove box and the pack of Pall Malls. Skeet walked around the back of the truck and retrieved the beer. "Black Label." he said. "Isn't there a whiskey called Black Label?"

"I think so," Edison answered. "So this must be good beer."

"You know what we should do? We should slip in and get a tent and some sleeping bags. We'll set up the tent and then we can smoke and drink all we want, and then fall asleep out here," Skeet suggested.

"If we build a fire, we can blame any cigarette smell on the fire."

"What if we wake up someone when we go in the house?"

"Maybe we should. I'll go tell my folks that we're sleepin' out here. That'll keep them from coming out to see where we are."

"And save any questions in the morning like, 'Why didn't you tell us where you were?'" Skeet grinned. "You finally came up with a good plan, ol' buddy. By gosh, I believe smokin' has made you smarter."

Both boys let themselves into their houses, gathered their gear, spoke to their folks, and were back in under ten minutes.

"My mom said, 'Oh, that'll be fun.'" Skeet said.

"My dad said, 'Don't do anything stupid,'" Edison laughed. "Who does he think we are?"

It took another fifteen minutes to get the tent set up and the fire going.

"I always knew that being a Boy Scout would pay off someday. We got camp set up fast."

Edison gave Skeet a cigarette as they found seats around the fire. Edison watched as Skeet lit it, gagged, floated, coughed, and then sucked again. "You're right," he said, "that is weird. Maybe somebody smoking for the first time coined the phrase 'awfully good.'" He coughed, and both boys laughed.

Edison lit up. He raised his eyebrows in appreciation of the sensation. "Not bad, when you get right down to it."

"Okay," Skeeter said, "let's do the beer."

They pulled two of the red cans out of the box and cracked them open. "To you and me, pal," Skeet toasted. They sipped cautiously.

After the effects of his first drag on a cigarette, Edison was a bit trepidatious about how the beer would hit him. The first sip went down easy enough, so he took a long pull. "Hum," he mused, "not at all like a cigarette."

"Except," replied Skeet, "that it tastes like lukewarm pee."

"Yeah, that's true. It might be better cold."

"I heard that Europeans drink it warm."

"Maybe that's why the Pilgrims came over here."

When they'd finished their first beers Skeeter belched. "Well, I'm not sure I feel any different. I don't guess I'm drunk, anyway."

"My tongue hurts," Edison said, "but I think that's from the smokes, not the beer." He belched.

"Well, there's something."

They chuckled, and then Skeeter belched again. "Ten to go," he announced.

"And," Edison tried to look into the pack of cigarettes, "I'd say this pack is still more than half full."

"See that, smoking has not only made you smarter, but you've become an optimist as well."

They started on their second beers and lit more cigarettes.

"What are we going to do with these cans?" Skeet asked. "We can't burn them, can we?"

"Maybe we can recycle them, build duck houses with the money."

"For what?"

"Ducks, of course."

"No, moron, why build duck houses?"

"I don't know, just a thought. Ducks need houses. We need a project to do, to complete our Eagle Scout stuff. So, let's build duck houses."

Halfway through the third beer Skeet said, "Boy, I gotta pee."

"Me, too."

Somewhere during their fourth beers the boys quietly fell asleep beside the fire. Edison woke suddenly, cold and soaked with dew.

The sun's early work could be seen off to the east. The fire had long since died away. Shifting his head a little he saw beer cans, cigarette butts, and Skeeter, strewn about the backyard. Edison's head was rock hard, his neck stiff, his bladder swollen, his tongue fat, his mouth filled with ash, and his eyes sore.

He poked Skeeter.

"Are we dead?" moaned Skeet.

"Can't tell. It could just be cancer."

"Well, we're gonna be dead if we don't get this stuff cleaned up, and us into our houses without getting caught."

"What time is it?"

"About six, I think."

"Then we'll just clean up, but we don't gotta go in 'cause we got this tent and these nice warm sleeping bags to sleep in. Too bad we didn't think of that last night."

"Indeed," Skeet affirmed.

Moving with care, the boys peed, collected the cans, pulled a few logs from the firewood stack and hid the rest of the beer and the empty cans behind the pile, buried the cigarette butts, and crawled into the tent.

Edison didn't see Skeet again until late that afternoon.

"What happen to you?" he asked when they saw each other.

"I woke up about eight, crawled into the house, took a shower, and then I took a nap."

"Still bleary?"

"Yep."

"Let's just forget beer for a while."

"My stomach, which feels like a rotten grapefruit, agrees," said Skeeter. "Cigarettes, too."

"Why do people do that to themselves?"

"Got me."

"You reckon we learned an important lesson?"

"I doubt it."

"We gotta get those cans from behind the wood pile. What'll we do with the ones that're still full?"

"Throw them out. Maybe shoot them. Or hang on to them, hide them, in case we need them later."

"You know, if we treated anybody else like we treated ourselves last night they'd put us in jail for abuse."

22

Edison's jealousy of Charolais was like a cicada, coming up only after long periods of dormancy to chirp for a brief interval, and leave nothing behind but an empty shell that was easily crushed and carried off by the evening breeze. He wasn't threatened by Charolais anymore, but Halfdollar could be a dull place. And harboring a sterile seed of jealousy gave him something to do for which he could be neither arrested nor beaten. In that sense, it was one of his more constructive hobbies. Charolais' iron tenacity and her unflinching devotion to the idea that all wrong needed to be righted finally tore even that empty shred of resentment away. Charolais was Halfdollar's own little Mother Theresa with, as she would gladly add, looks that would give St. Paul a thorn somewhere other than his side.

The threesome were walking home from school one day, cutting through a few backyards that they didn't normally trespass through, when they saw a dog tied to a tree. It lay on the ground, its ribs showing through its skin. The dog's coat was matted and greasy with no sheen. Charolais walked over to the mistreated beast and stretched out her open hand.

"Watch it Charolais," Skeet warned, "that dog is mean."

Charolais rested her hand on the dog's head. The dog sighed as she rubbed gently. The dog, a female, rolled over, whining happily. "This dog is sick. Look at her. Her eyes are all filled with pus, and the water bowl is empty. Not just dry, but dusty. I'm going to find this dog some food and water."

She marched across the yard toward the house, water bowl in hand.

"Charolais, what are you doing?" Skeet asked, more than a little nervous.

She just kept on going. She started banging the water bowl on the backdoor of the house. It made a hollow metal sound. The door opened and a big, fat guy filled the frame. He had at least two-hundred pounds on Charolais.

She straightened her shoulders, looked the guy in the face and said calmly, "You're mistreating that dog. Fill this bowl with water and get me something to give her to eat."

"Who the f…" he started.

"I don't want a discussion about it," she demanded, slapping her little foot down on the packed dirt of the backyard. She thrust the bowl into the guy's belly. He was totally perplexed. If it was Edison or Skeeter poking him with the bowl the guy would have known what to do. He would have told them to bug off or even hit them, but he couldn't hit this tiny figure before him. The guy took the bowl and turned into the house. Charolais stood at the open door tapping her foot. The guy came back carrying the bowl of water carefully in both hands. He handed it to her and then pulled a stick of beef jerky from his pocket.

Charolais sighed heavily. "Oh for Heaven's sake you peckerweed. That dog is starving. What do you think one piece of jerky is gonna to do?" She put the water bowl down and pushed past the guy, right into his house.

"Charolais!" Skeet and Edison yelled her name at the same time. Edison was laughing when he said it. The boys raced forward, left the fat guy in his dirty shirt standing in the doorway. The guy just couldn't get his head around all of this. Three kids bursting into his house.

Skeet and Edison heard Charolais before they saw her. The boys turned toward the noise. She was in the kitchen. The kitchen smelled rancid. Dishes sat in the sink, unwashed and shrouded in bugs. The fridge was open. Charolais was skinning a loaf of liverwurst, an open can of SPAM sat on the counter beside her. She pulled a plate from a pile of molding kitchen items in the sink and swore under her breath. Edison couldn't tell exactly what she'd said, but she'd meant it. She turned on the hot water and while she waited for it to get hot, she rummaged around the kitchen until she found a bottle of dish soap. She washed the plate until it sparkled. Only then did she put the liverwurst and SPAM on it.

"Get that water bowl," Charolais ordered Skeet. She turned without another word and left the house. Edison and Skeeter followed her dumbly.

The fat guy just stood in his doorway, way out of his depth.

Edison knew this had to be a crime of some sort, but it was fun. Charolais was hell on wheels. Ninety-eight pounds of pure Panzer tank.

"What's the dog's name?" Charolais asked the guy, without turning around.

"Huh?" the guy said.

"The NAME of the dog, you moron."

"Sloppy," the guy said.

"Sloppy?" Charolais turned toward the guy. The dog looked up, sick. What kind of half brained name is that for a dog? Do you know what that does to her self-esteem?"

"Self-esteem? She's a dog. What does she care?" the guy asked.

Charolais was furious. She turned back to the dog, put the plate of food down and said to Skeet, who was standing with the water in his hands, "Well? Put the water down!" Then she marched over to the guy.

Sloppy, still laying down, ate the SPAM in two bites, the liverwurst in three. She started in on the water and drank the whole bowl down, without stopping to breathe.

Charolais stopped right in front of the big guy, who was trying hard to get some dignity flowing through his bones. He had very little to work with. Charolais kicked him in the shin before he could do anything. The guy hopped up onto foot and spun around.

"You little brat!" he screamed.

Sloppy jumped to her feet. Now she was alive and vicious, straining at her rope and showing her teeth.

The guy got his shin back in order and adjusted his full weight on both feet, towering over Charolais. She never flinched, never looked around. She said to Skeet and Edison, "Let the dog off her rope."

Skeet stuttered, looked at the dog, and complained, "Charolais, this isn't our dog. You're attacking her master. She'll tear us to pieces."

Charolais was cold, quiet, slow, and direct. "Let. The. Dog. Off. The. Rope. Now."

Skeet shrugged, mustered his courage and stepped toward

Sloppy. The fat guy was drawing an arm back over his head, his hand open. Skeet grabbed the dog's rope. He was having trouble because of the tension the dog was putting on the knot in the rope. The fat guy was glaring down at Charolais.

"You brazen little runt," he said, waving his open hand above his head, "coming into my yard and telling me how to raise my own dog." The guy tightened his face, drew his hand back a little further, made his open hand rigid and said, "Get out of my yard."

Charolais just stood there.

Skeet pulled out his pocketknife, opened the blade, and cut the rope holding Sloppy.

Sloppy took two bounds, flew into the air, brushed Charolais' shoulder, and caught the fat guy's forearm as it was descending toward her rescuer. The guy spun around under the weight of the dog and the momentum of the strike. There was a sharp crack. The dog let go and sat down next to Charolais. She patted Sloppy's head. The fat guy was holding his obese arm, blood running onto the dirt. His arm was obviously broken, and he was crying.

"I'm taking this dog," Charolais informed him.

The guy was crying like a kid. "You can't take my dog. She's mine," he sobbed.

"You mistreated this dog and therefore you are a peckerweed, and peckerweeds don't get a say."

The guy was really crying now, not from the pain in his arm. "But what if someone took your dog?"

"If I was mistreating my dog, well, than I would be a peckerweed, and it wouldn't matter." Charolais answered.

"I'll call the cops."

Charolais looked him straight in his ugly eyes and said, "My name is Charolais Fester. Trust me, Sheriff Hasbro knows right where I live."

The guy choked back a sob. He started to say something, thought it over, started again, then just lay down, holding his arm and crying.

Charolais turned to the dog, "Come on Ruth."

She and the dog left the yard, followed closely by Edison and Skeeter.

Edison said, "Holy Crap. That was cool! But I been thinking about it, and I just don't think peckerweed is a word, is it? I mean, we use it often enough, but is it a word?"

"It's like peckerwood, only less hard," Charolais said. "I made it up a long time ago."

The foursome walked a few hundred yards and then Skeet asked, "Did you call that dog Ruth?"

"Yep."

"Isn't her name Sloppy?"

"It was."

"How do you know," Edison asked, "that she wants to be called Ruth?"

Charolais stopped and turned toward Edison. "She doesn't want to be called Ruth, she is Ruth."

"What?" Skeet asked.

Charolais looked at the dog and said, "Sloppy, lie down." The dog just stood in place. Charolais then said, without changing her tone, "Ruth, lie down." The dog lay down.

"I don't get it," Skeet said.

"Me neither," Edison added.

The dog looked at the boys without emotion.

Charolais explained, "It's Biblical."

"Like a prophecy?" Skeet asked.

"No, you complete dolt," Charolais answered hotly. "Don't you listen to your best friend's father when he preaches? This dog is Ruth. My people are now her people."

"Which people? Me and Skeet? Or your dad and brothers?"

"Jeez," Charolais snorted. "I wouldn't rescue a dog just to have her become a Fester."

"Well, it is nice to know who you are," Skeet affirmed.

Edison agreed with Skeeter about not understanding the name, but he wasn't going to risk getting on the wrong side of Charolais. He stood watching his friends and the dog. In a sudden flash he knew more about friendship and loyalty than he'd ever known before. He took the sterile seed of jealousy he had been harboring toward Charolais and tossed it into the wind. And then he started looking for a new, mildly distracting hobby.

23

Skeeter and Edison had left beer alone after their first experience, but Angus Sr. loved his beer and always bought it at the little market cattycorner from Skeeter's house. As luck would have it, the window in Skeeter's attic opened onto a perfect, unobstructed view of the market's front door. Even without a scope the two pals could hit a soup can with a BB gun from 40 yards, and a soup can is just about the same size as a beer can. The parking lot of the store where Angus bought his beer was only thirty yards away.

The boys, after first noticing that Angus Sr. showed up at the market every evening (on the days that he wasn't in jail or in the hospital) between 7:20 and 7:35, set up a stake-out in the attic window. "Here's what we know," Skeet said, reviewing the notes he and Edison had scratched on a pad, "every evening, like clockwork, Angus Sr. drives his beat up pickup into the parking lot, parks, goes in, buys a six pack, carries it outside, lays it on the hood of his truck, and then walks over to the bench on the far side of the lot where the old men sit and smoke. Angus puts in a chew, folds his arms, and chats a bit."

"I say we do it tonight. We know all we need to. And we might not get another chance for a long time. Tonight's six-pack could be the six-pack that lands Angus back in jail," Edison replied.

So there they were, peeking out the attic window, watching Angus Sr. pull into the parking lot right on schedule. They watched him go in, come out, and lay a six-pack on the hood of his truck. "Now he'll go talk to the old guys," Edison whispered.

Skeeter slid the BB gun out the window as carefully as a sniper. He drew a bead on the six-pack sitting on Angus' hood. There was the fump of the air gun going off, and then, a few seconds later, the tink of a brass BB impacting a full aluminum can. A beautiful stream of pure white foam arced out from a can and splashed onto the sidewalk with a distinct whizzing sound.

Skeet handed Edison the gun. Edison aimed at the six pack. Fump. Tink. Whizzzzzz.

"It ain't deer hunting, but it'll do for now." He handed the gun back to Skeeter.

"And, it rhymes with deer hunting," Skeet chuckled.

Angus Sr. had placed his six-pack, almost surely unintentionally, so that the boys had a clear line of sight to three of the cans and then a side view of a forth can. Two cans were already leaking, and two were hidden behind the other four. That left two cans to be shot. The first can was an easy one since most of the can was visible. The second can left was the one that was partially hidden by the other cans. Skeet opted for the skill shot. "Fourth can, side shot," he announced. He drew a deep breath and then let out half of it. Fump. Tink. No whiz. The boys waited a moment, ears alert. "Well, I must have just winged it."

"Yep. I heard it hit. Hand me the gun."

Just as Skeeter handed the gun to Edison, Angus Sr. started saying his good-byes to the old fellas at the bench and walking toward his truck. "Too bad," Edison whispered, pulling the rifle back in the window. Angus walked around the front of his pickup and paused to look at the beer on the sidewalk, and on the hood of his truck. He picked up the six-pack and could obviously feel that it was about 24 fluid ounces light. Angus jiggled the six-pack, a perplexed look on his face. He pursed his lips, scowled, and lifted the cans to his ear. He shook them. He must have heard the BBs rolling around inside the cans because he scowled again. He was holding the defective six-pack right beside his ear. He gave the cans a mighty shake, listening closely.

Sometimes the world is a perfect place. Angus Sr. had no love for the law and Sheriff Hasbro had no love for Angus Sr. Angus had spent more than a few belligerent nights in the county jail for various offences involving beer. Now, Angus was standing beside his truck, facing the street, and while he was shaking the six-pack next to his ear Skeeter and Edison saw Sheriff Hasbro come around the corner of Main Street in his cruiser and then pull into the parking lot of the store.

Suddenly the can Skeeter had winged burst open. Apparently the BB had jammed into the side of the can. Vigorous shaking had caused the pressure in the can to build and the BB was the weak spot. A stream of foam shot straight out of the can and into Angus' ear. The beer quickly soaked his over-alls and shirt. He spat out a few quick obscenities (Angus' ability to swear was about his only redeeming quality) and then he deftly aimed the stream of beer away from his ear and into his mouth. Just then he must have spotted Sheriff Hasbro because he quickly dropped the six-pack to his waist and spun away from the street.

Sheriff Hasbro, the boys had learned from experience, had a cop's keen eye for picking up sudden movements. Hasbro was used to people frantically trying to hide themselves or their actions at the very sight of his police cruiser. When Sheriff Hasbro saw Angus lower his arm and spin around he must have figured that he ought to investigate.

Angus, his back to the street, had both hands down around his mid section and was looking over his shoulder, a panicked expression creasing his face.

Later, Sheriff Hasbro would tell folks that he thought to himself, "Naw. Couldn't be. I mean the guy has no class a'tall, but in the parkin' lot? At 7:30? Takin' a leak?"

It was a cool evening and a breeze blew from the direction of parking lot, across the street and up into Skeeter's attic. Carried on the breeze was a clear whizzing sound emanating from Angus, and the smell of cheap beer. Growing around Angus' feet, and running in frothy streamers down the gentle slope of the parking lot, was a puddle of fizzy, yellowish liquid.

The sun was setting at an angle that suited Skeeter and Edison. It lit the front window of the store so that they saw a perfect reflection of Angus' front side. Angus was looking over his shoulder at Sheriff Hasbro, almost crying. All the while the boys could see him was unzipping his cover-alls and trying to shove the six pack inside.

Sheriff Hasbro got out of his car and approached Angus slowly, a hand on his nightstick. "Angus," Sheriff Hasbro said slowly but loudly, "what the Sam Hill're you doin'?"

"Nothin' Sheriff, honest." Angus' panic caused his voice to rise.

"You ain't been drinkin' beer?"

"No, Sir, honest."

"You smell like beer. You realize that public ur'nation is a crime, right?"

"Sir?" Angus sounded utterly shocked at that accusation.

"Angus, turn 'round."

The stream of beer ceased to splash onto the sidewalk. Angus fiddled with his zipper. He lifted his left foot and jiggled his leg. He turned around slowly. A dark, wet stain emerged from his belt line, and grew steadily down both thighs. Angus smiled awkwardly. "Is there a problem officer?"

A crowd had gathered and Angus did his best to act like there wasn't a leaky six-pack in his pants, and his best to pretend that he didn't know that it looked like he had wet himself. The crowd was snickering and Angus was turning bright red.

"Okay, look," he said, as he undid his zipper. There was a gasp from the crowd as Angus started to pull out the six-pack.

"Now, jist you take it easy there," Sheriff Hasbro yelled.

Angus made it clear that he was pulling out the six-pack, and nothing else. He redid his cover-alls. Angus held the six-pack above his head as an explanation. He shook it gently so that everyone could hear the rattling sound. He pointed out the holes in the cans to Sheriff Hasbro. The sheriff looked at the holes and rubbed his chin thoughtfully. Angus put the cans back on the hood of his truck just as they had been when he had first put them down. Skeeter and Edison heard the words BB and Trajectory as they ducked beneath the windowsill. They lay perfectly still. The temperature in the attic doubled, then started to triple. Everyone knew where Skeeter lived, especially the sheriff and Angus.

Careful not to reveal their position, the boys lay on the unfinished floor of the attic, tears of laughter washing down their cheeks. The sheriff's words drifted up to them, "Why don't we let's walk 'cross the street and visit young Skeeter Barth an' see jist what he's up ta this evenin'?"

Footsteps grew louder as the crowd crossed the street and started up Skeet's sidewalk. There was a thumping on the front door so loud the boys heard it both through the house and through the window. They didn't dare look up or move, and with the window open they had to struggle to keep from laughing aloud. Their stifled mirth seemed to shake the whole house.

"He can knock all evening," Skeet managed to whisper. "We're the only ones home and I'll be derned if I'm going to open the front door!"

This made them laugh all the harder.

They let the sheriff knock and knock, and with each thumping of his fat fist on the front door the boys convulsed ever more with laughter. They could hear Angus yelling all sorts of curses, threats, and demands, but the sheriff kept his cool. The sheriff, knowing that Skeeter and Edison weren't coming to the door, said, "Well, I'll catch 'em sooner er later at somethin', and when I do, well, I'll jist be twice as mean."

Later that evening Charolais showed up at Skeeter's house. "My dad can get himself into trouble without you boys tryin' to help him!"

"What'd we do?" Skeet asked, smiling.

She was angry, but she was laughing, too. "I know he's a peckerweed, but just leave him be!"

24

Bow hunting for deer was not one of Edison's favorite things to do, but Skeet loved it, so Edison went along. Just after noon Edison tripped on a log and dropped his bow. "Crap," he said, picking it up.

"Break it?"

"Yep. Not too much though. I just tore the rubber thing that holds my sight straight. So, now I can't aim too well."

"You couldn't aim well when you had the sight. Now you'll never hit a thing."

"Piss off peckerweed. I'm going to knock off. Go back to the camp."

"I'll go with you, maybe eat some lunch."

After lunch Skeet lay down for a nap and Edison went to get a fresh pair of socks from the back of his dad's Bronco. He set his bow on the hood of the Bronco and took his quick release off his wrist. He opened the back of the truck, grabbed some socks out of a bag, and sat on the bumper of the truck to unlace his boots. Movement caught his eye off to the left. He looked up and saw a black bear coming down over the ridge. They'd hunted out here for nearly a decade and had seen very few bear, and those were way back in the woods, never near the parking area. Because bear season ran concurrent with bow season Edison, Skeeter and their fathers always bought bear tags, but they never seriously hunted bear.

Now a bear was walking not thirty yards from Edison. He tied his boot up quickly and then stepped to the front of the Bronco and picked up his bow. The bear hadn't noticed him. Edison knocked an arrow and drew the bow back. It was then that he remembered the broken sight. Shooting a bear with a bow was a tricky thing. Bear are tough beasts. Edison realized he didn't want to do this alone. Better to have backup. He moved as quietly as possible to the tent were Skeet was sleeping and said, "Skeet! Bear!"

Skeeter came out of the tent in a flash. He grabbed his bow

and followed after Edison. The bear had stopped by the creek at the bottom of the hill. Edison pointed it out to Skeet, and then drew his bow back. Without the sight it was tricky aiming the bow. Edison didn't know how the Indians did it. He looked down the shaft of the arrow and aimed the tip one foot above and just behind the bear's front shoulder. That would compensate for the arrows arcing flight. Then he realized he wasn't wearing his quick release. How did the Indians do it?

He let go of the arrow. The arrow soared toward the bear and hit right where Edison had aimed. One foot above and just behind the bears shoulder. The arrow hadn't dropped like he had hoped. "Shine-olla," he hissed. The bear heard the arrow thunk into a tree beside him and, startled, jogged off into the deeper woods.

"What now?" Skeeter asked.

"Let's follow him. See if we can get another shot."

"He's gone."

"No, he's not. He's right there. Looks like he's headed for those apple trees."

Skeet scanned the woods and sure enough, there was the bear. It was lumbering along as though it didn't have a care in the world. The boys followed a parallel course, staying as low and as quiet as possible. They watched the bear climb an apple tree and then sprawl lazily in the branches.

"He's eating apples. He couldn't care less that we're here," Skeet whispered. "Is this a good idea? Shooting a bear with a bow from forty yards away? I mean, we're on the ground. We should be up in a tree stand or something."

"No. It's not a good idea, but when will we ever have the chance to do it again?"

Skeet smirked. "Now that is pure logic. Even though it's a dangerous and a bad idea we should do it because we might not have the chance to do it again?"

"Exactly."

"Sounds good to me."

"It's good to know who you are."

The bear lay in a tree at least forty yards away and was mostly obscured by the apple tree it was lounging in. Edison drew back. He looked at Skeet and said, "Cover me." Skeet knocked an arrow and drew on the bear. Edison's shot went way wide. And then Skeet let loose a shot. It hit the bear square in the shoulder. The bear dropped out of the tree.

"What the hell?" Edison said to Skeet, dropping his bow. Anger seized him. Edison punched Skeeter right in his victorious smile. "That was my bear!" Edison shouted.

Skeeter dropped his bow and swung back at Edison, hitting him hard on the jaw. They locked arms and fell to the gound exchanging punches. "You said, 'Cover me.'" Skeet managed to say while swinging.

"Cover me," Edison grunted, blocking a blow, "not 'steal my bear.'"

And then they remembered the bear. The wounded bear was forty yards from them and thrashing around in the brush. The boys pushed off each other and stood quickly. They scanned the woods through teary eyes. No bear. Skeet hunched over. Edison squatted.

"What'a we do?" Skeet asked, wiping blood from his nose and trying to be sensible, since there was wounded bear very near.

"Wait and see what it does. Just like with a deer."

"Why'd you punch me?"

"It was my bear."

"I thought you wanted cover."

"I did!" Edison said angrily. "But you shouldn't have taken that shot."

"How 'bout we finish this later? Right now we should save our strength in case we have to fight that bear," Skeet said sharply.

"Oh, we'll finish it later alright."

Frank was coming down the path toward them. "What's going here? You two have a fight?"

Both boys looked sheepish. Skeeter's nose had stopped bleeding but there was crust of blood on his upper lip. Edison took a deep breath and said, "We shot a bear," and then he started to explain.

"Wait! Where's the bear?" Frank asked.

"Over by that apple tree. He's been down about five minutes. We were going to give him time to die."

"Good idea. While we're waiting, tell me about it."

Edison did.

"Well," Frank said, not wanting to look like he was taking Skeet's side just because Skeet was his son. "Well, we've always hunted as team, right? I mean, we help each other out, and we share each other's victories. Right?"

"Yes," Edison said, "but I was going to shoot again."

"Then you should have shot. Instead of punching me," Skeet blurted.

The urge to hit Skeeter seized Edison again, but he held himself back. "Okay," he said, "I shouldn't have hit you. Sorry."

"And I shouldn't have shot. Sorry."

Both boys were quiet, surly.

"Now, let's give it another ten or so minutes and then go look for that bear," Frank said.

The bear was gone. They found Skeet's arrow at the base of the tree. It had a little bit of blood and fur on the tip, but nothing on the shaft.

"Looks like you hit the shoulder and the arrow bounced out. Bears have thick skin and tough bones. Hard to kill one from that distance with a bow."

"Bad shot," Edison said, a note of satisfaction in his voice.

"At least I hit it," Skeet retorted.

"Boys," Frank said sternly, "that is enough. Cut that crap out. We have a bear to find. Start looking for a blood trail."

Skeet and Edison started looking for blood in different directions.

"Here's a drop," Edison said. "Not much at all."

"Look," Skeet yelled, "quit riding me about my bad shot. Okay, I barely hit him. I accept that, but get off it!"

"I wasn't riding you. I'm just saying that the amount of blood is small. Just a drop," Edison said as civilly as he could.

Frank came over and looked. "Sure enough, that's just a drop. You hardly hit him. Just poked him, really."

They tracked the bear up a small hill and across the road, where it appeared to have headed up the bank and toward the ridge line. They fanned out and headed up the ridge, looking for blood or signs of the bear's passing.

"There's nothing here," Skeet said. "I just didn't hit him hard enough."

"Well," Edison said as earnestly as he could, "it was a nice shot."

Edison's dad emerged from the other side of the ridge, dragging a deer. "Holy cow," he said when he saw his three partners. "A big black bear just went running by me at about a hundred miles an hour. I was dragging this deer and didn't have a chance at it. You should of seen that thing go!"

"Well," Frank said, "I guess that settles it. That bear ain't hurt too bad."

By time Edison finished telling the story to his dad, the adrenalin was out of his system and he was feeling ashamed.

He looked at Skeeter and said, "Sorry. I acted like a moron."

"Same by me. I should have asked about the shot."

"Alright then. If we say any more about it folks'll think we're gay."

On the way home Frank said, "Some day fellas, some day we'll go hunt bear in Montana. Only I don't want no fist fights."

"Right now," Skeet chuckled, "that bear is sitting in his den telling his friends, 'So there I was up in an apple tree, and then these guys reached out and poked me! Hurt so bad I fell out of the tree.'"

FOUR

25

Ron Green moved to Halfdollar with his family three days before Edison's junior year began. At dinner that night Rev. Janzen said, "The new funeral director moved in. Nice guy. Randall Green. He's got a kid about your age, a boy, name's Ron, I think. His wife is Justinia. I invited them to dinner next Monday."

"He bought Benton's Funeral home?" Mrs. Janzen asked.

"Well, a company bought it, some big tri-state funeral home franchise. They buy up funeral homes, leave them with the old name and hope nobody notices," Rev. Janzen explained.

"That company obviously doesn't understand Halfdollar," Edison added.

"Yeah," said Chris, who was home from college for the weekend, "I'm pretty sure that folks here will notice a funeral home that has been owned by the same family for a hundred years is no longer family owned."

"Considering that the Greens are black, I think that you are more right than you imagine, Chris," his dad answered.

"Black?" Edison asked

"Yep," Rev. Janzen said. "I hate to admit it, but I think the Greens will have trouble here. Maybe not, probably not violence, but certainly business-wise. Benton buried a lot of the families in this area, but I doubt those families'll want to be buried by a black man. Old stereotypes are going to surface."

Strange as it may seem, there was not one single black family in Halfdollar prior to the Greens moving into town, except over on the other side of the ridge.

"I don't get it," Chris said. "This town isn't racist."

"This town," Rev. Janzen pointed out, "isn't racist against blacks because no blacks live here. But it is racist against the folks on the ridge, and over the hill. In fact, Benton wouldn't bury the ridge people because 'towns folk' didn't want to lie dead on the same table as the 'ridge people. This town is plenty racist."

"So," Edison asked, "where do the people who live on the ridge go for funerals?" He had never thought about it before.

"The families either drive into Beckley or down to Bluefield. It costs a fortune for them," Rev. Janzen answered.

Edison's Mom wiped her mouth and said, "Maybe Mr. Green can get their business. I mean, there's just as many people dying on the other side of the mountain as there is on this side. Gosh, it would even be a public service. Those people are all so poor. Mr. Green could bury them for a lot less cost and inconvenience." She looked at her husband. "George, you tell Mr. Green that not only is he and his family welcome for dinner anytime, but that you will personally provide pastoral services to anyone who needs it at his funeral home."

"Honey," Rev. Janzen chuckled, "I already told him."

"And you tell him our church will pay for anyone who can't afford a proper funeral," she ordered.

"Already done." And then he added, "It's times like these that it would be useful to die. I mean, I could really make a statement about racism if I died right now and you took my body to Green's to be buried. Folks would say, 'Well, the preacher got buried by him. Reckon I can, too.' I bet Randall Green would appreciate that sort of effort to make him feel welcome."

"George," Mrs. Janzen said, smiling, "I'm sure quite a few people in town would appreciate it if you died, no matter who buried you."

When Edison told Skeet about the Greens, Skeet said, "I'm not sure I like black people."

"I'm not sure you ever knew a black person. Not many in our community."

"I don't know, it's just something inside me."

"You're a moron. You know better than that. You got no reason to be prejudiced. If you prejudged people do you think you would have ever started dating Charolais? I mean, based on her family?"

"Not really a fair question. I've known her since we were kids, since before we knew how to prejudge."

"Good point. Anyway, just give them a chance. We'll treat this new kid like everybody else. Give him equal chance to prove if he's a peckerweed based solely on his actions and personality, not on race, creed or religion."

"Fair enough."

Skeet and Edison met Ron Green a few days after he moved in. Ron was standing beside his car, on the shoulder of Route 60, about three miles out of town. His car was up on a jack, the rear left tire removed, the spare leaning on the fender. Three Fester boys were grouped around Ron, their pickup pulled up close in front of Ron's car. Ron Green had a tire iron in his right hand, ready to go. Skeet u-turned and pulled up behind Ron's car.

"What are you doing?" Edison asked.

"Going to help that guy."

"Why? You told me you didn't particularly care for blacks."

"And you said I should give folks a chance. Plus, it looks like we might get to fight the Festers."

"You enjoy fighting your girlfriends family?"

"Yep. Plus, I haven't been in a fight since I whipped you after I shot that bear."

"Whipped me? Other way around pal. And you poked that bear. You didn't shoot it."

Skeeter pulled the truck to side of the road.

As Edison and Skeeter walked up to the group, Ron said, "Two more racist rednecks? Never mind to me, I'll kick the crap out of all five of you. One at a time or all together. You choose."

Edison believed it. Ron wasn't big—maybe 5'11—but he looked quick and fit, the tire iron grasped firmly in his hand and bouncing off his thigh.

"Nope," Edison said, "just one undecided racist, and me. I don't prejudge. It just looks like you are about to fight these three Fester boys and, if you don't mind, my buddy Skeet and I would like to help you."

"Don't need no help," Ron growled.

"I reckon that's so," Skeet agreed, "but still, it'd be nice if you let us get a few licks in. Except for their sister and their mother, the whole bunch of them ain't worth nothin'."

"You leave my sister and momma out of it," Malvi Fester said. "We done taught you a lesson once about messin' with our sister."

Skeet sighed. "Yeah, in elementary school. And though the three of you are probably still in elementary school, Edison and I are now juniors in high school. And I have been dating your sister ever since you taught me that so-called lesson."

"Well, we ain't here to fight you, Skeeter. We're here to fight this boy."

"All the same," Edison said, "we'd like to fight against you Festers, if no one has any objections." Edison looked at Ron Green.

"Suit yourself. My name's Ron. We can shake hands and make nice in a minute."

"Deal. I'm Edison."

Malvi Fester, trying hard to follow the exchange, finally said, "Edison? You and Skeet nigger lovers, too?"

"Too?" Skeet asked. "That means 'also,' Malvi. It's an inclusive statement. Do you mean to suggest by your question that you love niggers as well?"

"What? Shut-up Skeeter. You geek," Malvi said.

"Geek? Oh my, now that hurts."

Malvi was tired of the game. He swung a huge fist toward Skeet's head. Ron swung the tire iron up from his thigh and crashed it into Malvi's ribs. Malvi expelled a great burst of dry air and fell face first onto the road. Jersey and Beefalo looked at their brother and then dove at Ron, Edison and Skeet. All five were trading punches good and hard when a siren shouted twice. All the fighters stopped and looked over at the sheriff's car, idling in the road. Sheriff Hasbro looked out his car window and said, "The hell you five," he glanced down and saw Malvi sprawled on the shoulder, "six, doing?"

"Sheriff," Jersey started, "we was…"

"Shut up, Fester," Hasbro commanded. "Get yer brother and get the hell out'a here."

Jersey and Beefalo didn't wait to be told again. They threw their brother into the bed of their truck and took off.

Sheriff Hasbro smiled at Ron and said, "You mus' be Ron Green."

"Yes, Sir," Ron answered. "I know this don't look good…"

"Forget it, Ron. Jist don't judge the whole town by them maggots. And, by God, don't judge the whole town by the two dipstick troublemakers standing beside ya, neither." Hasbro smiled at Edison and Skeeter. Ron laughed.

"I didn't need it," Ron said to Hasbro, "but they saved my life."

"Yeah, well, they have their uses. You boys get 'at tire fixed and get back ta town 'fore the Fester's marshal their troops."

"Thanks Sheriff," Edison said.

"All in a days work."

"Sheriff?" Skeet began, "you going to do anything about this?"

"Not ta y'all. I believe you was prob'ly in the right, this time, Skeeter. But, I 'spect that by now 'em Fester boys is speedin' down the road an' drinkin' beer. I'm gonna turn 'round and go catch 'em. None of 'em have valid driver's licenses, and they're all under age. I believe I'll spend the rest of my day doin' the paperwork on ah impounded 1977 Chevy Silverado with 'xpired plates and no reg'stration. Have a nice day." Sheriff Hasbro drove off.

Ron watched as the sheriff drove away. "Was that what you call country justice?"

"That," said Skeet, "is the man who swallowed country justice, whole."

"You guys act like you know the sheriff pretty well," Ron said.

"Better than our folks' wish we did."

"You guys really dipstick troublemakers?" Ron asked with a smile.

"I am," Edison said. "Ol' Skeeter here, he is just trying to bridge his inherent racism by giving you a chance to live long enough to see if he hates you. And if he does hate you, he wants to know if he hates you because you're black, or because you're a peckerweed."

"Thanks," Skeet said to Edison. "Someway to start a friendship."

"Well, it is nice to know where we stand." Ron said with a smile. Considering them both, he added, "It just so happens that some of my best friends are dipstick troublemakers. Mind you, I wouldn't want my sister to marry one, but maybe we can be friends."

"You deer hunt?" Skeet asked.

"Yep."

"Okay then. I don't see why we can't at least try to be friends," Skeet said.

Ron nodded. They shook hands all around.

Charolais showed up after supper. Skeeter and Edison were sitting on Skeet's porch.

"Here we go," Skeet whispered to Edison.

"She's pissed," Edison agreed.

Charolais stomped up onto the porch, shaking her finger first at Skeet, then at Edison. He eyes were dark, her face tight and bitter.

Edison and Skeeter were trying hard not to giggle.

"You peckerweeds!" she spat.

"We were just trying to help our new friend," Skeet argued. "Your brothers were going to beat up a lone guy."

"You just don't know," Charolais hissed, "the sort of trouble this causes at home."

That sobered Skeet and Edison.

Edison said, "You're right. We didn't think in those terms. But your brothers had already picked the fight."

"Oh, I know," Charolais admitted. She sat down between the boys. "And you boys didn't make them drink, and you didn't put them in a truck with no registration or insurance. Or make Hasbro come along. But you did fight them. Now my mom has to deal with the tickets, and probably go to court. My mom likes you two, but, for the love of Pete, it makes things uncomfortable around the house when my boyfriend beats up my brothers."

"I helped," Edison added.

She punched his shoulder.

"Hasbro take the truck?" Skeet asked.

"No. He followed my brothers home, and he and my mom had a quiet talk. We need that truck."

"Hasbo's alright," Skeeter acknowledged.

"He tries to be," Charolais said, "but I think the Law costs the poor more than it does the rich."

26

Girls voices' drifted over the fence and out into the night.

"Come on," Skeet urged, "we're already here, and no one is ever going to know. Besides, it was your idea."

"You'd better hope Charolais never finds out. We don't have what you would call good intentions," Edison whispered.

"No one will find out. We'll just peek in, and that'll be that. Besides, if the road to Hell is paved with good intentions, maybe the converse is also true. Maybe the road to Heaven is paved with bad intentions."

"Nice," said Edison. "That is just good thinking."

They crept out of the bushes by Emily O'Neal's house and toward the fence that surrounded the pool. The pool was on the side of the house, and anybody passing on the street would be hard pressed to miss the two figures creeping toward the fence. The late August night was cool and dark, the moon having waned away to nothing earlier in the week.

When Edison again voiced his concerns, Skeet said, "It's midnight on a Wednesday. No one is going to be out. Again, this was your idea."

Emily O'Neal was a tall, blond beauty in their class. She played center on the girl's basketball team, and she was a dancer. Her legs were muscled and tan, her shoulders broad and bronze, her neck long and thin. But Edison knew where her neck went. Every boy—and most girls in town—knew where that neck went. It drifted down beneath her collar and toward the best pair of knockers Edison had ever seen. Perfectly proportioned. Attendance at basketball games had tripled since Emily's sophomore growth spurt. And while there were rumors, no boy in school could provide reliable proof that he had seen those breasts bare.

But Skeet and Edison had a plan.

Charolais was spending the night at Emily's, as were several other girls from school. They were going to have a pool party. Edison had been intrigued by the information and had asked Skeet, "You reckon they'll skinny dip?"

"Why would they?"

"I don't know. They're girls," Edison argued hopefully.

"And therefore they'll skinny dip?" Skeet raised an eyebrow questioningly.

"Sure. Remember those magazines we found in that shed, down by the railroad tracks?"

Skeet nodded.

"Remember those letters in them? They were all like, "Dear Sugar, I'm Sandy and I just had to write and tell you that the other day I was at the pool with my best friend, Bunny, and it was so hot that we decided to take off our swimsuits…"

"Did you believe those letters?" Skeet chuckled.

"Those letters," Edison said authoritatively, "were printed in an internationally published journal. You don't think the editors of that fine magazine would allow their readers to be lead astray, do you?"

"I think," Skeeter said, "that the editors and readers of that magazine are far more concerned about the photographic essays they print than they are about the credibility of the letters in the 'Dear Sugar' section."

"You don't say?" Edison shook his head disbelievingly. "Well, that notwithstanding, you reckon Emily O'Neal, Charolais, and the rest of the lovelies are going to skinny dip at Emily's overnight pool party?" Edison asked again.

"I kind of doubt it. I mean if you, me, and some of the guys had a pool party, you wouldn't want to skinny dip with them, would you?"

"No," Edison agreed, "I wouldn't. But I fall back on my original point. Emily and Charolais are girls. So they might get naked and skinny dip."

Skeet nodded. "You know what? I suppose you are right. It could happen. I doubt it will happen, but it is not impossible. Why do ask?"

"Well," Edison cleared his throat, "I was thinking that maybe we should go over to Emily's and look over the pool fence."

"Why?"

Edison thought about it for a long time, but all he could come up with was, "To make sure Charolais is okay?"

Skeet nodded. "Okay. Sounds like we should. Just so long as we are clear on the fact that we are not going to look over the fence in hopes of seeing Emily O'Neal's boobs."

"What?" Edison asked, mocking shock. "What would even give you that idea? At the very most, I am simply motivated by the fact that it is August and thus we are nearing the end of the swimming season. We should enjoy the pleasures of summer while we can."

Skeet shook his head again. "You mean girls in bathing suits?"

"It is a pleasant sight."

"Nice to know who you are. But, what if they see us?" Skeet asked.

"We say we came to say hello," Edison offered.

"And what if they are naked?"

"Well? That would be something."

"Best we keep this to ourselves. I don't think I'll tell Charolais we are planning to drop by."

"Good thinking."

They had been in the bushes just over an hour, waiting for the girls to come out of the house and to the pool. After deliberating for just a moment longer, Edison got up from where he was laying and stood beside Skeet. They crept across the mowed lawn and ducked beneath the top of the fence.

"You look first," Skeet said.

Edison raised his head until he was looking over the fence. The girls, all of them dressed in swimsuits, were seated at the far side of the pool.

"They're all dressed," Edison reported. "But wait, what's this?"

Skeet looked over the fence.

Emily stood, her back toward Edison, and then bent at the waist to pick up her towel, stretching the material of her bikini bottom tight across her butt. Edison could see her vertebrae rising nicely beneath the smooth skin of her lower back.

"My God!" Skeet said. "That is lovely."

Just then, Edison heard tires squeal to a stop in the street. Skeet and Edison jerked their heads toward the road just in time to see Sheriff Hasbro's car slamming into reverse.

"Piss!" Skeet yelled.

All that the sheriff saw when he flipped on his spotlight were two backs disappearing around the corner of the house. Edison heard Hasbro yell, "Hey!" They didn't stop. The boys jumped the chain link fence in a neighboring backyard, and cut through a second yard. Skeeter motioned Edison to slow to a walk as they came out on Alaska Mountain Road. The boys were breathing hard, and laughing while they walked briskly toward Main Street.

"Hasbro has screwed up quite a few of our adventures, but I think I hate him most for screwing this up," Edison said. "Emily has a nice fanny."

"Why don't you ask her out?" Skeet asked.

"Cowardice. She's pretty much got her choice of guys. What do I have to offer?"

"You could ask."

There was another screeching of tires as Hasbro's cruiser rounded the corner. Edison and Skeeter started running again. They turned left down the alley that ran parallel to Main Street. It was a narrow, cluttered alley that the sheriff would have a hard time driving down. There were also several places where the boys could cut through yards and come out on Main, so Hasbro wouldn't be able to just drive to the other end of the alley and wait for them. Tires barked behind them and they heard a car door open.

"Dern it, you two!" came Hasbro's booming voice, "Stop!"

They quickened their pace until they were sprinting. Footsteps pounded the pavement behind them. Edison could hardly believe his ears. Big and fat as he was, Hasbro was chasing the boys on foot. Surely there were more important crimes going on in the county than two boys looking over a fence.

"Is he following us?" Skeet asked, not turning around.

"Yep," Edison gasped, conserving breath.

"If he's chasing us on foot? Maybe he really needs us for something. I mean, maybe he wants something. Maybe this isn't about Emily's?"

"I'm not stopping to find out."

Edison followed Skeet through a backyard. They crossed Main Street at a dead run, slipped through another yard and came out on Williams Street. They turned the opposite direction of their houses and bolted around the corner of Williams and onto Berentson Road. Edison ran into Skeet when Skeet stopped abruptly. Thirty yards in front of them, and coming like an oil tanker, was Sheriff Hasbro.

"Stop, dern it!" he huffed.

"Where'd he cut through?" Skeet asked.

Edison and Skeeter turned back toward Williams Street, the sheriff thirty yards behind them.

Sheriff Hasbro came around the corner too fast. He was too fat to be running full out, especially in chase of two teenage boys. It was late and dark, and he stepped off the curb onto a drain grate which shifted under his weight. He toppled over onto the pavement and even from twenty yards away, Edison heard the bone in Hasbro's ankle snap, and then his curt yelp. The boys stopped running. Edison looked at Skeeter and said, "You take off, I'll go check on the sheriff."

"Bullcrap. He already knows it was us. We might as well both go help him. You and me, pal"

"Boys, help me." It was Sheriff Hasbro. His voice was raspy, strained. Edison and Skeeter jogged back to him and, as they drew closer, the seriousness of the situation became more and more clear. Hasbro's leg was jammed in the grate, there was a huge gash down the side of his head, and he was clutching his shoulder. He was gasping for air and croaking like a landed catfish. They boys knelt beside him. "Don't move, Sheriff." Edison said.

Hasbro smiled, "I'm supposed ta say that to y'all."

"Dern, Sheriff. We're sorry about this. We didn't figure you'd run after us," Skeet said. While he talked, Skeet checked out the sheriff's leg. His ankle was bent backwards but the bones were not sticking through the skin. And then the sheriff's huge body shuddered. He grabbed his neck and went pale. His eyes rolled back in his head.

"Edison, the big bastard is having a heart attack. And all because you thought we'd be witness to a naked swim party!"

"Okay, that's true, but we can't let him die. Roll him over on his back as best you can, but watch his ankle. Now, just like we learned in Scouts with that doll, Annie."

Skeet lifted the sheriff's arm and checked for a pulse. He did the same thing under the sheriff's jaw. "No pulse. His heart is stopped. Unbutton his shirt. Find his sternum," Skeet talked out the instructions for CPR to himself as he located the proper spot on the sheriff's meaty chest to start compressions. Meanwhile, Edison tilted the man's head back, put his cheek just above Hasbro's open mouth, and looked at his chest. The chest was not rising and Edison could feel no breath. It was a cool evening and Edison could see his and Skeet's breath. Not one wisp emitted from the sheriff's gaping mouth.

"Piss. He's not breathing either. Do five compressions!" Skeet pushed the sheriff's chest down and counted as he had been taught in Scouts. "One and two and three…" While he was doing that, Edison was screaming for help at the top of his lungs. There were a number of houses very close by. When Skeet finished compressions, Edison pinched the sheriff's nose shut and breathed into his mouth. Skeet took up screaming for help. Edison counted out his breaths and checked to see if Hasbro's pulse or breath had started up. Then the boys started the cycle over again. Edison was sweating and it was hard to get his lips to seal around the sheriff's slick, cold lips. During their fourth round of CPR a man finally ran up to them.

"It's Sheriff Hasbro," Skeet said to the guy. "He's had a heart attack and he broke his ankle. Go call an ambulance!"

The guy looked at Edison and Skeeter, who were steadily administering CPR. "Now look here boys," the man said, "this is no joking matter, you should let…"

Edison finished giving Hasbro the required breaths, and Skeet started pumping. "Damn-it!" Edison shouted, "You're right. It's no joking matter. You're wasting time. Go call an ambulance. We ain't doctors and he's gonna die if you don't go call." The guy ran off. He returned in sixty seconds telling the boys that an ambulance was on the way.

Halfdollar was a small town, but the citizens were keen on healthcare. The hamlet paid for a professional ambulance to be in town every night, the nearest paramedic station being forty minutes away. The town rented a little apartment for the ambulance crew to stay in, and paid them overtime to be there. Sheriff Hasbro had been one of the main forces responsible for getting the ambulance stationed in town.

It rolled up about three minutes after the guy told Edison he'd called. The paramedics took over for Skeeter and Edison, warmed up the defibrillator, and blasted the sheriff's chest with electricity. Hasbro's body jerked and his eyes fluttered. The paramedics freed and immobilized Hasbro's ankle, loaded him up on a gurney, and wheeled him into the back of the ambulance. Just before they closed the doors, one of the paramedics stuck his head out the door and said, "Good job boys, if you hadn't been here, he'd ah died. You probably saved his life."

The neighbor walked off, muttering about having been the one who called the ambulance.

Skeet and Edison stood and watched the lights of the ambulance disappear over the hill. "Shoot," Edison said, "if we hadn't been here, he wouldn't have had a heart attack. And all because of girls!"

"Maybe it wasn't supposed to be tonight," Skeet reasoned, "but come on, he's built for a heart attack. We didn't cause his heart attack; we just hurried it on. And then there's these." Skeet held up a pack of Pall Malls. "I took them out of his pocket so they wouldn't get crushed. I don't reckon he'll be needing these in the hospital. And I doubt he'll even miss them, given his condition."

"You stole cigarettes from the man we killed, while we were saving his life?"

"Hey, the way I figure it, we are gonna be in a load of trouble when this story comes out so we might as well live it up tonight. What is one more small crime going to mean, compared to giving a lawman a heart attack?"

Edison couldn't argue with that. "Well, let's go steal my dad's car and go to the hospital. See how he is."

Skeet looked at Edison and nodded. "We saved his freakin' life."

"This whole night is like when we shot that bear. It was a bad idea from the beginning but we did it anyway because we figured we might as well."

"Me and you pal, me and you."

27

Skeet's truck was in the shop, so the boys pushed Edison's dad's car down the driveway, started it in the street, and headed toward Beckley. Edison lit one of Hasbro's cigarettes.

The pack of Pall Malls they had lifted from Hasbro must have been a pretty new one because there weren't more than three or four cigarettes missing.

"You gonna smoke in yer dad's car?" Skeet asked.

"Man, we gave the sheriff a heart attack. I expect we'll do a spell at Pruntytown for that. I reckon the next, say, four hours of our lives are our last hours of freedom for a long, long time. Let's live it up, and damn the torpedoes."

Skeet lit up, blew out a lungful of smoke and said, "Strangely liberating, knowing that it's our last night on earth. Goodbye future, goodbye Charolais. I can't think of any self-redeeming way to explain this to her." Skeet was quiet for a second, and then he said, "He died you know—just for a few seconds—but the sheriff was dead. He might die for good later on because of this. Reckon that's manslaughter? Screw it, I say we either keep on driving 'til we get to California, or maybe Vegas, or knock over a convenience store on the way to the hospital. I mean, why not?"

Edison nodded. "Maybe you're right. We could go out in a blaze of glory. We'll be ruined, but folks will remember the night that Skeet and Edison went bad. Then, later, we can get out of jail, turn our lives around, and impress everyone when we overcome the odds. What'd ya say? Maybe they'll make a movie about it. You could cast some hot starlet to play Charolais, and she could stand by your side throughout the whole thing. Or, Emily O'Neal could be so moved by the story that she runs away with you. No, check that, she runs away with me."

Skeet coughed on his cigarette. "Keep that fantasy alive for when we're in the can."

"I don't like the term the can. It sounds too much like the

bathroom. I don't want people thinking I spent a few years in the bathroom. I think we should say the joint. Or up the river."

"But Pruneytown isn't up the river," Skeet noted. "It's just down the road."

"I'm not sure the geography matters."

"Well," Skeet threw his cigarette butt out the window and lit another. "If I get five years, I'm telling everyone that I'm doing A nickel in the skull."

"Oh, yeah, that's cool. If we do time, I guess I hope it's at least five years. 'Three pennies in the skull' just doesn't have the same ring."

"And to think, people say that you and I don't ever think about our futures."

"You know," Edison said, shifting subjects, "girls are a lot of trouble. I got beat up because of you and Charolais. Now I'm going to jail because I wanted to see if those girls were going to skinny dip."

"We're gonna look real tough to the cons when we go down for looking over a pool fence."

"Think they'll let us out to hunt?"

They rode in silence for a few miles. Edison pulled off on the Sandstone exit and made the left toward Hinton.

"What are you doing?" Skeet asked.

"There's that Shell station just over the rise."

"Do we need gas?"

"Nope."

"Then what?"

Edison turned right into the gas station parking lot. He stopped way out on the edge of the lot, in the shadow of a semi.

"What are you doing?"

Edison looked at Skeeter for a moment and then said, "Exercising my right to make bad decisions." He pulled his bandana from his back pocket, folded it diagonally, and tied it around his face, like a bandito.

"What are you doing?" Skeet nearly screamed.

"I'm thinking about the movie. It's gonna be great." Edison reached in the glove box and came out with his dad's .38 pistol. Strange thing for a pacifist to have in his glove box, but there it was. Rev. Janzen always claimed that he carried it in case he hit a deer and had to put it out of its misery. Edison's mom hated it. She said guns were trouble, that if one was around, sooner or later somebody would do something dumb with it. Edison chuckled at the thought.

"You coming?" Edison asked as he leapt from the car. He ran across the parking lot at full speed before Skeet could try to talk him out of it. Edison heard a car door slam and then Skeet was running up behind him.

Skeet had his T-shirt pulled up over his face. He jogged a few steps after Edison. "Hey! Stop!" Skeet was torn. He didn't really want to be part of this. He wanted to tackle Edison. They were in deep enough trouble already. And he wanted to get in the car and go. But he couldn't leave his pal stranded. Not even like this. Skeet started running after his friend.

Edison saw the cashier staring out the window. He also saw his and Skeet's reflections in the window. He thought he looked pretty cool, though he figured he'd look cooler playing the part of the good guy, or at least some sort of Robin Hood character. But this was just a country gas station, not the evil king's castle. And he was just being an adolescent dipscrew, not a hero. He'd work on the story before he told his fellow cons about it. And Skeet, running back there with his T-shirt up over his face, he just looked dumb. He looked like a guy caught on the outskirts of a teargas barrage.

The girl in the store was pretty, and she looked confused and afraid. She had the most wonderful red hair running over her shoulders. When Edison got to the big glass doors he could see her hands lying flat on the counter. She wasn't going to resist. "If only I was here to save her," he thought, "now that would be something." He felt the .38 in his hand. It was heavy and hot. He had it down by his thigh, out of sight. But the bandana was a dead give-away. His intentions were obvious. He got to the door and stopped.

Skeet, his shirt off his face now, caught up to Edison. He pushed Edison out of the way. Edison spun around and tripped on a trash can. He almost dropped the gun. Only then did he think to look for security cameras. He didn't see one, and he couldn't remember there ever being any in the store.

Skeet burst through the door like a fast drunk. He looked back at Edison, saw his pal turn so he could stuff the gun away, smiled, and said to the cashier, "Do you sell gum?"

Edison hurried back to the car while the very legal transaction took place.

When Skeet got back in the car, Edison tore out of the parking lot.

"Good Lord! What was I thinking?" he was shaking, coming off the adrenaline rush. "What was I going to do if I got in there?"

"Well," Skeet said, "I told her that I'd bet you a pack of gum that you wouldn't run up to the door with a bandana on your face." He tossed Edison the pack of gum he'd bought. "You win."

"What'd she say?"

"She said that was dumbest thing she'd ever heard. She said we should be glad that regular night guy wasn't working 'cause he'd have shot us."

"Makes sense. I couldn't do it though. I got cold feet about ten feet from the door. I could see her, and she was so nice looking, and pretty. I didn't figure I had the right to scare her, mess up her life, just so we could go down in a blaze of glory."

"She was pretty, that's for sure. And, she's one girl who actually kept you out of trouble. You should keep her in mind."

"Well, too bad I tried to stick her up. Now I'll never be able to pick her up."

"Nice," Skeet said sarcastically. "Why not try that line on her?"

Edison laughed.

28

Visiting hours at the hospital didn't start until 9:00 a.m., but Skeet told the nurse that he and Edison were Hasbro's kids. "Honey," the nurse smiled at him, "that's Sheriff Hasbro in there. Everybody knows him. And everybody knows he ain't got no kids 'cause his wife—the tramp—left him long before either of you were born. But I did hear that two boys about your age kept him alive until the ambulance showed up. I reckon you are those two boys? So y'all can go on in, but don't let me catch you lyin' no more. And I'll skin you both if you give him a cigarette."

Sheriff Hasbro was okay. It had taken a long time to for the boys to smoke the seventeen cigarettes they had stolen from the man they might have killed, so by the time Edison and Skeet got to the hospital, Hasbro had been assigned a room and had had his ankle set. The morning light broke through the cracks in the blinds like floodwaters seeping through sandbags. He didn't have a roommate.

Hasbro was pale white like the dust that settles around a quarry. He was asleep, but was still croaking like a landed catfish. "Still looks tough as a mother though, don't he?" Edison said.

Skeet nodded, "It wouldn't surprise me at all if he jumped up outta that bed and whipped us both."

The boys sat down in the cold plastic chairs beside Hasbro's bed.

"I expected he'd be hooked up to a lot more stuff."

The sheriff had a single IV tube stuck in his hand, and he was hooked up to a heart monitor, but that was it.

"You'd think they'd a least have to pump oxygen into him."

They sat in silence for a few minutes, watching the big man in the bed, before Edison asked, "Explain to me again why we're here, and not running like hell?"

"You're a bad criminal," Skeet explained. "You can't be trusted to hold up stores where pretty women work. No sense going on the lam with you."

"Oh, right. Well, nice to know who you are." Edison stretched out his legs, rearranged his chair so he could rest his head on the wall, and closed his eyes.

"Hey," Skeet whispered, nudging his friend. "He's up."

Edison looked over at the sheriff, who was smiling down at the boys from his bed. "Well, looky who come to see me. I reckon I had me a lil' hart'tack, an' broke my ankle." Hasbro rubbed his chest while he talked.

"Yeah," Skeet mumbled, "Um, sorry about that."

"Sorry 'bout what?"

"You're leg and your heart."

"Way I un'erstand it," the sheriff said, "you boys happened 'long an' saved my life. Doctors told me 'bout it 'fore they sedated me."

"Yeah, well it was our…" Edison started.

"Yer pleasure?" Hasbro broke in. "Why, thank ya boys. Don't know how I stepped in 'at drain. Couldn't say. I was jist walkin' down the road an', well, stepped in, I reckon. As fer the heart, well, that's been my fault fer forty some years."

"You don't remember?" Skeet asked doubtfully.

"I remember WALKING down that street for NO particular reason, is what I r'member." Hasbro looked at the boys, long and hard.

Edison nodded, smiled his thanks. It was all the boys' fault, the whole thing. And now Hasbro was saving their lives, depending on them to not make a fool of him. Tonight they hadn't just strayed into the gray area that existed between good kids and bad kids, they had crossed the line altogether. But Hasbro was giving them the benefit of the doubt. Maybe for the last time.

"Now," Hasbro said, "here's what you boys are gonna do. Y'all git me the phone so I ken call yer folks an' explain why y'all never come home las' night, an' then yer gonna fetch me a cigarette from somewhere. Derndest thing. There was a whole pack, near new, in my shirt pocket las' night, but I reckon it fell out. Er them doctors took it. Sorry bastards. Where do doctors 'spect to get paid from if folks like me quit smokin'? I'm their ironclad retirement plan an' they done stole my smokes! How um I s'posed to keep havin' hart'tacks if I don't eat bad, an' smoke?"

"Well, at least you can't take up jogging anytime soon," Skeet muttered.

"Watch it, kid," Hasbro warned.

"Sheriff," Edison said while getting the phone, "I don't reckon they'll let you smok…"

"And I don't reckon a man's mind can ferget properly if it is deprived of nic-o-teen fer too long," Hasbro nearly yelled. "Yep, sure enough, I ken see two boys tryin' to look inta a windah…"

"Ahh," Edison said, "right. Any kind of cigarette in particular?"

Hasbro was dialing. Edison was amazed that a guy who had had a heart attack like Hasbro's would feel as good as he seemed to. He was even starting to look better. The sheriff said into the phone, "Mr. Barth? Sheriff Hasbro. No, no, they're fine. 'Fact, they saved my life." He looked at Edison and mouthed, "Pall Mall." Then back to the phone, "That's right, they ain't a'rested, they just come to the hospital with me. I had a lil' hart'tack and they found me on the street, did a l'il CPR and got an ambulance. Could you call Edison's folks?"

Out in the hall Edison looked at Skeeter. "Holy Smokes, Batman," Edison exclaimed. "Can you believe that?"

"I believe the man is serious about wanting a cigarette. And I ain't gonna push it past that." Skeet shook his head. "What trips me out is that he said he talked to the doctors before they sedated him last night. I mean, that's one tough guy. The guy broke his ankle, had a heart attack, died, and then by the time he got to the hospital he was alert enough to talk about the night, and then they had to sedate him! Maybe we better quit messin' with him."

"Well, like you said, he's serious about the cigarettes. Let's find some. Pretty inconsiderate of us to smoke all of his. I think I saw one of those cigarette machines down by the front doors. You got any quarters?"

29

Edison and Skeeter stayed with the sheriff until that night, serving as lookouts while he smoked and ate the fast food burgers and salt he had the boys smuggle in. It turned out that Hasbro did have some family, a sister who lived near Hinton. She and her husband came by around noon. Some other folks dropped in as well. When Hasbro had visitors Edison and Skeet would slip down to the parking lot.

The boys headed home when visiting hours ended at nine that night. Once home, they slept until the next morning.

About 10 o'clock, Edison found Skeet out back. "Let's go back and see Hasbro," he suggested.

They got Skeet's truck from the shop and headed toward the hospital. Skeeter drove for a long time without speaking.

"Did you tell Charolais?" Edison asked.

"Sorta. I left out the part about trying to see if they were skinny dipping. No sense mentioning what didn't happen. I told her we were just out and messin' around. She said not to let the fact that we saved Hasbro's life keep us from being ashamed of ourselves for killing him."

"Poor Emily. Her boobs caused all this. She's lethal and she doesn't even know it. What's gonna happen when some poor guy actually sees those things?"

They were quiet again for a while.

At the Sandstone exit Skeet pulled down the exit ramp and into the parking lot of the Shell station.

Edison asked quietly, "What are you doing?"

"I want to see if that girl with the red hair—the one from the other night—is working."

"What for? You think Charolais wants you to get a second girlfriend?"

"No. But that girl is hot, and I think she was interested in you."

"In me? For the love of God, Skeet, I was going to hold the place up. I hope she never even comes close to recognizing me. Oh, and thanks to you, she thinks I'm dumb enough to rob a store for a pack of gum."

Skeet looked out the windshield. "She's in there. I can see her. Go buy some chips or something. And see if she'll sell you a pack of Pall Malls for the sheriff. He's likely to hold all of this against us, us killing him and all, and the more smokes we can bring him, the better off we might be. We ought to get him a Big Mac, too. He'll like that."

"Skeeter, are you a moron? Don't you understand that you should never return to the scene of the crime? We got away with it. Let's just go."

"Nope. Just get out. I ain't movin' this truck until you get out and buy some chips and a pack of Pall Malls."

They sat there for eight or nine minutes, crickets chirping, gas fumes drifting, the truck's motor humming. Realizing Skeet wasn't going to move, and feeling stupid and conspicuous sitting in the truck, Edison opened the truck door. "Give me three dollars." He held out his hand to Skeet.

"Why?"

"Because I don't have any money."

Skeet gave Edison a five, and Edison walked into the store. Edison could feel Skeet watching him through the truck's windshield, and the redhead watching him through the window of the store. He felt, even though he was the one out in the open, like he was in a fishbowl. He open the door, head down, and walked into the store.

She was pretty, no two ways about it. Nearly as tall as Edison, with broad swimmer's shoulders. And she had nice boobs. The sunlight coming through the window caught in her hair, making the tips of the individual hairs glow orange and yellow. Edison studied the gum for a long, long time and then picked a pack of Big Red. He walked to the counter and showed her the gum. "This, and a pack of Pall Malls."

She smiled a devious grin, her thin, pale lips drifting back for ages. She had a nice smile, even if it was devious. Edison had nothing against deviousness. "You going to rob me? Or do you just need more gum?" she asked. There was a coolness to her words and Edison was a little frightened she might call the law. He considered running, but he couldn't move. He was too intrigued by her. He suddenly had to know what she was going to do.

Edison stared at her. His gaze consisted of one part shock, one part anticipation, and two parts shame. She suddenly flinched her shoulders and slapped her hands down on the counter, like she was about to vault over it, and yelled, "Boo!" He took a quick step backward, ready to sprint. She didn't vault the counter. Instead, her eyes brightening, she laughed. Edison caught his breath and smiled too, a tentative smile, not knowing how this would end. She laughed the way people do when they've intentionally, and effectively, scared the stuffing out of someone. Edison laughed the laughter of the relieved.

"Sorry," she said. "I couldn't resist. You looked like a little kid who peed in his classroom."

"Little do you know," Edison said. "I should apologize, too. For robbing you the other night. I'd, well, there's no best way to say this. I had just killed a man earlier in the evening, and I was feeling a little buried under."

"You seem awful free for a guy who just killed a man."

Edison couldn't believe it. She was flirting. "Yeah, well," he said, "turns out he lived. And it was an accident. And I saved his life. After I'd killed him. It was a big night for me. The Pall Malls are for him. He's in the hospital."

"You trying to kill him with cigarettes? Rather slow way to kill a man."

"No. He's killing himself with the Palls. We are just trying to keep him happy so he forgets that it was us who killed him in the first place."

"How'd you kill him?"

"Well," Edison began, "it is both a long and an embarrassing story."

"More embarrassing than trying to rob a poor, helpless girl?"

"Helpless? You near scared the pee out of me just now. And, so long as we seem to be flirting…"

"Are we flirting?"

"Seem to be. Anyway, from the look of your marvelous shoulders I'd say you're strong enough to hurt me, if you put you mind to it."

"You saying I look like a body builder?" she mocked a frown.

Edison was amazed at the ease and familiarity between them. Did he know her? Had he seen her before? He'd been to this store before, before the other night, that is. No. He was sure he'd have remembered her. "I'm saying you look like a swimmer, and that you keep yourself nicely fit."

"Thank you for noticing. I am a swimmer. So. Tell me the story."

"Do I have to? We seem to be doing so well. Getting along just fine."

"In for a penny," she said. "Maybe I'll understand, and then maybe we can keep getting along well, and then you won't have this big secret murder to complicate things later on."

"Okay, but the story involves trying to spy on some skinny dipping women, a storm grate, and a bad heart."

"You don't," she began, "seem like that kind of guy. The spying, I mean. Your eyes are better than that."

"Yeah, well, it was just one naked lady in particular we were trying to see, a girl from school actually, and we was just lookin'. And, to top it all off, we never did see her naked. Fact is, we had no real reason to believe there'd even be any skinny dipping at all. It was just a harebrained I'd had." Nothing like honesty.

The redhead blushed, surprising Edison. She wasn't nearly as self-assured as she wanted to let on. But then neither was he. She looked down and cleared her throat, waited until the heat left her cheeks, and said, "So, why didn't you rob me?"

"Why didn't you report me?"

"You didn't rob me."

"I couldn't."

"Why?"

"I saw you through the window," Edison said. He took a deep breath, blushed a little himself, and asked, "In for a penny?"

She looked pleasantly expectant. "In for a pound."

"Your eyes were too clever, too open. It sounds terrible, I know, but if you had been grievously ugly, or a man, or just dumb looking, I might have done it. But I could see that you were going to let me take the money. I could see that you had made up your mind not to be too scared, and that you would look me in the eyes the whole time and make me feel guilty for the rest of my life, just because I robbed you."

She smiled, offered her hand. "My name is Lynn."

"Mine's Edison." He took her hand, hoping to feel a little electricity.

Lynn said: "Sheriff Hasbro is my uncle."

Edison felt faint. He got ready to run, all over again. But she was smiling that nice, devious smile, and still holding his hand. "He's my mom's brother. I guess my parents met you yesterday at the hospital. They said two nice young men saved Uncle Hasbro's life." Lynn let go of Edison's hand, reached above her head, and found a pack of Pall Malls. "I never charge him for cigarettes, but you tell him I said 'Quit yer dern smokin', you fat lawdog.'"

Edison couldn't even blink for a long moment. This was a powerful does of information. He finally managed to say, "I think that I will not tell him that." He coughed and asked, "You call him 'Uncle Hasbro'?"

"He doesn't like his first name. Everybody, even my mom, calls him Hasbro."

"I call him Sheriff, thank-you very much."

Lynn smiled and said, "You stop back by here on your way home and maybe we can catch a movie."

"Sorry," Edison said.

"For what?"

"For killing your uncle, and for robbing you."

"You didn't do either, and besides, if you had not done either we wouldn't be going to a movie later."

Edison reached across the counter, and Lynn met his hand halfway. "Who knew that the fastest way to a woman's heart was the notion of a naked pool party, manslaughter, and armed robbery," he said.

"You just remember that you are starting in a hole. Don't screw up any more. Oh, and I won't tell my mom you killed her brother."

"Thanks, it's sort of a secret," Edison said quietly. "Oh, and how 'bout not tellin' the sheriff we're going on a date?"

"See you later." She smiled one more time.

Edison climbed back into the truck and Skeet grinned. "Took you long enough."

Skeet started the truck.

Edison waited until they were accelerating up the on ramp, a vicious incline with a wicked curve that Skeet loved to take too fast. When Skeet had the steering wheel held so tightly that his knuckles were white and his forearms flexed, fighting the forces acting on the truck, Edison said, "She's Hasbro's niece and she knows who we are."

Skeet jerked his head toward Edison, eyes white, and the truck slid off the road and onto the grassy shoulder. He muscled it back under control and said, "WHAT!"

"Yep. She and I, her name is Lynn, we're going to a movie later."

Skeeter shook his head and watched the road especially carefully.

30

"It's a sin, you know. A cardinal sin," Skeet said to Edison five weeks later. They were sitting in Skeet's room discussing Edison's relationship with Lynn, and the upcoming football game between Dry County High and Faybour County High, where Lynn attended.

"What is?"

"Dating a girl from another county. Lynn's a great girl— don't get me wrong, but she is from Faybour."

"I know. I always did hate guys from other counties dating our girls. But it can't be helped. She's too good to let go just because she was born in a foreign county. Besides, I tried in this county. Asked out just about every girl in Dry County—the pretty ones, anyway. And if it is a sin, you have to admit that it's one of the lesser sins we've sinned. I'd say it's worth it. I mean, Lynn's beautiful. And hot. And smart. And hot."

"Very hot. Can't be denied." Skeet acknowledged. "But what do we do about the football game next Friday night?"

Edison shrugged. "That's a toughy, but I gotta sit on the Faybour High side. It's their homecoming, you know. Lynn and I are going to the dance afterwards. So, I'll sit there, under their colors, but I'll be secretly rooting for the Dry County High Buckdogs to destroy the Faybour County High Divine Bovines. Lynn doesn't care, too much. So long as I go to the dance with her and don't start any fights. Then, when we have our homecoming, she'll sit on our side of the field with me, you and Charolais."

"You realize," Skeet mused, "that if Charolais went to Faybour, she'd be a Lady Bovine."

"You call her a Lady Bovine and she'll sic Ruth-dog on you. Anyway, we can all meet at the snack bar—neutral territory—and hang out most of the game."

"I'm just glad that Charolais likes Lynn," Skeet said. "I mean she likes her a lot. They sort of palled up right away."

"Fortunate," Edison said. "Okay, I'm leaving. We'll meet you guys for dinner about seven. Does that work?"

"Yeah, me and Charolais are going to see a movie, then we'll meet you guys. She's coming over in a bit."

"You've never been to her house, have you?"

"Nope. Crossed that cow pasture a thousand times headed over to Skitter Creek, but never to see Charolais. I don't think it's a very nice place to be."

"That Angus, what a peckerweed. He ever hit Charolais, you think?"

Skeet snorted. "Do you? She's pretty dag on tough."

"But, I mean, she's so small. Angus could hit her. Or her brothers."

"Three things stop them all from trying anything. Skeet ticked them off his fingers. First, her mother would kill any of them that tried. Literally. Like Easter Boggins did to Angus Jr. Second, Charolais is made of the same stuff that they make foundry vats out of. She told me she broke Malvi's arm recently, but not why. Third that dog, Ruth. We joke about that dog, but you saw her attack it's own master for Charolais."

"Why don't they leave? Mrs. Fester and Charolais? Or do something about it?"

"I don't know. I don't know. I think Mrs. Fester is concerned for the boys. Most of them still live at home."

"Well, on that happy note," Edison said softly, "I'm off to a swim meet."

"Lynn swimming today?"

"Yep."

"I'd like to go to one of those swim meets."

"Why?"

"Because I enjoy seeing women compete."

"In bathing suits."

"Naturally."

"Nice to know who you are."

"Yep."

Lynn had borrowed her mother's car to pick up Edison at his

house. She came in and talked with his folks for a while, and then she and Edison headed toward Elkins.

"Nice," she said, "how Halfdollar seems to be within thirty minutes of everywhere we want to go in West Virginia."

"It does come in handy," Edison agreed. "And, by the way, you look absolutely fantastic."

"You're lying. I've got no make up on, I'm wearing a sweat suit, and my hair is pulled back too tightly."

"Still, you look amazing. Natural. Like a flame."

"A flame? Your metaphors are often weird. Explain that one."

"A flame. Raw energy. Heat. Potential. Beautiful curves. Light, as in without weight, yet powerful. And Light, as in Illumination. Subtle, yet precarious if neglected or ignored. Ravenous. Insatiable. And the ability to refine that which it encounters."

She blushed. "That's why I give you the benefit of the doubt Edison Janzen. Lean over here and kiss me."

He did.

"Why don't you tell people you're so smart?"

"I'm not. And it's not nice to brag."

"You are smart. You and Skeeter both. About the brightest boys I ever met. And remember, I'm from Faybour County, where folks are generally smarter."

"We're not smart. We're morons."

"You only want people to believe that. That's why you get the grades you do."

"Easy now. We get poor grades because we're lazy. We act like morons because it makes being lazy easier."

"Boys are so stupid."

"You got your swimsuit on under that sweat suit?"

"None of your business."

"Some of my business."

"None." Lynn smiled, and then said, "Kiss me again, but remember I'm driving, and I have to compete in an athletic event in the very near future. And quit checking to see if I'm wearing a bathing suit." She slapped his hand.

"Geezle. Remember all that? And kiss you?"

"Just do it, moron."

At the swim meet, Edison sat in the bleachers by himself. Lynn swam for the Faybour County YMCA, and they were at the Y in Elkins now. There were not a lot of people on hand to watch the meet. Mostly parents and younger siblings. Lynn came out of the locker room and headed toward Edison. She had a towel over her shoulders and she wore a blue swimsuit. It was a suit designed for competitive swimming so it wasn't like she was wearing a bikini or anything, but Edison's eyes bulged nonetheless.

"Stop looking at me like that. You'll embarrass yourself. And me." She leaned over and kissed him on the cheek.

"We been together weeks and weeks, and I still look at you that way every time I see you. You should be flattered."

"I am. But now I gotta go swim."

"Break a fin," he said, patting her on her lower back as she turned to go.

She glanced over her shoulder and smiled at him. He smiled back, knowing he had patted her in an appropriate place given her outfit, and their present location. Sometimes, he got things right.

Edison watched as Lynn warmed up. She stretched and pulled on a swimming cap and goggles. She joked with her teammates, of both sexes, with an easy manner. It was a Y team, so the ages of her teammates varied widely, from little kids to retired folks. She got along with them all. She offered support and advice, and deftly avoided any overly flirtatious team members. Edison watched one older guy—he was maybe twenty-five—get a serious punch in the gut when he tried to pat Lynn's rear. After she punched the guy she looked over her shoulder at Edison and winked a powerful wink at him.

Later, Edison watched Lynn as she climbed onto the starting block and went through the motions of starting a race. Up on her toes, knees bent, fingertips gripping the front edge of the starting block, neck bent, head up. He didn't even try for a metaphor. She was just beautiful. Muscular, but not like a Soviet hammer thrower. And smooth. Not so tan, but then it was autumn and she was a redhead.

When the gun sounded to start her final race of the day Lynn left the block as straight as an arrow, slicing into the water a body length from the starting block. Her shoulders were taut as she surfaced and started swimming the butterfly. Two lengths of the pool, and none of the other women ever came close to catching her.

"Amazing," Edison said later. "You should go out for the Olympics."

"I'm trying to get a scholarship to WVU, or someplace. Texas and Stanford have the best swim teams. Then, maybe the Olympics."

"Really? Are you that good? I mean you look fantastic, but are you that good?"

"I might just be," she said as modestly as she could. "Now, let me get changed. Then you can take me out for dinner with Charolais and Skeeter. I'm as hungry as a flame." She winked again.

"Lord, I love that wink. I'll be right here."

31

"It is a racist town," Ron Green argued as he, Edison, and Skeeter walked down the hall to the pep assembly. You're a racist Skeet- said so yourself first time we met."

"Actually," Skeet corrected, "Edison told you I was a racist. Not me."

Ron continued, "All towns are racist to one degree or another. Some folks here, the Festers for example, except Charolais, hate blacks because they feel like they are supposed to. You can see it on their faces. I walk in a room and they think, 'At last. Someone folks hate more than us.'

"Your dad, Edison, he doesn't hate anyone because he truly is into that Jesus he preaches. And your dad, Skeet, he's willing to accept anyone until they prove themselves full of crap. Except you. He knows yer full of crap but you're his kid so he's kind of stuck. I'll give you Sheriff Hasbro, too. He's not a racist.

"But other people in this town, they feel superior, but don't want to admit it, even to themselves. They are ashamed to be racist, and I guess that's good except that they cover for it by being especially overbearing, nice, pleasant, whatever you want to call it. They are so polite about racism that they do anything to sweep it under the carpet. Not fight it, not join it, just not see it. That's why they pretend the people over the ridge don't exist."

"That's bull," Edison asserted. "Plenty of people here would be up in arms if there was a racist attack."

"That's because attacks are impolite. But ignorance is deniable," Ron retorted.

"That's crazy. Nobody here cares," Skeet argued.

"Then how come not one white person has used my dad's services as undertaker? It's 'cause he's black."

'That's not true, man, he's just new in town. It takes a while. If I died, I'd let him bury me," Edison assured him.

"Why don't you?" Ron asked.

"Got stuff to do, I guess. I finally got a girlfriend."

Skeet wasn't finished. "Look Ron, I bet if someone did something to you at school, even verbally, there'd be heads rolling. The teachers would go crazy trying to find out who did it. They care."

"They'd ignore it as soon as they could. In fact, I bet I'd get in trouble."

"No way," Edison said.

They entered the gym and found seats about halfway up the bleachers. The student body was packed into the bleachers and everyone was loud and rowdy. They sat down beside Charolais.

Ron leaned over to Edison and said, "How much?"

"How much what?"

"How much you want to bet that it's ignored and I end up in the principal's office."

"What are you going to do?" asked Charolais, dubiously.

"How much?" Ron said to Edison.

"Ten bucks."

They shook on it.

"Whatever it is, I'm moving." Charolais kissed Skeet on the cheek and went to sit with some girls.

The pep rally noise climbed higher and higher as the cheerleaders got the crowd signing and repeating rhythmic chants. Lights flashed, music blared, and then, suddenly, the lights went out, the music stopped, and the cheerleaders took a knee. The big moment. The coach was making his way to the stage to rally the troops before the football players charged into the gym. The room was dead silent as the coach walked to the microphone.

Ron looked at Edison, winked, then jumped from his seat. He leapt up onto the bench, eyes flashing and fists curled. He shouted, "WHO SAID NIGGER? WHO SAID NIGGER!" The words echoed off the walls.

Edison looked at Skeeter. Skeeter gaped, same as Edison.

The coach stopped in the middle of the floor. The room stayed silent, all eyes on Ron.

"WHO SAID IT?" he asked the crowd again, looking around at the awed faces all around him.

"Now, son," Principal Hundfoos was making his way toward the bleachers, "Let's just calm down. I'm sure nobody said a thing."

"I heard it!" Ron yelled.

"Well, maybe you misunderstood."

"Yes," put in one of the teachers, "no one here would say such an awful word."

Edison pulled out his wallet out and counted out ten dollars.

Hundfoos made his way up to Ron. "Let's just go to my office, Ron. Well talk about this."

Ron started walking down the steps, turned, gave Edison an 'I told you so' look, and marched off. At the base of the bleachers Hundfoos stopped, turned up toward Skeeter and Edison and said, "Edison. Skeeter. You two better come, too."

"What'd we do?" Skeet asked, forgetting the rule never to question Hundfoos.

"We didn't say it," Edison protested. "Ron's our friend."

"We'll see," answered Hundfoos.

As the four left the gym the noise started up again—the world got back to order just as soon as the trouble left it.

In his office, Hundfoos said, "You boys, all three of you, are troublemakers! I mean, for the love of God, this is 1988. There is no racism in America anymore. We put that to rest in the '60s! And there never was any racism in Halfdollar, anyway! We are a progressive community. And you two," he pointed at Skeet and Edison, "and your new confederate in crime," he pointed at Ron, "are just stirring up trouble!"

"Confederate?" Ron asked. "Who are you calling a Confederate? I sure ain't no Confederate! I'm from Akron, Ohio."

Skeet glanced at Edison. It was never a good tactic to speak in Hundfoos' office—better to just listen, agree, and go about your day. Ron had not only spoken, but challenged Hundfoos. Edison mouthed, "Oh crap," to Skeet.

"Ron," Skeet said, shaking his head to indicate that silence was the best policy.

Ron had turned his head away from Hundfoos when Skeet spoke, and thus Hundfoos could not see his face. Edison and Skeeter could. And the wink and quick smile Ron flashed them shook them. A whole world of dung was about to hit the fan.

"Now, now," said Hundfoos, making calm-down motions with

his hand, "I didn't mean Confederate like fighting for the South, I meant confederate like a friend or co-conspirator. Of course you're not a Confederate."

"What?" screamed Ron, "what makes you say that? Why wouldn't I be a Confederate, like for the South? Who says I'm not?"

"Well," Hundfoos was confused, "you said you weren't."

"That's right, I did. But what makes you so sure I'm not pro-Southern?"

"Well," Hundfoos couldn't get the angle, "you're black."

"Oh my God!" Ron shouted so loud that the secretary outside the closed door peered in through the window. "So now it's a race thing! You just said there was no racism in this town and then you just pointed out, clear as day, that I'm black. I suppose you are going to treat me different than these two," he said, gesturing to Edison and Skeeter.

Hundfoos tried, "I was just making a point."

"So now you're going to make a point of the fact that I'm black?"

"Jesus, son, just calm down." Hundfoos was starting to sweat. Edison couldn't believe it.

"Please," Ron pleaded, "don't take the Lord's name in vain."

"Right, sorry," Hundfoos said, sitting down. He shook his head. "You boys, ah, gentlemen, can go." He motioned to all three of the boys.

Skeet and Edison got up, but Ron just sat there, looking perplexed. "Go?" he asked. "You called us down here for a reason, aren't we going to do something about it?"

"Yes," Hundfoos groaned, "I'll look into it. Until I do, you bo..., gentlemen, head back to the assembly."

"You'd better look into it. Or my daddy will call the NAACP!"

"I'll get right on it," Hundfoos said softly, thoroughly exhausted, "Right on it."

Outside the office, Edison handed Ron the ten dollars.

Skeeter shook his head and said, "I've never seen anybody run Hundfoos in circles like that. Nicely done, Ron."

"You seen in the downstairs bathroom where somebody wrote 'Hundfoos is an asswhole' on the stall wall?" Edison asked.

Skeet and Ron chuckled. "Yep," Ron said. "I saw that. This whole place is full of stupid hicks. I suppose it was one of you two who wrote 'better to be an asswhole than an asshalf' under the graffiti"

"Actually," Skeet said quietly, "Charolais wrote that. But don't tell her I told you."

32

Edison was just finishing up a phone conversation with Lynn about going to a movie when his mom came into the kitchen. Edison said, "I'll ask if I can borrow the car, then call you back." He hung up the phone.

His Mom snapped at him "You can't borrow the car."

"What?" he asked, taken aback. "Why?"

"You can take your own."

"Real funny, Mom, I don't have a car."

Mrs. Janzen smiled and tossed him a key. He could tell, as it flew across the room, that it was a Ford key. It had a huge, black, triangular head. He caught it as he jumped out of his chair and ran to the window. There was a gray Escort parked in the drive. He had been hoping that it was going to be an F-150, or at least a Ranger, but he wasn't going to complain. Edison turned and hugged his mother, who had come up beside him.

"You like it?" she asked.

"Heck yes!" he shouted. "It's beautiful! Where'd it come from?"

"Your father and I figured it was time you had one of your own, that's all."

"Did you win the lottery?"

"Let's just say that you'll have to get a job if you want to go to college."

"And if I don't want to go to college?"

"Then I'll take your car back, and beat you," she answered, smacking him on the back of the head.

Edison hugged her harder. He ran to his room, showered, got dressed, and ran out to his car.

After he had checked it out from fender to fender, which, considering the size of the car, didn't take long, he went in and called Lynn.

"My folks gave me a car!" he shouted over the phone.

"Then come and get me!" she shouted back. "We'll take a ride, like Skeet and Charolais do. Down by the river someplace. Why don't you see if Charolais and Skeet want to go. That way, they can sit and relax while you drive, and I'll sit close to you in the front seat. We'll pay them back for letting us ride in the bed of their truck when they went for rides," Lynn suggested.

"Okay, I'll do that. See you soon."

"See you soon, too. You can just pick me up at the store. I'll drive down and meet you."

"Great, give us twenty minutes."

Edison walked next door where he found Skeeter and Charolais sitting in the living room. "Let's find a waterway and drive into the sun," he told them.

"Okay," Skeet answered, "I'll get my keys."

Charolais got up and headed out the door.

"Won't need 'em," Edison grinned. He held up his key.

"A Ford!" Skeet yelled. "F-150 or Ranger?" Then Skeet walked to the door, looked out, and chuckled. "Sweet. An Escort."

Edison punched him in the arm. "Well, it's my car, anyway. Hatchback and all."

Charolais, who was standing on the porch said, "Oh. It's cute. And it's so small."

Edison hip-checked Charolais, playfully bumping her out of the way, and smirked, "My car might be cute..." He turned and looked directly at Charolais' chest. He put his hand on his chin, obviously and openly studying her breasts, and said with a mischievous grin, "...but it ain't small. It's perky. Isn't that the word you use, Ms. Fester, to describe cute little things?" And then he started running.

"Run for yer life," Skeeter shouted.

"Peckerweed," Charolais laughed and threw a shoe at Edison. "You're lucky Ruth ain't here. I'd have her chase you down, tear something perky off of you."

As they got into the car, still laughing, Edison smiled. "Just go ahead and get in the back."

Charolais hesitated. "Oh, I forgot to ask. We are going to get Lynn, right?"

"Yep. She'll meet us at the store."

They took the turns to the highway. Edison had fun with the

new car, testing everything from acceleration, to breaking time, to the windshield wipers. Skeet and Charolais talked softly, giggling occasionally, in the backseat. "You better not be laughing at my car," he warned them.

"You sure you and Lynn want to take us along for the car's first ride?" Charolais asked.

"Actually, it was her idea. To pay you guys back for all the rides you've taken us on."

"I just love Lynn," Charolais said. "And it's so romantic how you two met. Killed a man, robbed her. So sweet."

"And saved the man's life. Don't forget that part," Skeet reminded her. "Very chivalrous to kill a man, and save him. We're a full service operation."

"Well, she's a sweet girl. And, you, Mr. Skeeter Barth," Charolais said coolly, "you will be unhappy to know that Lynn told me everything that Edison told her about the night you killed Hasbro."

There was a long silence before Skeet said, "Oh, crap."

Edison knew that Lynn and Charolais were getting along well. The four of them worked well together. He left the highway and pulled into the gas station parking lot. Lynn was standing beside her car. When she recognized Edison, she ran toward his car. She jumped in and said, "Wow, hot wheels."

"Watch it," Charolais told her, "he's sensitive about the size of his car."

"I meant," Lynn said, kissing Edison's cheek, "that the car is cool. Not that it looks like a Hot Wheels car, but now that you mention it...."

"Hmmph. Better than walking." Edison pulled out of the parking lot and headed toward the river.

"I was just telling Skeeter," Charolais told Lynn, "that you had filled me in on the facts of the night you met Edison."

"Opps," Lynn said. "Sorry Skeeter. Serves you right though. Peeping. I mean, really!?"

"Edison did it, too!" Skeet laughed.

"I mean, really!?" Charolais echoed. "Emily O'Neal? She's such a good person! How could you try to spy on her?"

"Honest," Skeet defended himself, "it was Edison's idea, and we didn't see a thing. Besides, I just came along to look at you."

"Piffle," Charolais snorted. "You've seen me. You came to check out the other girls. And it killed Hasbro," retorted Charolais. "That's a pretty serious consequence."

"Well," Edison added helpfully, "everybody said that Emily's boobs would kill somebody, some day. Who knew it would be a third party that got hurt? Besides, Hasbro's okay. And I met Lynn. Good or bad, all things work out in the end.

"This is exactly what my dad is always rattling on about. If we look at the situation on the surface it looks bad. Skeet and I up to no good, Hasbro breaks his ankle, has a heart attack, we nearly rob a store. We should be in jail. We could label that set of circumstances as Bad. But, on the other hand, Hasbro lived, he's healing well, I met Lynn, and the four of us are here now, happy. We could label those circumstances as Good. So, which is it?"

"If I tell Emily, she'll tear your arms off. That'll be bad," Charolais said. "I'll tell you what, though. I've seen them boobs in the shower, at school. And, if I may speak freely, I took a second look. Would 'knockers' be an appropriate word to describe them?"

"See that? Even you looked. And, yes—technically speaking—'knockers' will do fine," Skeet declared triumphantly.

"You shut up," Charolais warned. "It was a good thing I didn't find out right when it happened. I would have killed you. Just never lie to me again."

Edison left the hardtop, bumped over the railroad tracks, and drove beside the sparkling water, headed west. Lynn got as close to Edison as she could, but the car had bucket seats in the front. She lay her head on Edison's shoulder and put her hand on his thigh, then whispered in his ear. He put his right hand on top of hers, kissed the top of her head, and looked at her reflection in the rearview mirror.

Lynn was stunning. Long and thin, like a snake. And, like a snake, she was muscle from head to toe. Except snakes don't have toes, and Lynn had very unsnake-like hips. And those swimmer's shoulders. When she curled up next to him and embraced him, he could feel her power. Lithe, flexible, ready to spring like a rattler. It was an imperfect metaphor, Edison knew. He hadn't yet shared it with her. Snakes, after all, are cold-blooded, scaly things that eat live rodents and are sometimes venomous. The metaphor needed more work.

Edison could hear Charolais whispering to Skeeter. He figured he had the two prettiest girls in the world right there in his car. Not bad for a perky, gray, hatch-backed Escort driving down a dirt road in Dry County, West Virginia.

He chuckled.

"Why are you chuckling?" Lynn asked.

"A ridiculous thought just crossed my mind."

"Seems like you'd be in a perpetual state of chuckle if ridiculous thoughts did that to you," Skeet joked from the back.

"What was that thought?" Lynn asked.

"Well, I was thinking that I probably have the two prettiest girls in the world in this car."

"What's so ridiculous about that?" Lynn and Charolais asked.

"That's not the crazy part. First, I thought maybe I could name my car the The Hatchback of Notable Dames."

"Better be Notable Dame," Lynn informed him, "not Dames. Unless Charolais is with us."

"Right," Edison agreed, "but that's not what made me chuckle either. See, after that, I imagined that, well, you know how people talk about The Forces of Evil trying to destroy Goodness?"

He paused. Everybody agreed that they had heard of such things.

"So, I was thinking, what if there was The Forces of Ugly out there somewhere, bent on destroying beauty? We'd be in a real pickle. I mean we're in the most beautiful place on earth, with the two most beautiful women in the world. We could be ambushed by The Forces of Ugly at any minute."

"Me and Lynn might be in danger, but I think you and Skeet may already have been ambushed," Charolais quipped.

"We have the most beautiful spirits in the world," Skeet asserted.

"You and me, pal," Edison agreed.

"Close, anyway," Lynn agreed.

"Well, let's just keep our eyes peeled for The Forces of Ugly," Skeet counseled.

Everybody fell into an easy silence.

And then rain began to fall.

"Lord," Skeet exclaimed, "it's really coming down."

"Isn't there a picnic shelter down here somewhere?" Charolais asked.

"I think so," Skeet answered.

"We could stop there, feel the rain blow in, watch the river get bigger."

Edison spotted the shelter a few minutes later and pulled the car up next to it. The four jumped out of the car and under the shelter. Charolais stood at the edge of the shelter, spread her arms, closed her eyes, and felt the cool rain blow onto her face. The other three joined her. Water and light flowed out of the sky and down the valley as the four passed the afternoon beneath the shelter.

"I'm hungry," Lynn spoke softly into the damp dusk.

"Let's go eat," Edison urged them, clapping his hands.

As they drove, the rain redoubled its efforts. Edison drove his new car as carefully as he could, trying to remember all the rules for wet weather. He took Lynn's exit cautiously, gearing down, but dark water flowed across the ramp. The car started drifting toward the guardrail. "Piss," he shouted, turning into the slide. He got the nose of the car pointed down hill again but had to give the car gas to keep moving in the direction he wanted to go. The car was fishtailing a bit, but they had nearly reached the bottom of the ramp when the car's headlights flashed across a pickup, on its side, laying across the bottom of the ramp. "Hold on tight," he yelled. He floored the accelerator. Dodging the front of the tipped truck with inches to spare, the Escort splashed hard into water deep enough to drown a goat. The car jerked as it hit the water, roared in an effort to move, seemed to float for half a second, and then shot out of the streaming water and up onto the higher and drier asphalt of Route 20.

"Holy crap!" Skeet shouted. "This car walks on water! This car is a gray Jesus! This car is Gray Jesus! Forget The Hatch Back of Notable Dames. This car is Gray Jesus!"

Edison pulled onto the shoulder, the four of them laughing at the sacrilege.

"Well, you two manly disciples of Gray Jesus, why don't you go see if everyone is alright back there," Charolais suggested.

"I don't know," Lynn warned, "it could be the Forces of Ugly setting up their ambush. Do be careful."

"On our way, fair maidens," Skeet laughed.

Edison got out of the driver's side door and waited while Lynn leaned forward and let her seat up so that Skeet could scramble out the passenger side. The guys ran in knee-deep water and drenching rain back toward the up-turned pickup.

"There better be someone in serious peril inside that truck," Skeet shouted over the water.

"Yep," Edison agreed.

There wasn't anybody in peril in the truck. In fact, there was nobody in the truck at all. The boys were arguing about which one of them should walk up the off-ramp to warn oncoming traffic about the danger, and which one should go find a phone, when a state trooper rolled off the highway.

Edison waved his arms in warning.

The Trooper's car approached the boys and then the cop lit them with his spotlight. "This your truck?" the trooper shouted from his window. The boys both shook their heads.

Skeet called, "No, Sir. We just about hit it though. We're parked up on Route 20. Came back down to see if anyone was hurt."

"Is there?"

"Nope, truck's empty," Edison answered. "Could be a trap. The Forces of Ugly are after us."

Skeet laughed. The officer didn't.

"The Forces of what?" the trooper asked.

"Ugly. The Forces of Ugly."

The trooped glared at them. "You positive it ain't your truck, and maybe you boys are just drunk? Don't want to say so?"

"No, Sir," Edison shouted. "It ain't our truck, and we ain't drunk."

The trooper got out a pen and a pad, and asked, "What's your names and addresses?"

They told him and he wrote it down. Then he said, "Step over here and show me some ID."

They did. The trooper seemed satisfied, but he made the boys stand in the rain while he called in their information on the radio. "Got a couple of smart alecks here in the rain," he snapped into the radio. The trooper found out from his dispatcher that neither of the boys owned a truck like the one in the road. He said, "Okay, you boys can get out of the rain. Thanks for helping out. I find out this is your truck though, I'm coming knocking."

"Yes, Sir," Edison said. "It ain't our truck."

"Well," Skeet said when they were back in the car, "we got soaked for nothing."

"Not for nothing," Lynn said. "Now we know this car's name. Gray Jesus. That's something. It's good to know a thing's name."

"I gather," Charolais commented, "that The Forces of Ugly have been vanquished?"

"Right. That cop though, he acted like he had never heard of them," Skeet told her. "Might be he was working for them. He looked qualified."

"You didn't say it to him, did you?" Charolais chided him.

"Of course not. Edison did."

"You two just can't help it, can you?" asked Lynn.

"Don't reckon," Edison shrugged. "But we are sworn to protect you two maidens. Come ugly or high water."

Skeet joined in, "The ladies probably think we are heroes now that we have saved them."

"Right," said Lynn and Charolais with the same sarcastic inflection.

"I'm still hungry," Lynn announced.

"Food it is."

FIVE

33

One day, in the summer before their senior year, Edison was underneath the church laying plastic sheeting. You wouldn't call it a basement, just the space between the earth and the bottom of the floor. The church was an old structure. Well, compared to Edison it was old. There were still men in the church who had built it. The church had aged better than they. The joists were of wormy chestnut, hand hewn, three inches thick and twelve inches wide. A real three-by-twelve inches, not two and three-quarters by eleven and one-half. All the logs had been donated, all the milling done for free, all the construction done for the cost of several covered-dish, cornbread-and-bean dinners for the workers. Along the center of the floor, running perpendicular to the joists, was a huge solid oak beam. The joists tied into the beam every sixteen inches. The beam was sixty feet long and eighteen inches square and still sported the half-moon marks the broad axes had made. It would take a man six weeks to do that work with power tools, and the story was that the local people had done the whole beam in a day, with handsaws and axes. The beam rested on hand-chiseled stones, cut and stacked to make the floor level. The foundation was built of the same hand cut stone. Edison couldn't help but think that was a how a church should be; cornbread fed, handmade, sturdy, and just perceptibly elevated.

A trap door in the back of the sanctuary gave access to the area beneath the church. The trap opened onto a set of steps that led down into a wide, deep, stone-lined room that had been dug for the furnace. The furnace, a great iron monster that had burned coal and needed constant attention, was gone now, the church having installed a centralized, electrical heating unit. The original furnace had been donated to the church by an old sinner who found religion late in life. Before that, the gentleman had owned a brothel that serviced several coal camps. The furnace had first served the brothel, then the church. In a way, the furnace itself had been a prostitute, heating up anybody that fed it.

The battle over the furnace, and its installation in the church, was a legend still recounted in Halfdollar. The coal-eating monster had been brought to Dry County by a Mr. Rudolph Samson, who came here from Pittsburgh in 1913. At that time Dry County was nothing but logging camps and coalmines. Most of the county's citizens were young, strong, single, immigrant men, largely from Eastern Europe and Great Britain, who had been lured there from Ellis Island with promises of high wages and easy work. In Dry County, they found neither. They also found a notable lack of lasses. Mr. Samson, who believed that men ought not be denied the company of women, provided that the men who were willing to pay for the pleasure of a woman's company, established the Dry County Refuge. The Refuge was staffed with many, many beautiful women who were both pleasant and willing to ease a man's woes, provided of course, he could pay.

The house that Mr. Samson built was a monster of a mansion; three stories high, and decorated with the finest accruements money could buy. The first floor housed a kitchen, a dining room, a large living room, a bar, and an office. The top two floors were nothing but bedrooms. In the basement, Mr. Samson installed a huge, coal-burning furnace to heat the place. The coal he got free, though his women paid for it via gratis service to the owner of a local mine.

Mr. Samson did a whopping business for about eighteen months before he ran into a snag he should have foreseen. Certainly, the men enjoyed the pleasure of the women, but the men and women being all young, strong, and pretty, started to fall in love. The men saw love as a way to save money; the women saw it as a way to narrow the field on which they were called to play. Within two years of opening his house, Mr. Samson had lost twenty-four of the original thirty women to matrimony. That left him six women to satisfy the rest of Dry County. It was too much to ask of the women. So, Mr. Samson faced two financial problems—losing his customer base and the base for which the customers came.

To solve the problem, Mr. Samson traveled back to Pittsburgh regularly to recruit new women, paid their passage to Dry County, outfitted them for their jobs, and then set them loose, only to see them fall in love and leave. He was a decent enough brothel owner, as brothel owners go, and never forced the women to stay. And he'd take them back if the marriage didn't work out. Nevertheless, it soon became clear that he was doing nothing more than running a matchmaking service, all at his own expense.

With the ladies going out the door almost as fast as he could bring them in, Mr. Samson decided to fight fire with fire. He turned to religion. He didn't, mind you, turn religious, but rather he became a preacher, authorized to perform marriage services. The Reverend Samson turned the living room of his house into a chapel, and gladly, for a price, found wives for the local men, and then, for another price, married them. He bought a number of nice suits and three or four wedding dresses, all of the latest styles, which he rented to the couple. Mr. Samson also found and employed a baker who baked nothing but wedding cakes. By happy circumstance, the baker was also a photographer. Rev. Samson then turned the third story of his house into an entire floor of honeymoon suites. He kept the second floor reserved for those seeking pre, post, or extra-marital enjoyment.

Men came from all the surrounding counties, and again business boomed. But then a curious thing happened. Rev. Rudolph Samson actually got religion. He had a dream that he was rotting in Hell for his sins, that demons assailed him from every direction, that his limbs were pulled free from their joints and left to dangle by tendons alone. And so Rev. Samson changed his ways. He closed his house and lived a quiet life on the edge of Halfdollar.

When the church was built, in 1933, it needed a furnace. Mr. Samson, who no longer called himself a Reverend, was now a faithful member of Halfdollar Methodist Church. He generously offered the furnace from his old house. The church dived into controversy over the issue. Many of the folks in town, the older folks, had been married, even introduced, by Mr. Samson. They were not ashamed of the services he had provided, or of the house, and certainly not of the furnace. "How could a furnace be sinful?" they asked.

Another large segment of the church, however, did not take kindly to the idea of a whoremonger's whore-heating furnace heating their bodies on cold Sunday mornings. The pastor, a convert from a life of dedicated sin, was all for the furnace. One blustery Sunday morning he preached from the third chapter of Daniel. "Nebuchadnezzar," he is reported to have shouted, "built an idol and commanded everyone to bow and worship it whenever the music sounded. People in his kingdom obeyed the order from the King, all except three Jews named Shadrach, Meshach, and Abednego. These three Jews refused to bow to any false god and so they told Nebuchadnezzar that he could do what he wished, but they would not worship his god. They had their own.

"Old Nebuchadnezzar, he was a mighty king and used to getting his way. He told those boys to bow down or be thrown into a furnace! A FURNACE!" the pastor had emphasized. "Now this was the furnace of a sinning king who had no respect for our beloved God. This was the furnace of a man who broke commandments as regularly as he broke wind. He murdered. He worshiped false gods. He was likely an adulterer. He lied. He coveted. He did it all! And the furnace he was going to throw Shadrach, Meshach, and Abednego into belonged to this sinner.

"Those boys said, 'Put us in. Our God will protect us.' That made Nebuchadnezzar even madder, so he heated that old furnace up seven times hotter than it was supposed to be, and threw those boys into the glowing flames. They walked right through that furnace! Right through the sinner's furnace! Not a hair on their heads was burned because they were faithful and loved God. Nebuchadnezzar was so impressed that he ordered those boys freed and said that anyone who persecuted the followers of the God of Shadrach, Meshach, and Abednego would be torn limb from limb.

"That furnace, which belonged to a sinner, ended up being the tool that made freedom of religion possible in a pagan kingdom. That sinner Nebuchadnezzar's furnace made it possible for the Jews to live in peace!

"Now I ask you, if God can use that sinner's furnace to save His people and make their lives comfortable in a harsh land, don't you reckon God could use the furnace of our Mr. Samson, a repented sinner and confessed Christian, to make our lives more comfortable on a harsh winter morning?

"Let the furnace in. If it is a sinful furnace, and if it casts a sinful heat, then you who are saved need not worry. Just as those three boys passed through the fires unhurt, so shall you. If some of you are right, and the furnace is sinful, then we will know who is righteous and who is not by the way the sinless shiver in their seats from the cold, untouched by the heat even if the furnace is heated seven times too hot and bursts into flames! The rest of us will continue to worship in comfort, praying for forgiveness and the day that we will no longer need to feel the heat."

Following that service the matter was put to a vote. The furnace won by the narrowest of margins.

Some of the more proper women in the church refused to admit that they felt any heat at all from the furnace. On the coldest Sundays, when the furnace glowed red and kept the church toasty, those women refused to take off their coats. They'd complain all morning about the cold and say "Isn't it time we bought a heater?" But, at least two of the most proper women in the church took off their coats gladly, leaned back in their pews and fanned themselves with a bulletin, sly smiles creeping across their faces as the old familiar heat crept over their bodies.

Now, with the furnace gone, muddy water crept into the old furnace room when it rained. The concrete floor was stained red, as were the bottom blocks of the wall. Once a cat got under the church and died on the floor. By the time the church folk pinpointed the source of the awful stench, the dead cat's carcass was in horrid condition. Decomposition had rotted its body through in places. The cat was half submerged in filthy water. Skeet and Edison had watched as one of the trustees shoveled the cat out of the basement. The trustee set up a pump, drained the furnace room, and dumped two fifty-pound bags of lye all over the floor. The room had flooded since then, and now the lye lay thick in places, like wet flour.

Lynn, having been in the furnace room on only one occasion, steadfastly refused to ever even so much as look through the trapdoor again, much less make out under the church floor. "Girls," thought Edison, "are just strange."

The trustees had recently decided they needed somebody willing to crawl around on the moist dirt under the church and roll out black plastic to keep the moisture from setting into the wood. It was a miserable job, but the trustees were paying five dollars an hour.

Honest work, really any work, was tough to come by in Halfdollar, so Edison had taken the job. He was saving up to buy a new hunting rifle. He wanted a .300 Weatherby magnum, just in case Frank ever did take them to hunt bear in Montana.

It was cool underneath the church, and out of the sun. Edison had a Walkman on and was listening to music way too loud. Rolling out the plastic wasn't the greatest job ever, but it beat throwing bails of hay onto a trailer or digging fence posts. Skeet was out there somewhere in the sun with a posthole digger and a sunburn. Edison chuckled to himself. Being the preacher's son certainly had its advantages.

34

As he slid under a low joist, Edison knocked the earphones of his Walkman off of his head. He realized that he was under his dad's office when he heard his dad's voice. Rev. Janzen was saying, "Well Helen, God doesn't want people to get beaten either. What Jesus is condemning is divorce for stupid reasons, for what we would call 'incompatibility.' There was just no excuse for that sort of thing two thousand years ago. A divorced woman had no rights and no way of providing for herself. God didn't want women in that day and age left destitute. But nowadays, there are options for women. You could get out of here, get a job, take care of yourself."

Edison knew the conversation was none of his business. He knew he should just keep on pushing the plastic, but Helen was Mrs. Fester. Charolais' mother. It was a poorly kept secret that Angus Sr. abused her. He abused everyone. His whole life was a cycle of beating up smaller people, why not his wife? She tried to hide it. And she kept the farm running, mainly just so she could feed and clothe Charolais and the boys, but the abuse was wearing on her.

"Look," Edison heard his dad say, "your boys can all kick his tail, and Charolais probably can, too. But if he hasn't started beating the boys and her up already, he will. I know you don't want me to call the cops, but I will soon. I just can't stomach it anymore. I will give you the money to go to your sister's in California, or anywhere else, but just get out of here."

"I think," her voice grew quiet, but remained strong, "that you are right. I've waited long enough for him to change. And really he's never tried. My father was a real bastard, too. When I was seventeen, all I wanted was to get out of my father's house. I met Angus at a football game when our team was over here playing Dry County High. He was tall, drunk, and handsome, but he offered me a way out. I snuck out of my parents' house four nights later and walked all the way here from Greenbrier County in the middle of the night. It was good for about three days, but he knew he had me, knew I couldn't go home and couldn't go anyplace else. And he let me know it.

"Angus'd bring other women home, fat, nasty, old drunk sluts, and make me sleep on the couch. 'Go wherever the hell you want to,' he'd slur, 'go back to yer daddy, just get the hell out of this bedroom. This here woman said she was gonna show me some things I ain't never seen a'fore, and I aim to have that look.' He's really just a numb-cocked skunk. And the boys are tough. But Charolais is a fine-looking girl and I'm afraid he'll come home drunk one night and, well," she paused, "well, it's time I got her out of there. He's getting worse."

"I'll go. And I'll take Charolais with me, but I'm gonna screw him in the process. I don't need your money, I got some stashed away. And tomorrow is the livestock auction over at Braggs in Lewisburg. I was going to take a few head over there anyway. I'll load up all the cattle the trailer will hold and sell the lot of them. Big John will give me the cash on the spot. And then we'll go. Angus won't know I'm gone 'til he gets out of the county jail next Thursday, and by that time I'll be long gone, me and Charolais both. Not that he would come after us. And the boys'll be okay. They're not boys anymore, really. Some of 'em are out of the house anyway, or should be."

A long moment of silence followed, and then Edison heard Rev. Janzen say, "It's the right thing to do. I'll keep an eye on the boys. Now let's pray." Edison bowed his head out of habit. "Father God," his dad began, "you are the God of those in need. You sent your Son to the woman at the well, you blessed those who suffer, you befriended the hopeless and revealed your Glory to them. You also give strength. We ask that you send that strength to Helen and Charolais as they start down a new road. We ask that you be with her boys and we ask especially that you be with that, uh, skunk Angus. His heart is still twice as hard as his liver, but somewhere there must be good in him. Lead him to you. Amen."

"Amen," Mrs. Fester repeated. "Thank you, Reverend."

"Amen," Edison whispered.

"God speed, Helen. And don't tell anybody. Oh, and if you aren't going to take that dog of Charolais', leave her with us."

"Nope, Ruth goes. I'll be taking enough away from Charolais as it is."

Edison's heart sank. Skeet would be crushed. Edison miss Charolais himself. He liked her. But Skeet, Skeet would grow a hole right through his heart and down through his stomach. Edison knew he shouldn't, but he was going to have to tell Skeeter. Edison knew Skeet'd run over to the Festers' house and do something stupid, but Edison had to tell him.

Edison lay in the cool dirt until he was sure his dad and Mrs. Fester were out of the office. He didn't want to make any noise. When he finally did come up through the trap door and into the sanctuary, his dad was standing there.

"Son," Rev. Janzen said, "it's a secret. I know you want to tell Skeeter, but you can't. Not tonight. But I'll make you a deal. If Charolais doesn't sneak through his window tonight..."

"How do you know about that?" Edison interrupted, astonished.

His father waved his hand in dismissal, then continued, "If Charolais doesn't sneak through his window tonight, you can drive Skeet to Lewisburg first thing in the morning. You and Skeet can ditch your jobs for the day. I'll clear it with the guy he's working for. I know him pretty good. Once you're in the car, you can tell him. Deal?"

Edison looked at his father wide-eyed. "Yea, thanks Pop. It's a deal." And then he asked, "How do you know Charolais crawls in his window? Wait! Don't answer that."

"Okay," Rev. Janzen smiled, "I gotta call Bragg and tell him to pay top price for Fester beef."

As Rev. Janzen walked away, he said, "Next time you eavesdrop, try not to bump your head on the floorboards."

It was 4:30 in the afternoon. Skeet never got back from work until after six. Edison would just have to wait and see what happened. Skeet'd be pissed that Edison hadn't told him as soon as he found out, but Rev. Janzen was right. There would be plenty of time. Edison shrugged his shoulders. His dilemma was nothing compared to Mrs. Fester's. He looked up at the altar, closed his eyes, prayed for the Festers, all of them, and then went back down under the church. He had at least two hours until he had to worry about avoiding Skeet, so Edison figured he might as well roll out black plastic.

There was only one permanent light under the church and it was just a bare bulb in the furnace room, but there was an outlet wired to the light socket that worked if the light was switched on. Edison had borrowed an one-hundred-foot extension cord and a work lamp from Mr. Barth. He didn't need much light to roll out plastic—he wasn't a complete moron—but it was nice to have some light. The problem was that he had to drag the light around with him everywhere he crawled. He'd unroll a few yards of plastic and then crawl back and get the light. On and on, all day. Edison figured that one-fifth of the money the church paid him for that job went toward fetching the light.

He worked steadily for another two hours and then rolled over on his back to rest, contemplating what he would do about Skeet and Charolais. Skeet and he lied to just about everyone when the circumstances called for it, but not often to each other. He considered just telling Skeeter straight out, as soon as he saw him, and then making him promise to keep his mouth shut, to not do anything stupid, but that was too risky. As he debated his options, he heard footsteps on the floor above him. He lay against the front wall of the church, under the doors, on the opposite side of the sanctuary from the trap door. The footsteps moved down the length of the church and then the trapdoor squeaked open. He quickly shut off the work light. After a few seconds he could see Skeeter in the furnace room, but Edison was completely concealed.

"Edison? You in here?"

Edison didn't answer.

"Edison?"

Edison decided he would just avoid Skeet for the rest of the day. He'd have to. It was the only way. And so he just lay there and watched his friend try to see into the darkness. Finally, Skeeter turned and started up the stairs. Figuring that Edison had forgotten to turn the furnace room light off, Skeet threw the switch at the top of the stairs. Suddenly it was utterly lightless beneath the church. Edison dropped his head back down to the earth and said, "Peckerweed." And then he fell asleep.

35

Edison woke with a start. It was still pitch black underneath the church and, as far as he knew, it was midnight. He adjusted his position and dug out his pocket watch. It was so dark that he couldn't even tell if he was looking at the front or the back of the watch. He thought, "It's so dark I can barely hear the watch tick." He chuckled at his joke and shoved the watch back into his pocket. He started crawling toward the furnace room and the trap door. Upstairs he checked the clock in his dad's office. 7:30. That meant he was late for dinner. His mom would have a fit. Mrs. Janzen didn't like anyone or anything to mess up the family meal. And now that Gerry and Chris where out on their own, Edison and his father bore the responsibility of being home and on time for dinner.

He dusted himself off outside the church and then checked to make sure Skeet was nowhere around. Edison didn't want to run into him. The coast clear, he walked over to his house. When he opened the kitchen door he saw his mom standing over the sink. She glanced over at him, obviously mad. "Where were you?" she demanded.

Edison had already thought this through. He tried to look surprised. Rev. Janzen was sitting at the kitchen table, trying to look stern. Thankfully, his dad had obviously not thought it through. His dad would be more convincing because of that. If Edison was going down for missing supper without letting his mother know about Helen Fester, then his dad was going down with him. It was, after all, largely his father's fault that he had had to stay locked up under the church all day. "Dad knew I was going to miss dinner. Didn't he tell you?"

His dad, catching on, said sort of sheepishly, "Oh yeah, sorry, I forgot." That was nothing new. Rev. Janzen often forgot to tell his wife things. Her ire shifted away from Edison.

"George, I asked you specifically if you knew where Edison was and you said, 'Nope.' Sometimes I believe you are just plain ignorant."

Rev. Janzen shrugged. He couldn't argue that point.

Edison's mom turned toward the boy and said, now with less vinegar in her voice, "I'll heat something up for you. Wash your hands and sit down. Where were you, anyway?"

"Just laying plastic, trying to get it done." She seemed satisfied with that and Edison went to wash up.

While he ate, his mom told him that Lynn had called.

After supper Edison went to his room and read. He knew he should call Lynn back but then he'd have to tell her about Charolais, and he couldn't. He read until he noticed the light on in Skeeter's bedroom. Edison turned his own light off and lay down the book he was reading. It was As I Lay Dying, by William Faulkner. Edison loved the book for the line "I am a seed, wild in the hot, blind earth." Or something like that. The line was erotic, he thought. The seed full of potential, about to explode the surface and change the world. He sat in his dark room thinking of that seed. Then he got up, took the screen out of his window, and sat in the opening.

Edison's eyes were open and he could see through the hedgerow separating his house from Skeet's. Mrs. Crankberry had planted the hedgerow before Edison was born. His dad said that when he and Mrs. Janzen moved into the house with Edison's brothers, who were little then, Mrs. Crankberry had told Rev. Janzen that kids were a nuisance. Rev. Janzen agreed that children could be loud, but were only a nuisance to people who didn't have love.

Edison listened to the crickets while he thought. Crickets know the world and all that is in it. They feel emotion on the breeze as easily as he felt the breeze caress his skin. Crickets always scratch out a similar song, but the rhythm they strum often reflects the atmosphere in which they play. It is one clear and natural example of art reflecting society, or maybe it was the other way around. The crickets must have felt his melancholy over Skeeter, Mrs. Fester, and Charolais, he thought. Their song was sad tonight. And then the crickets stopped.

Edison Charolais came soundlessly to Skeeter's window, like the shadow of a cloud drifting over a mountain field. The night paused with her as she stood before the window, waiting for Skeeter to sense her. Edison saw Skeet come to the window and pull her in, causing his mind to jump backwards like the arm on a jarred record player.

"Boo," came a whisper from Edison's right side.

He jumped, hit his head on the window frame, and swore. Lynn stood there giggling.

"Lynn?! What are you doing here?"

"Aren't I welcome?"

"Oh, yeah, of course, I just…"

"When you didn't call, I knew."

"Knew what?"

"Knew that you knew."

"Knew what?"

"About them, about Charolais, leaving."

"How do you know? Wait," he said. He reached out and pulled her through his window.

Inside, she hugged him close. "Charolais told me. Last week. We knew we couldn't tell you two knuckleheads. You'd do something stupid."

"Lord, I'm just glad Charolais showed up. I didn't want to tell him. How did you get here?"

Lynn said, "I brought Charolais. I thought you might need someone to be with, too."

"Thanks." He kissed her.

After a while Edison said, "The first time I saw Charolais at Skeet's window wasn't all that long ago, maybe four years ago? Skeet told me that he was busy one night, that he couldn't come over or go out. It was a Friday. Skeeter had been vague about what he had to do and it had pissed me off. I knew that it must have had something to do with Charolais, but Skeeter wouldn't just come out and say it." He smiled at Lynn, a little embarrassed, and said, "Back then, I had a hard time with Charolais sometimes. I'd known her forever, but I was jealous, I guess. Not that I wanted her, but I worried that she would take Skeet. Pretty gay, right?"

"No, not at all," Lynn assured him.

"Course you'd say that, you're a girl. Anyway, that night I was sitting at my desk reading, and around midnight I heard Charolais laughing. I looked out my window and there, in front of Skeet's window, was Charolais. Skeet unhitched his screen, and then he helped her through. I switched off my bedroom light. I was bitter that night."

"Because they were gonna make out? Or because she was invading?"

"Invasion. How long had that window been mine and Skeeter's escape? Our secret passage into the night. And then he pulled Charolais into the window. Then he put the screen back in the frame, and shut the window. I felt hollow. Locked out."

"What'd you do?"

"I pulled my own screen out and crept over to Skeet's window. Skeeter and Charolais were sitting on his bed, kissing. I remember Charolais was saying something to Skeeter, and that he had looked away, embarrassed a little." Edison chuckled. "They were being so serious. I couldn't, for the life of me, fathom what those two could be discussing. Duh."

Lynn smiled. "It's sweet. You used to be innocent."

"Not so. Never innocent, but naive. Anyway, then they leaned toward each other, talking quietly. And then all of the sudden Charolais grabbed the bottom of her shirt and BAM! pulled it up over her head. She wasn't wearing a bra."

"You seem to have a knack for seeing boobs."

Edison blushed. "I only saw boobs I wasn't supposed to see that once. I never saw Emily's. And I wasn't trying to see Charolais' either. I was just bitter at Skeeter. And when I saw Charolais' boobs, nobody died. Though I think all three of us nearly did, from shock. But Hasbro was okay that time. Doubt he even knew about it"

"Tricky little girl, that Charolais. Not wearing a bra. That's premeditation."

Edison laughed. "I never thought of that," he said. "More naiveté. Boy was that something. Hers were the first boobs I'd ever seen. Outside of a magazine, anyway. But, Charolais' whole torso blushed. Skeet's mouth dropped open and his eyes bulged.

"Skeet, Charolais and I were all three staring at Charolais' breasts like they were alive, and dangerously unpredictable. Her eyes darted from her boobs to Skeet's hands, suspended three inches out, roving like orbiting satellites." Edison helped the story here by gesturing with his hands three inches from Lynn's chest. She pushed his hands away. "So, Skeet was focused on the boobs. His hands no longer under his control. They were shackled three inches from Heaven. It was like Skeet's hands and Charolais' blushing breasts were opposite poles of powerful magnets. Dad would say something about grace here. I wanted to yell for Skeet and Charolais to get moving. Honestly, I'd had never been so proud of my two best friends. And then I realized I was peeping. Intruding. As soon as I realized that, I turned to go. I took two steps away from the window. Then, overcome, I looked back, just one more time, at those breasts."

Lynn smiled. "You learn anything?"

"Charolais has a nice little rack. Perky, she calls them."

Lynn hit him. "No, I mean it. Did you learn anything important?"

"It was the first time that I really understood that Charolais was a girl, and that therefore she was different. She needed different things from Skeeter than I did. She wanted emotional and physical things from Skeeter that I had neither claim to, need of, nor desire for."

Lynne smiled. "See, that's called being introspective. You learned something about your relationships. I bet it was nice to know who you all were, and where you all stood." Lynn kissed Edison's cheek. "That's a nice story. A little creepy, but endearing. Did you ever tell them?"

"It was nice to figure out our roles, and no, I never told them."

"Tonight," Lynn said, holding Edison tightly, "is different, huh? There's no sense of awakenings, of beginnings tonight. We'll stay over here, give them some time together, then maybe go see them."

"Thanks for coming by, Lynn. Please don't leave, like Charolais."

"She isn't leaving Skeeter. She's leaving her peckerweed dad."

"I know, but God… It must be bad over in Skeet's room."

"I think Charolais has planned on making it as happy a night as possible."

"Really? They're not just talking?" Edison asked, feigning astonishment.

"Spoon full of sugar, you know," Lynn said, smiling wickedly.

She grabbed the bottom of her shirt, and pulled it up over her head.

"No bra," Edison noted.

"Premeditation," Lynn whispered, dropping her shirt to the floor.

"Nice to know who you are," he whispered.

At around 2:00 a.m. Edison woke up and noticed Skeet's bedroom light was still burning. He woke Lynn, pulled his shoes on. Being a girl, she'd long ago put her shirt back on. He pulled his screen free of the frame. Edison hopped out of his window, helped Lynn through, and they walked through the shrubs toward Skeet's window. Edison stopped just to the side of the window and whispered, "You look."

"Not me." Without looking in, she knocked on the window frame. The bed creaked. Skeet's head came to the screen.

"Hey," he said through the window. His eyes were swollen. "You guys knew?"

"Yeah. I heard Mrs. Fester telling my dad this afternoon. I wanted Charolais to explain it to you," Edison said, looking at the leaves and grass beside the wall of Skeet's house.

"Yeah. That was good. Once Charolais told me your dad knew, I figured that's why I couldn't find you."

"It seemed better that way."

"Coward," Skeet snorted. Skeeter pulled the screen out of his window and laid a hand on Edison's shoulder. Skeet was bare-chested and his hair was mussed. His cheeks were red, his eyes teary. "Come on in."

Edison helped Lynn through the window and then climbed into the room. To his surprise, Skeet hugged him. He returned the hug. When Skeet let go of Edison, Charolais was standing beside them. She hugged Edison too, and said in his ear, "Hi Edison. You'll take care of Skeeter for me?"

Edison nodded, his head beside hers, and said, "Ever since we were five."

She laughed, choked back a sob, and let him go.

Lynn was crying. She hugged Charolais.

"Listen," Edison told Charolais as he sat down in a chair, "I was under the church, in the cellar, and I overheard your mom talking to my dad. My dad knows I know. He said I could drive Skeet out to Lewisburg to see you off."

"Crap," Skeet said, "my boss said if I miss another day he'll fire me. But I don't care about that, I guess." He looked across at Charolais sitting on the bed. She smiled at him.

"No," Edison responded, "my dad said he'd call your boss and clear it for you. They're old friends."

Skeet was still staring at Charolais. "What time are you leaving?"

"Mom said about 5:30."

"Okay," Edison said, "well, we'll leave you two alone. We'll meet you in the driveway about 5:15, Skeet."

"Sounds good. Thanks, Edison."

Lynn hugged Charolais, then Skeeter.

Lynn and Edison climbed back through the window. Skeet left the screen open behind them. Edison and Lynn went to his room and lay down on his bed. He reached over and set his alarm clock for 5:00.

Lynn said, "I already said my good-byes to Charolais. So, I'm not going with you in the morning. I'll let you and Skeet be alone tomorrow. He'll need you."

"How's Charolais getting home?"

"She said she'd walk."

Edison kissed her. They lay close for a long while. After Edison drifted off to sleep, she slipped out the window, leaving behind a love note and a promise to return.

36

"Edison. Edison."

Someone was calling him. It took Edison a moment to rise out of slumber and organize which sensations were dream induced and which were real. He recognized the voice as real; it was Skeeter.

"Edison!" The nudge was real, too. "Get up."

He came more fully awake and saw Skeeter standing over his bed. Jumping up, Edison grabbed the alarm clock. Sleep still held him. He couldn't make out the numbers, but he didn't feel like he'd overslept. It was still dark outside. "Am I late? Did I oversleep?" he asked, a little panic in his voice.

"No," Skeet shook his head and sat down on Edison's bed. "It's a little after four. Charolais had to get back to her house."

"Yeah. I guess Lynn took off, too," Edison mused, looking around. He found her note, read it. Smiled.

Skeeter sat on the edge of Edison's bed, head down, hands folded in his lap. "What is wrong with Angus Fester? Why does he have to be such a bastard? I mean, he just screws up everybody's life."

"I don't know, man. He's just a peckerweed. No two ways about it."

"I wish he would die. Get drunk and die. Turn yellow from a rotten liver and keel over. Drive his truck into a tree. Say the wrong thing to the wrong guy. Why would God even plant the seed for that sod?"

"You know how it goes," Edison told him. "Without Angus, there'd be no Charolais. As crazy as God is, you gotta admit that Charolais is one of the more awesome of God's creations. All things work out in the end, as my dad would say."

"That's just weird. I mean, why put the world through all the trouble. Couldn't she have been born to your folks?"

"Then she wouldn't be Charolais. She wouldn't be as pretty, she wouldn't be as good. She wouldn't be as strong. And she sure wouldn't be able to charm animals and make grown men cry for mercy and forgiveness."

"And she wouldn't be named after a cow." Skeet laughed in a short, loud burst. "My girlfriend is named for a cow. It always gets me."

The boys sat silent for awhile. Edison was thinking about Lynn, how he would feel if she had to leave under the cover of darkness. And he thought of Charolais. There were days when Edison wished that he had recognized how great she was, before Skeet had noticed, but there weren't many of those days. He and Charolais might have been made from similar fabric, but Charolais and Skeeter were the same piece of cloth.

Skeet sat, just letting his mind slip through the fissures of reasons and answers. He could find no solid evidence of either.

"What are you going to do?" Edison finally asked.

"I don't know. I love her, she loves me. But we're seventeen. And we'll be half a country apart."

"Where's she going?"

"Sioux Falls."

"South Dakota?"

"The one and only."

"Why there?"

"Her mom likes the idea. Helen likes winter."

"Winter?" Edison asked. "We got winter here. They got winter in Cleveland. Cleveland is a lot closer to Halfdollar than Sioux Falls. Why not go to Cleveland?"

"I think," Skeet answered, "that might just be the point. Angus could drive to Cleveland without getting lost, drunk, or distracted. Same for Pittsburgh or Baltimore. But Mrs. Fester figures Angus couldn't make it all the way to South Dakota, even if he wanted to."

They sat in the quiet for a few more minutes. "Well, I reckon I'll get up. You ready?"

"Yeah. Let's go. We can stop and get some coffee."

Edison had slept in his clothes so it wasn't long before they were headed out the door and getting into Gray Jesus.

"It was nice of Lynn to come by last night, too," Skeet said. "Charolais told me to watch over you two."

"She told us to watch over you."

"Well, there you have it." Skeet choked, blinked at some tears. "That doesn't leave her with anybody." He turned his head and wiped his eyes.

Edison started the car and turned the turns until they were on the way to Lewisburg. They stopped briefly in Elton for coffee and doughnuts and then drove I-64 headed east. Skeet was as quiet as a weed. The steam from the coffee lifted above the cups and hung in the car. The sun was just up ahead, turning the world blue.

"I just don't get it," Skeet finally said.

"Look," Edison tried for a Dad-like voice, "Angus is such a peckerweed that Mrs. Fester has to go. She told my dad all kinds of horrible stuff, about beatings, and sex with other women, and just honest to God sin. She said that Angus hadn't ever tried to molest Charolais, but that she figured he might try any day now."

Skeet flinched. "I'd kill the bastard."

"No, you wouldn't."

"Yes I would," Skeet argued.

"Nope. Charolais would cut his prick off just like Easter did to Junior, and then feed it to the cows."

"Yes, she would do that. But why Sioux Falls? Why South Dakota?"

"I guess that it's just brand new, totally different. Like you said, far away, too far for Angus to bother."

"Fresh. New." Skeet whispered. "Peckerweed."

They rode the rest of the twenty-odd miles in silence. They were going away from Lynn, but only for the day. When Charolais headed west, it would be forever.

37

The sun was full up by the time they got to John Bragg's livestock auction. Edison parked Gray Jesus in a grassy field, and he and Skeet headed toward the gate. Charolais was standing by a booth, and when she saw Skeeter she ran over to him. They fell into each other's arms. Edison thought that if it wasn't so ridiculously sad, it would have been utterly embarrassing. Useless and impotent to aid his friends, he left them to their parting, and went in search of a sausage biscuit. Skeet would find him when he needed him.

Edison found it astonishingly easy to find a sausage biscuit at a beef sale. He unwrapped the biscuit and prayed, like Jesus in the garden, that God would lift this cup from Skeet and Charolais. The cup, as always, stayed on that great, hallowed coaster that is God's plan.

John Bragg, the owner of the auction house, in his quiet way, let the circumstances of Mrs. Fester be known to the crowd. The crowd, mostly old men in faded shirts and Levi Garrett hats, whispered among themselves that Mrs. Fester was fed up and leaving Angus. She was selling off the cows he farmed, but that she had worked for, to fund her flight. Everybody hated Angus Fester, even all the way over in Lewisburg. Mrs. Fester got a fantastic price for her cows. John Bragg paid Mrs. Fester in cash, and, though she protested, he would not his accept his auctioneer's fee.

Mrs. Fester sold the cattle trailer in which she had hauled the cattle to the auction, pocketing an additional handful of cash. Tears slid down her cheeks as she looked on the turned faces of the men who had bought her cows and trailer. The men, for their part, blushed, and felt forgiven for various sins.

Edison even caught a glimpse of Sheriff Hasbro. He was talking to Mrs. Fester, leaning in toward her. Edison figured he was just making sure Angus didn't show up and cause problems.

When it was time to go, Charolais and Skeet hugged one last time at the truck door. Ruth-dog sat in the middle of the front seat, sullen. Skeet kissed Charolais and she got in the truck, shutting the door behind her. Mrs. Fester beckoned Skeet to her side of the truck. He walked around the front of the pickup while Edison hugged Charolais good-bye through the open window. Edison said: "I'll miss you, too. Almost as much as he will." Edison smiled, but it was false. His jaw quivered. "And I'll miss that dog." He reached over and patted Ruth's head.

"I'll miss you, too," Charolais replied quietly. She was crying again. "These tears are just for you," she whispered, wiping her cheek. "I've cried a lot of tears in the last twenty-four hours. For Skeet, for Mom, for Lynn, but these are just for you."

Edison held her tighter and said, "You're one of the best friends I have."

They let go of each other. Charolais kissed Edison softly on the lips and then said, "You and me, pal."

Edison grinned.

Mrs. Fester leaned out her door and hugged Skeet. "I'm sorry. But come see us. You're a good boy, and you and Edison are welcome anytime. Thanks for being such good friends."

Skeet sobbed once, returned the hug, and said, "No. Thank you. Thank you for her. Thank you for getting her out of here."

Mrs. Fester started the engine. They all waved, and then Mrs. Fester and Charolais drove off into the afternoon sun.

Of all the words in the world, Edison couldn't sling any combination of them together to say anything worthwhile to his friend, so he abandoned all words and left Skeeter standing in the settling dust with his hands deep in his pockets and his head sinking as if he were reading a commentary on the Book of Numbers, the smell of cows thick and all about them.

Edison walked over to Gray Jesus and, when his best friend at last joined him, he threw him a cigarette. "I bummed these."

Skeet nodded and said, "Care to take me by Rex's? I already feel like I did when we woke in the backyard after the first time we drank beer. I figure if I am going to feel this bad anyway, I might as well drink beer."

"I think," Edison laughed, "that is the American middle-class attitude in a nut shell."

"Drive on," Skeet instructed, pointing in the general direction of home.

Edison drove.

"If there is a bright side to all of this, at least I can go deer hunting as much as I want, and not have to worry about fitting my hunting life around my love life."

"Good God, Skeet. You better never let Charolais hear you say that. But, it is nice to know who you are, deep down."

38

After Charolais was gone, having Skeet for a best friend was like having a nagging head cold for a best friend— Edison couldn't get rid of him. Skeet was always there, and he just made Edison's head hurt and his eyes water. It was a hard autumn and winter. Edison had mixed feelings when he went to see Lynn, knowing Skeet had no one to go to. Lynn, so far, was cool with the situation.

Mr. Barth saw Skeet blooming into a perfect, morose, desert cactus and decided to attack the problem head-on.

Frank, Skeeter and Edison were sitting in the Barths' basement watching TV. "Skeet," Frank began, "you're really turning into ninny. There's only one cure, so far as I can tell. We're finally going to Montana to do a little black bear hunting. I reckon you need some serious therapy and I ain't paying some shrink thousands of dollars to tell me you're a heartbroken pup, when I can spend two grand to go bear hunting."

Edison's head jerked up. Mr. Barth looked at him and said, "Don't worry, boy. You're going, too. I already asked your folks. You're dad can't get away because of sick people and funerals, curse of the ministry, but he said I could take you to Montana, too, if you want to go.

"I even talked to Principal Hundfoos over at the school. Lord that man is a piece of work. At one point that officious twit said, 'I don't know if you are aware of this, Mr. Barth, but I'm a Major in the United States Air Force Reserve.' I couldn't help myself. I said, 'I don't know if you are aware of this, but I can tell.' Lord, he was pissed. I had to backtrack after that, smooth his feathers, but I finally told him that I wanted to take you two out of school for two weeks. He said he'd be pleased to let you boys take your final exams early. I couldn't figure if he was glad that he could finally be rid of you, or if he just wants you to fail so he can have you for another year."

Mr. Barth paused to give Skeeter and Edison a serious, fatherly look. "Don't fail your exams. You fail, in fact, let's say, you get less than a C on any one exam, either of you, and we don't go to Montana? Deal?"

Edison nodded. Skeet muttered, "Sure. Not really much of a choice."

Mr. Barth went on, "I know you two aren't dumb, you're just dipsticks. Peckerweeds. Isn't that what Charolais says? You two are smart as Hell, too smart for that school anyway, I'll say that. You both read more than me and your mother ever did. If I put a gun to your head you could probably recite the complete works of Faulkner. But you'd only do it if I put a gun to your head. And you're crafty. If I put a gun to one of your heads, the other one of you would run me through. Anyway, you'll be back in time for graduation. Your mommas wouldn't let you miss that. Like bear hunting isn't more important than some ceremony? So, you both have to take your exams next week. Pass your exams."

Edison smiled and looked across the room at Skeet. For the first time in months Skeet smiled, and his eyes flickered. "Montana?" he asked in rhetorical way.

"Yes," Frank said, gently. "And to answer your next question, we'll spend the night in Sioux Falls on the way out. If you know anybody out that way, give them a call. Maybe you can get together with them."

Skeet ran out of the room. Edison guessed to the phone in the kitchen.

Meanwhile, Frank walked to a cabinet and pulled out a dozen maps. He laid them if front of Edison and, opening one of the United States, commented, "I figure we'll take I-64 over to I-77, then we'll…"

Frank was a map addict. He'd open a map, look at the lines, and get map drunk. Edison had learned to tune Frank out when he was in this condition. Skeet's dad was likely to point to Kansas and then explain that at one time the whole of the central United States was covered by huge wetlands. Edison simply nodded where nods were necessary. Frank was explaining the route they would take, the extra gas that would be burned when they entered the Rockies, the surfaces of the various highways they would be driving on…

Edison, knowing Frank was too consumed to think of anything

but travel and maps, asked, "Can I have a cigarette?"

Frank shook one out of his pack and handed it to him. He lit it with Frank's lighter and then nodded again, as if he were paying attention. By the time Skeet came back into the room Frank had a topographical map of Flathead County, Montana, open on the table, and was explaining where he thought the bear were most likely to be. He was buried in the details. Skeet motioned his head toward his father, then pointed at Edison's cigarette, silently asking, "He's map drunk, ain't he?" Edison nodded and threw the pack of cigarettes to Skeeter. Frank was tapping the map and saying something about the natural formation of mountain lakes and ponds. Skeet nodded, blew smoke, and then said, "Geomorphology."

Frank grunted, "Right, right. Geomorphology." And then he went right on with his lecture. The boys chuckled. They'd learned over the years how to throw certain words into Frank's lectures. If they pretended to listen, and used a few good words here and there, they could drop Frank deeper and deeper into a map drunk. It was like a hypnotist offering suggestions to influence and induce a deeper trance.

"We can stay with Charolais in Sioux Falls," Skeet beamed.

Frank looked up from his maps and said, "Good. Good. 'Course we'll be pushin' through. Can't spend too much time."

Skeet winked at Edison, got three beers out of the fridge, and said, "They'll meet us near the highway, and then lead us to their house."

SIX

39

Frank had a minivan and he, Skeeter and Edison spent a few days outfitting it for the hunt. They removed the third row of seats and the passenger side bucket seat from the second row. That left enough room to pack in all the gear on the left side of the van and lay a sleeping bag on the floor across the right side. Packed like that, the driver and the first passenger could sit up front and the third person could sleep or sit in the back. With one person sleeping, one resting, and one driving at all times, they planned to make the trip out west in three days.

Frank, Skeeter and Edison left Halfdollar just after four in the afternoon, on the first day of May. Frank was driving, Skeet sat up front with him, and Edison sat in the back. They had four rifles, a box of sandwiches, and a John Denver tape in the player. Halfway across Ohio, Edison pulled the sleeping bag over his head and tried to go to sleep on the road-humming floor of the van. He figured to take the late night driving shift and had left strict orders to be awakened when the crew got to the Mississippi River. As he dozed off on the Ohio plains he conjured up the Mississippi in his mind. America's river. The aquatic home of Mark Twain, the site of cities and battles, the highway for the steam driven paddle boats. A huge, mighty, muddy vein feeding, cleaning, and flooding the heart, war, and commerce of the country.

Big waters and famous rivers fascinated Edison. He wanted to see the Jordan for all the reasons anybody does, but he wanted to see the Mississippi because it was the greatest river of them all. Edison reckoned that the Mississippi was the antithesis of the Jordan, and that maybe that was why the Mississippi captured his imagination so completely. He thought to himself, in the back of the van, "I am full of piss, and driven by pride. I want to be great and to somehow take part and leave my mark on history." But he had heard countless sermons from the mouth of his very own father about humility, and service, and turning the other cheek. The Mississippi would cotton to none of that. He thought, "If you live in the world of the Mississippi, you either have to move fast enough to navigate, or be swallowed by the current."

As he lay there, in the back of that van full of guns headed west, Edison knew that he was living on the American pioneer spirit, not the spirit of a child of God. The Jordan might be a fine river to drop a hook and sinker into or get baptized in, but he had discovered one day, while reading through an encyclopedia of the Bible, that the Jordan was nearly as shallow and narrow as Skitter Creek. Mark Twain, Edison had learned in Innocents Abroad, claimed that the Jordan is not any wider than two American streets. Twain didn't mentioned exactly which two streets. But Edison knew a man could get swept away in the mighty Mississippi. The Mississippi swallows ships and drowns cities; it drains the North and fertilizes the most fertile cropland in the world. The Jordan is a creek in an arid land. The Jordan is famous because a peaceable man dipped his head under its waters, and because a dove descended upon that man, there at the river. That man was killed on a cross. The Mississippi is famous because it birthed a nation that cannot, it seems, be killed. Edison's last thoughts before drifting off were of commerce and communion, of deep, powerful flowing forces, and of subtly spoken words preached from a mountain, words that lit on a weak river's current and flowed into a dead sea, but which never lost their nerve, their truth, or strayed from their course—words which eventually flooded the world.

"Hey, Dork. Hey, Stupid!" Skeet's voice seeped through the down sleeping bag. "Get up. We're at the river."

And then there it was below him. Edison awoke in the dark, having slept across Ohio, Indiana, and Illinois. The van was filled with cigarette smoke. Frank had developed a way of not looking when Skeet and Edison smoked, especially since they had killed the sheriff. Edison sat up in the glare of street lamps, bright and sterile, rushing by at fifty-five miles an hour. He could tell that they were on a bridge, crossing the big water. Giant steel beams loomed above and the great, murky, unlit waters moved beneath. Edison could see a glint here and there off the water. He couldn't tell if the river flowed or oozed. Nevertheless, down there, maybe fifty yards below him, alive and brown and powerful, flowed the mighty Mississip.

On the other side of the river, just inside Iowa, Frank pulled into a rest stop. Skeet and his dad moved off toward the restrooms but Edison said, "I'm gonna try and get down to the river."

"It's your nickel," Frank said.

Edison found his way to the edge of the parking lot. The asphalt ended at a narrow stretch of dew-covered grass that shone like a crown in the spring night under the street lamps. On the other side of the grass was a short fence. He jumped the fence and slid and skidded down the steep and tangled bank, filling his low shoes with pounds of gravel and cutting his arms on countless thorns. And then he was there, standing on the west bank of the Mississippi. The bridge sat above him like a skyborne leviathan, looming above in the lights. His feet sank into the sandy mud as he drew ever nearer the flowing waters.

At the water's edge he could hear the cars above him, the bridge fighting its condition and the lapping of the waters on the shore. The river itself was much quieter than he had expected, it hummed rather than roared. Edison knelt in the unnatural light and touched the water. He thought of jumping in, of Huck Finn, of giant catfish that could swallow a man whole, of what Charolais must have felt when she saw the big river, of how the surface area of the portion of the river that he could see was likely more voluminous then the whole of the Jordan.

He knelt and let the water play around his fingers, and then he cupped a handful, brought it to his mouth, and drank deep of the waters. He could feel the silt on his tongue. The water tasted as mysterious as Lynn.

Edison sat crouched by the flow for another minute, feeling the water soak into his blood and shoes, and then he looked southward. There, on the wet sand, not two feet away, and large enough to cast a shadow, was a pile of human crap. There, beside this mighty, life giving, country sustaining river, by the waters from which Edison had just drunk, was human fecal matter. God bless America.

And thank God it was downstream.

Skeeter and Frank were waiting beside the van when Edison crested the bank, dirty and bleeding from scratches on both arms.

"Hell happened to you?" Skeet asked.

"I drank from the Mississippi."

"You're nuts!"

"Well," Frank said, "my philosophy on this trip is that if a man wants to do something and doesn't speak up, or do it himself, well, that's his own fault. We are out here not just to hunt bear, but to live a little. If Edison wants to drink from the Mississippi, well, it's his nickel. That's what I say."

"I still think yer a freak," Skeet said to Edison.

40

They got in the van and headed west again. It was nearing midnight, local time, and Edison was at the wheel of the van, piloting the trio across Iowa on I-80. Frank slept in the back and Skeet sat in the passenger seat looking out the window. The quiet of the post-midnight road enveloped them, and they each sat with their own thoughts.

The silence continued until well past Cedar Rapids when Skeet finally asked, "Did you see that K-Mart truck we just overtook?"

"Yep, I guess so," Edison replied.

"I've been watching the other side of the road, the eastbound traffic," Skeet continued, "and I noticed, maybe half-an-hour ago, a K-Mart truck heading east."

"So?"

"So?" If there is a K-Mart somewhere east of us, and a K-Mart somewhere west of us, wouldn't it be easier for the truck we just passed, which was headed west, to go to the eastern store, and the truck that was headed East to stay at the western store?"

Edison turned so he could see Skeeter. Skeeter smiled at him. "Think," Skeet grinned, "how much gas that would save."

Edison cleared his throat, started to call Skeeter a name he had in mind, but decided against it. It was a powerfully unpleasant name and thus shouldn't be overused. He'd save it a while longer. Instead, he turned his eyes back toward the road and opted to fight folly with folly. "What I was thinking," he started, "is that it is a tremendous waste for trucks that carry new cars to dealerships, you know, the ones that carry like twenty cars, to go around empty." Edison glanced at Skeeter.

Skeeter said, "Go on."

Edison did. "Let's say, for example, that a car carrier, or car ferry, whatever they call it, leaves Detroit with twenty new cars to be delivered at various locales in the greater Seattle area. Well, that truck is going to have to drive all the way back to Detroit empty.

What if those companies offered to let travelers load their own cars on the truck and be carried across the country piggybacked on the truck? I mean, people could still ride in their own cars, on the back of the truck, but they wouldn't have to worry about driving across the country, and when they got to where they were going, they wouldn't have to rent a car. It would be like a rolling land ferry."

"You," Skeet laughed, "are a rolling land ferry."

"It's no worse an idea than yours, and it saves more gas."

They sat silently again, driving away from the sun that would rise before long in the east, but toward Charolais, and then the bear. Skeet fell asleep and Edison played with the radio until they were just outside of Des Moines. A truck had jackknifed and rolled over into the oncoming lanes. The police were directing traffic around the scene. Several emergency vehicles, their lights flashing, were parked along the road. Whatever had happened, the worst was over. A huge tow truck positioned itself to haul the tractor trailer out of the way.

Skeet, awake now, asked, "You know what's wrong with the world?"

Edison shook his head to indicate that not only did he not know, but that he didn't want Skeet to tell him his opinion of what was wrong with the world..

"Words," Skeet went on. "Words and names. Everything is all wrong. That tow truck back there, it's called a wrecker, but it doesn't actually wreck anything. It does, in fact, just the opposite. It's really an un-wrecker."

"I liked it much better when you were asleep," Edison mumbled.

Undaunted, Skeet continued, "Now, what we, you and I, should do is start a real wrecker service. Skeet and Edison's Wrecker Service. If someone needed a car trashed, or a house torn down, or a barn burned, they could call us. We'd come out and wreck whatever they wanted wrecked."

Edison laughed out loud. "That, my friend, is the best idea you've had in years. Why didn't you have that idea in the eighth grade, when Mr. Martini was telling us about Einstein, Thomas Edison, and the Wright Brothers? We could have dropped out of school right then. You could have saved us three years of school.

That is a job for which no one could deny our suitability."

"Where are we?" came Frank's voice from the back.

"Just west of Des Moines," Edison answered.

"How long until we get to I-29?"

"I'd say about three hours."

"Well," Frank said, and then paused to light a smoke, "don't miss it, or we'll end up in Denver."

"Hey," Edison retorted, "I'm driving, and it is, if I am not incorrect, my nickel."

"Yeah, but it's my car. And if we don't get Skeet to Sioux Falls, and his beloved Charolais, by night fall I believe he will swoon and die the death of a lonesome, love-struck, ass-ugly, sonneteer."

All three laughed at that. Frank laughed loudest, proud of his little pre-dawn string of words.

"I believe your dad knows just who you are, Skeet."

41

Edison had been driving nearly seven hours by the time they got to the junction of I-29. "In nearly the same amount of time it took me to drive across Iowa," he said, "I slept through Ohio, Indiana, and Illinois."

Frank said, "Well, you've always been a proficient sleeper. Anyway, I guess it's time for you to quit driving."

Edison pulled the mini-van into a gas station and turned the keys over to Skeet. Skeet would lead the charge into Sioux Falls.

Edison woke up in the early afternoon as Skeet was pulling off the Interstate. The first sign he saw read, "41st Street." He had no idea where they were or where they were going.

Skeet had some directions scribbled on a sheet of yellow paper and he was following them. He pulled into a fast food restaurant parking lot. Edison was still pulling his boots on as Skeet jumped out of the car. Frank said, "There she is."

When Edison walked around the van, Skeet and Charolais were locked in an embrace tight enough to awe an anaconda. Mrs. Fester was standing beside her pickup, smiling and looking like Edison had never seen her look. She had on a sleeveless dress that hung just above her knees, and sandals on her feet. She wasn't wearing sunglasses. There wasn't a bruise on her. She smiled when she saw Edison and held her arms open for him. She gave him a motherly hug, and then hugged Frank. Ruth, the dog, bounded about happily.

"It is good to see you three," she said. "There's a nice little restaurant just down the street. How 'bout we all go eat something, if those two ever let go of each other."

The restaurant was good. They ate and chatted about Halfdollar, and the life of the Fester women in Sioux Falls. It had been nearly nine months since the women had left.

"The divorce," said Mrs. Fester, "came through without a hitch. Angus wanted to give me trouble for stealing his cows but I got a lawyer and threatened criminal abuse charges. Gaylord helped persuade him. Angus let it go. Do you ever see him?"

Edison answered, "No more or less than we did before you moved out here. Who's Gaylord?"

"Oh, I'm sorry. He hates that name. I mean Sheriff Hasbro. How are my boys?"

Edison, astounded, commented to Skeeter in a hushed voice, "Hasbro's first name is Gaylord? But Lynn said that nobody knows his first name."

Skeeter shrugged. He was paying attention only to Charolais.

"The boys are about the same," Frank said. "Some of them have jobs. Still living at the farm."

"I figured. Well," Helen changed the subject, "Charolais has been accepted on a full scholarship to South Dakota State, up the road in Brookings."

"That's great!" Frank nodded approvingly at the news.

The conversation went on like that for a bit. Mrs. Fester was working on an agricultural management degree at a small school in the city, and she had a job as a butcher in a slaughterhouse. As the meal ended and conversation wound down, Skeet and Charolais announced that they were going out; she was going to show him the city. They took Frank's van. Mrs. Fester drove Frank and Edison to her house in her truck. The three passed the evening in pleasant conversation. Edison called Lynn who asked a lot of questions about Skeet and Charolais. They talked about little things. After he hung up the phone, Edison went to bed. He didn't know what time Skeet and Charolais came back to the house. In the morning they both looked pleased and a little sad.

Mrs. Fester made eggs and pancakes, sausage and oatmeal for breakfast. "It is nice," she smiled, "to cook for a bunch of boys again."

Following breakfast, Skeet and Charolais took a walk around the neighborhood while Frank and Edison went to fill up the van. Frank could spend hours at a gas station. He didn't like places that just had gas pumps; he liked to have a garage attached to the outfit. He wanted a place that smelled of oil, brake fluid, anti-freeze, and free air. He liked a mechanic he could chat with. And Edison knew that if he suggested to Frank that he might have heard an odd tick or a suspicious rattle coming from beneath the hood, Frank would stay at the station for hours, until he had detected the cause, fixed it, and deemed the repair not less than outstanding. Edison wanted to give Skeet and Charolais a little extra time, but he didn't want to spend the whole day at a service station, so as he got out of the van at the service station he asked, "Frank, does this tire look a little low?"

Frank rushed over to the passenger side of the van. "Which?"

"The front one."

Frank got down on a knee and asked, "It looks low to you?"

"Yep."

Frank tapped the tire, ran his hands over the treads, then pushed on the top of the tire. "It shouldn't be low. Let me see." He pulled a pressure gauge from his pocket and went back to the tire. He checked it. "Nope," he said, studying the gauge like a mother examining a thermometer fresh from a sick child's mouth. "It's perfect. I wonder why it looks low. I'd better check the other tires. Maybe the others are over-inflated."

Frank circled the car, examining each tire. Edison knew he had won Skeet and Charolais at least forty extra minutes, though it would cost Frank a little anxiety. Worried about the tires, Frank thought he'd better check all the fluids. Then Frank filled the tank, pulled a notebook from the glove box, wrote in the number of gallons he had just pumped in, and then the mileage since the last filling. He did some calculations, compared the answers with other calculations from previous fillings, and finally said, "Nope. We're getting the same gas mileage, so the tire can't be very low. We'll keep an eye on it though, what do you think?"

"Seems prudent, but I imagine the tire is fine."

"Probably."

In all, they'd spent an hour at the service station.

Skeet and Charolais were sitting on the front steps of the house when Frank and Edison finally pulled up. Mrs. Fester came out and everybody hugged, then the three guys piled into the van and headed back toward the Interstate.

Skeet said, "Sure took you guys a long time to fill the van."

Edison winked at Skeet and said, "I mentioned to your dad I thought the front tire was low."

"Ah-hah," Skeet said. "Thanks."

"You and me, pal. No price is too high to pay for safety and good gas mileage," Edison intoned.

"I think," said Frank, smiling "that I've been had. That tire wasn't low, was it, Edison?"

"Looked low to me," Edison lied with a smile.

Skeet asked, "Dad, is it still my nickel?"

"It is."

"Could we drive north a bit, to Brookings? Check out the college up there, South Dakota State?"

"How far is it?" asked Frank.

"About an hour, maybe a little more. But straight out of the way, and there's no easy way back to the interstate except to come straight back down."

Frank said, "What do you think, Edison."

"It is his nickel." Edison sat in the backseat, now out of sorts, staring at the floor, not wanting to see the campus of a college he didn't want his friend to go to. A long conquered jealousy was rearing its head.

They rode up the on-ramp and headed north on I-29.

Edison let Skeet and Frank look at the campus alone. They found the admissions office and talked someone into a tour. Edison took a pack of cigarettes to a shaded bench and watched the girls of South Dakota walk by. He figured it must be exam time at the college since some of the girls looked nervous as they passed. He was sure it was exams, and not his appearance, which caused the girls to look upset as they walked by him. He had, after all, bathed that very day.

He sat on the bench for nearly two hours before the Barths returned, Skeet holding a file with the logo of South Dakota University embossed on the cover.

"Like it?" Edison asked as they climbed into the van.

"I think," Skeet answered, "that a school is a school. But this school was wise enough to accept Charolais, and she was wise enough to not mention she might be a package deal. I doubt they would have accepted her if they knew I might come, too. But, the admissions dork was very nice and gave me an application. And it is a public university. How hard can it be to get in?"

Frank said, "It's a hell of a lot further to here from home, than it is to West Virginia University. By that, I mean it will cost me a fortune just to get you back and forth to school."

"You always said, Dad, that I could go to any college I got accepted to."

"Yeah," said Frank, "but I didn't figure you would want to go any where but WVU. And I'm still not sure you can get in anywhere but WVU. They pretty much have to take you."

They found I-29 south, made the turns, and started on their trip again. The sun was just starting its downward slide as they traded southbound I-29 for westbound I-90, leaving the buildings of Sioux Falls glowing silver behind them.

42

"Trips west," Frank said the next day as they stood on the east side of the Missouri River, looking west at the rolling plains on the far bank, "don't really start until a man crosses this river."

They were in the town of Chamberlain, South Dakota. The Missouri River looked at least a half-mile wide, maybe more. The water was dark and deep. Edison could not imagine crossing it in a wagon. "How," he asked, "did the first guy out here ever get across that river with a wagon?"

Skeet chuckled, "My guess is that the first guy out here with a wagon was named Chamberlain, and that he just parked his wagon on this side of the river and said, 'That's far enough, I'll live here.'"

"Seems reasonable to me," his friend replied. "But what I don't understand is why the Mississippi River is still called the Mississippi after it flows into this bad boy. If you look at a map, it's pretty clear that the Mississippi flows into the Missouri, and not the other way around."

"I expect," Frank put in, "that the folks who named the Mississippi named it before they found and mapped the Missouri."

"You going to drink from it?" Skeet asked Edison.

"If I can find a place."

They got back in the van and made their way into the town proper. They found a restaurant and had dinner. After dinner they walked through the streets, and then down to the river. Edison looked for piles of poop on the bank and, finding none, had a drink.

They started the van under a dark sky. Edison thought about the brave men and women in wagons who had somehow forded the river, or ferried themselves across the expansive waters with all their earthly goods and hopes tied to an ox drawn cart, headed toward a dream land. If their wagons had overturned, or if the current was stronger than they had guessed, they could loose their things, their animals, family members, everything. It must have taken serious gumption. The Missouri river is a physical and spiritual divide that calls one to decide if he wants to live like Jane Austen or Jack London.

Edison, Skeeter, and Frank, being full of wanderlust, and with visions of black bears dead in their heads, did not let the threat of that little old river daunt them. They forded that fat, dark river at seventy miles an hour, via the I-90 bridge.

Frank sat in the passenger seat now, Skeet drove and Edison stretched out in the back seat. He had bought a pack of cheap cigars, called Backwoods, in Chamberlain. Their slogan seemed to be "Looks wild. Tastes mild." Edison studied the tinfoil pouch, examining the picture of the cigar on the front of the pack. It was rough looking. It looked like it would hurt to smoke it. He bought the cigars because he was on an adventure that seemed above mere cigarettes. Plus, the cigar on the package looked like something Clint Eastwood would smoke. Edison opened the pouch and took out one of the cigars. It looked and felt like a twig, with tobacco sticking out each end. Edison chose the narrowest end to put in his mouth. Before lighting it, he asked, "Anybody want a cigar?" Skeet and Frank both begged off the offer. Edison took a deep breath, pulled out his Zippo, and lit up. The cigar, Edison was surprised to find, was not at all bad. The taste and texture of the smoke was more bitter than a cigarette's, but a lot more full. "Yum," he muttered approvingly.

"Good?" Frank asked.

"As a matter of fact, it is."

"Well," Skeet said, "it smells like a sick cow's dried crap."

Frank had the road atlas on his lap. He was looking at the map of South Dakota, but had one hand marking the page for Montana, and a pencil holding Wyoming at bay. He flipped back and forth between the pages, measuring distances with a ruler on which he had marked the scale of the atlas. He had a calculator on his knee. He had been measuring, marking, and pecking figures into the calculator for about fifteen minutes, pausing only long enough to inquire about Edison's cigar. After another minute, Frank opened the glove box, put the calculator away, folded the map, and said, "Boys, we will be well inside Montana when the sun rises tomorrow." He smiled big. "Now, give me one of those cigars."

Edison obliged.

43

Frank found a cheap motel in Billings, Montana. They slept well and headed out early the next morning. They drove hard through the beautiful country, stopping only for gas and tobacco. A little after one in the afternoon, Skeet caught the first glimpse of Missoula.

"Look at that!" He pointed to a large white M on the side of a hill, just outside town. The hill curved away from the road and the guys couldn't tell if there were any other letters to go along with the M. The hill was covered in grass as green as jade. The M looked like it had been carved into the hillside and then painted. It was at least twenty feet tall, and nearly as wide.

"I wonder what that's for?"

"Maybe," Frank chuckled, "it stands for Missoula."

"That's crazy talk," Edison said. "I think some vandals went up there with the intention of writing 'Mother Scratcher' on the side of the hill, but they got busted. Or they realized they couldn't fit it all on the mountain, so they gave up the idea."

"You have a thing about vandals, don't you?" Frank grinned. "What did you call Mount Rushmore? Government sanctioned graffiti?"

"Yep, that's what I said."

The road turned and the whole hillside became visible. Skeet announced, "Nope, just an M. Must have gotten busted, 'cause there's plenty of room to write 'Mother Scratcher' on the side of that hill."

At the exit for Route 93 Frank headed north toward the town of Swan Lake, in Flathead County. Swan Lake is a tiny town with a small campground, a couple of farms, a dumpster with a grizzly trap, and a bar. The town sets on the banks of Swan Lake, and the lake is fed by the Swan River. At dusk, Frank pulled into the campground where he had rented a cabin.

The cabin was a small. It had a kitchen, a living room/dining room, and a small bedroom. In the living room there was a fold out sofa bed, a wood burning stove, and a wardrobe. In the kitchen there was a table, with a bench on each side. The whole place was done in knotty pine paneling.

The bathroom was a bathhouse and stood twenty yards away from the cabin.

"We could go pee on the side of that bathhouse," Edison suggested, "make it all ours."

"Naw," Frank said, "we'll just share."

"Dad," Skeet said, "you take the bedroom."

"Nice of you to offer, but I was going to take it anyway."

"We are, of course," Edison added, "giving it to you out of respect for our elders."

Frank walked into the bedroom and a light clicked to life.

"Smooth," Edison said to Skeet. "Frank gets the bedroom, but we get the wood burning stove."

"I ain't dumb," Skeet shrugged. "I expect it gets cold up here at night."

Edison sat down on the sofa bed. He lit a cigar. Skeet sat on a bench and lit a cigarette.

Edison blew out smoke, settling easily into the soft bed, and sighed, "Nice to not be moving."

Skeet looked at the end of his cigarette and replied, "That's the truth. Here we are, in Montana. A thousand miles from anywhere that makes a difference to me."

Frank came back out of his room, looked at Skeet and Edison lounging and smoking, pulled a smoke from his pocket, and began, "Boys, I'm going to be serious for a minute." He lit his cigarette with a wooden match, shook the match out, and continued, "I grew up poor. When I was sixteen my dad, Skeet's Grandpa, took me and my brother on a hunting trip to a camp in southern Pennsylvania. He told us he couldn't afford to do it often and therefore we should get the most out of it that we could. He said we could do anything we wanted, that it was our trip, our nickel, so to speak, and that he would treat us as men for that trip, and forever after. I am saying the same to you. If either of you has a piss poor time on this trip, it's your own dern fault. Agreed?"

The boys nodded.

"Good, now get off your butts and bring the gear in from the van while your elder sits here and smokes."

They obliged. The first thing Edison brought in was the cooler. They had picked up some bread, eggs, canned chili, bacon, milk, spaghetti, tomato sauce and the like to get them through dinner and breakfast. Frank stood when Edison brought in the cooler. He opened the cooler and fished out the chili. Frank was going through a collection of pots and pans under the sink when Edison went out the door again.

By the time the boys had all the gear in the cabin, Frank had the chili heated and some bread toasted and buttered. He found bowls and glasses, poured three glasses of milk, ladled out the chili, and then all three sat at the table. After supper they remained at the knotty pine table, on the knotty pine benches, and put together a plan for the next ten days. Frank had purchased several topographical maps of the area where they would be hunting, and all three hunters were hunched over the maps, trying to pick bear hot zones.

Long ago Frank had hunted black bear in this area, but had not killed any. Black bear lived in West Virginia as well, and Frank had hunted them a bit at home, but the beasts they sought now were western black bear, and thus more alluring. Somehow, hunting a creature far from home was more seductive than hunting the same sort of creature in your own backyard.

Edison did not want to kill a black bear, but he kept that a secret. When they hunted deer at home they always ate what they killed. But bear meat was less appealing than venison, and they had no way to get it home. If they could not find someone in Montana to eat the meat they killed, it would go to waste. Edison did not cherish that idea. Many black bear hunters wanted the pelt to make a rug or wall hanging. Edison didn't care about that, either. He was interested in the hunt though, and the fun, and the time away, and the West. He figured he would worry about not killing a bear when he had the chance. After all, his first attempt at killing a bear had ended with him punching Skeeter. He didn't want a replay.

He commented, "One reason I think I prefer black bear hunting to deer hunting is that bear, unlike deer, are creatures little concerned about predators and are therefore, like myself, inclined to stay in bed until the sun is way up, the day warm, and food at hand. I won't have to get up in the bitter hours of the dark morning to freeze my tail off waiting for a bear to come my way. Instead, he and I can meet on the field of battle at a mutually suitable time, well rested and content. Neither of us worrying about toes freezing off. I have little urge to stumble across a bear, cranky from lack of sleep and irritated by the cold. And I am sure most bears are equally unanxious to stumble across me, a gun-toting greenhorn, in a similar state. If one of us is going to kill the other, well, there's no reason either of us should be in a foul mood about it."

Frank lit a cigarette and inhaled. He blew the smoke out in a narrow stream, and then pointed at Edison with the tip of his cigarette, "The thing is, we have to be very careful not to shoot a grizzly bear by mistake. Grizzlies are on the endangered species list and so it is quite a crime to kill one. As I understand the law, you pay a huge fine and your weapon is confiscated if you kill one."

"What if we're being attacked?" Edison asked.

"I think," Frank said, "that there are various rules concerning that, but the best policy is to not kill a grizzly by mistake, and to avoid being attacked by a grizzly whenever possible."

"Sounds like a good enough plan to me," Skeet put in. "Tell me again how we tell the difference between a grizzly and a black bear."

"Good idea," Frank started. "First of all, black bears are not necessarily black. They range in color from very light brown, or cinnamon, to black…"

Edison listened eagerly. The sum of his pre-trip knowledge about grizzlies was what he had learned from reading about Jeremiah "Liver Eating" Johnson. Johnson counsels that when a grizzly attacks, the victim should ram his knife deep into the grizzly's chest, and then break off the blade so that the bear bleeds to death. Edison saw obvious problems with that scheme. First, it involved being attacked by a grizzly. Second, it required that a man be strong enough to break off a solid steel blade imbedded in the chest of a bear. Furthermore, Jeremiah "Liver Eating" Johnson ate the livers of the men he killed. He was, in short, a lot tougher than Edison.

Edison was not eager to employ the tactic of breaking off his knife in the chest of a charging griz- at least not before exhausting all other possibilities.

Frank continued, "Grizzlies are generally cinnamon, or blond. Grizzlies are bigger than black bears, but that isn't very helpful since it is doubtful that we will see a griz and a black bear walking side by side. The differences which will be most useful to us are that grizzlies have a hump on their backs, just behind the neck and above the forelegs. Grizzlies also have a dish-shaped face, and their claws are considerably longer than those of a black bear."

Edison remarked, "I expect that if we see the claws of a griz close enough to examine their length it will be a little late to worry about that distinction."

"Yeah," Frank said, "if you see the claws that close up, it's too late to care. But, you complete moron, if we were to find a set of bear tracks in the mud, or in the snow, we can tell what kind of bear left the prints by the placement of the claws. Black bears' claws, in a print, will be right up against the print of the pad. The claws of a grizzly show up about three or four inches away from the pad." Frank held his thumb and index finger apart to describe the distance, then mashed the butt of his cigarette in the ashtray. "And finally," he continued, "the scat of a black bear isn't much bigger than the scat of a large dog, whereas a pile of grizzly crap probably wouldn't fit into a standard safety deposit box."

Skeet looked at Frank and asked, "Dad, what about koala bears? What are their claws like, would their poop fit in a bank vault? And can we shoot one if we see one?"

"Koalas," Edison said helpfully, "aren't bears. They are marsupials."

Frank gave the boys the finger.

Later, Edison got a fire going in the wood burning stove, and everybody got into bed. Skeet was reading The Call of the Wild again, and Edison was trying to read Great Expectations. He wished he'd brought some London along instead.

44

Each morning Frank got Skeeter and Edison up. They ate breakfast, loaded into the van, and sought out a suitable spot to hunt bear. They hiked trails deep into the silent woods, through thickets from which they were sure grizzlies would spring, and out onto clear-cut mountainsides where every burned stump looked just like a black bear. In fact, one of the first things they learned in the wilderness was that not every large black object dotting a clear-cut hillside is a bear. Most of those objects were, in fact, stumps. And then Edison learned that no matter how long he stared at a bear-shaped stump through binoculars, the stump would never, ever become a black bear, not even when Edison tried to catch it off guard by turning away, feigning disinterest, and then snapping his focus back onto the stump. Stumps remain stumps; it is the Law of the Jungle. Edison further came to understand that honey-colored boulders, dark shadows, derelict cabins, elk, deer, Canada Geese and slumped-over pine trees were also not black bears.

One day they hiked up Scout Peak toward Scout Lake. They started at about ten in the morning and climbed steadily on the dry road for an hour before they encountered ankle deep snow. By 1:00 in the afternoon they were thigh deep in the white stuff. At the top of the peak Edison fell through the snow up to his chest. "The mountains of West Virginia are beautiful," he thought, "but the flat-out endless, vistas of the Rockies, with the sun far past its zenith, are worth chest deep snow in May."

After supper that night Frank said, "We've been here four days and we haven't seen any bears." They lounged in the cabin discussing, yet again, the physical differences between grizzlies and black bears as a substitute for actually seeing any bear. And then they discussed what to do if they stumbled onto a griz. They'd had that conversation every night. It was agreed that one should not turn and run from a griz, but back slowly away, all the while praying for luck and forgiveness.

That night Edison gave up on Pip and his great expectations. He just couldn't take the creepy old house and odd rich people. He put the book on top of the wardrobe.

On the fifth morning the three started up a messy peak. It had snowed hard during the night, and snow still fell as they set out. The three rounded a bend in the road and there, in the snow, sat a steaming pile of scat, enough to fertilize a Mississippi cotton field.

"It's still steaming," observed Skeet. "It can't be more than thirty degrees out here. That is either some very fresh, or very hot, scat."

The collective excitement level of the three hunters shot up until it too simmered and steamed.

In the snow around the scat were paw prints the size of compact car tires. The prints came down out of the woods, crossed the road, and then went back into the trees on the downhill side of the road. Skeet and Edison crouched over the prints trying to determine if they had been left by a black bear or a grizzly. Skeet argued that since the claw marks were so far in front of the toe prints, the brute had to have been a grizzly, a huge grizzly. Edison agreed. Frank had gone around the bend in the road to see what he could see.

At precisely the moment Skeet and Edison agreed on the size and species of bear, they saw Frank backing slowly down the road, crouched low, rifle at the ready. Edison slung his rifle off his shoulder and laid a thumb on the safety. Skeet did the same. Skeet and Edison had both managed to pick up .300 Weatherby magnums before the trip. They were powerful rifles. Frank backed up to the boys and pointed to the far side of the road.

"Is it a griz?" Edison whispered to Frank.

"I don't know. I just saw it lying there, and then I started backing up. It hasn't moved."

All three of them could see the curve of a bear's back rising out of the snow thirty yards up the road. The head and legs were hidden.

"Must be resting or something," Frank suggested.

They all gazed at the marvelous creature, watching the ends of the bear's fur sway in the breeze. It was a giant, at least eight feet long, but the heavily falling snow and the landscape obscured the creature's full form. Because the figure was obscured, the hunters could not make out for certain what type of bear it was. They could not determine if it had the characteristic humped shoulders and dish-shaped face of a grizzly. The prints and steaming scat Edison and Skeeter had studied on the road had obviously been made by a grizzly, but the bear ahead was not necessarily the owner of the tracks. The only other physical way the three knew to determine the difference between a black bear and a grizzly was by the size of its claws, and none of them were willing to get close enough to play manicurist. "Well," said Skeet after a whispered discussion, "at least we know that it's not a polar bear."

"Or panda," added Edison helpfully.

"And koalas are marsupials," Skeet reminded.

"You two peckerweeds are not being helpful. Either of you," scolded Frank, who was studying the bear with great care through his binoculars. "Stop your damn chatter."

"Such language. Do you kiss my mother with that mouth?" asked Skeet, trying not to laugh out loud.

Frank ignored the boys.

A grizzly, even starting from a prone position, can cover thirty yards in less time than it takes a grown man to whimper, "Mommy." The three hunters decided it would be prudent to back down the road and find a suitable spot from which to watch their quarry. The road was slippery and the footing unsure, but it seemed a good idea not to turn their backs on the beast in front of them.

They all started moving backward. Frank slipped as they were edging up the road bank in order to position themselves behind a boulder. Skeeter reached out to steady Frank, but succeeded only in grabbing the strap on Frank's binoculars. The effort caused Skeeter to loose his footing, and he too began to fall. Edison instinctively lunged for the pair, at the same time stepping backwards in search of better footing. Edison managed to grab Skeeter's hunting vest and jerk him backwards. Just then the bear reared up, throwing snow in every direction. Terror stricken at the sight of an eight-foot grizzly standing on its hind legs, Edison fell rump first into the snow, still holding Skeet's collar, and Skeet still holding Frank's binocular strap.

The great beast rocked back and forth on its hind legs as the hunters lay stock-still, staring; inaudible gasps locked their lips as they watched what would surely be their death rising out of the frozen landscape like a snow phoenix. Edison lay perfectly still, his rifle held awkwardly across his chest, sure the charging grizzly would be on him any second. Nothing happened. He waited. Still nothing. Skeet raised his rifle and sighted through his scope. Edison rose to his knees, bringing his rifle to his shoulder. He peered up the road.

The bear still stood where they had last seen him—only now the bear was a dark green pine tree recently freed from the snow.

Even though he knew that no amount of staring would turn the tree into a bear, Edison looked away quickly, hoping to squelch any sympathetic magic and mollify any bad mojo.

The snow during the night had been so heavy that when it built up on smaller pine trees, the trees bent toward the ground under the weight of the snow until they were half hidden. As the day warmed up, and the snow began to melt, the trees suddenly jerked up out of the snow, throwing the white stuff in every direction and looking very much like ten-foot grizzlies suddenly rising up onto their hind legs.

Frank told the story to some folks in a diner that night. Most of the locals admitted that at sometime or another they had made the same mistake. That was comforting. "It's nice to not be the only idiot in the room," Frank grinned.

"That's why Skeet and I hang out together," Edison noted.

"Nice to know who you are," Skeet nodded.

As they were leaving the diner, the waitress chuckled and called, "Fear the trees. They aren't just coniferous in these parts, they are also carnivorous."

By the sixth day, though Edison was loath to admit it, they were growing discouraged. After breakfast they rolled out the topo map and picked a destination for the day's hunt. They grabbed their rifles, walked out into the brisk morning air, and Frank unlocked the minivan. As they placed their rifles in the back of the van Skeet said, "I think I have come upon a possible explanation for our bearlessness."

"Well," said Frank encouraged seriously, "let's hear it."

Skeet cleared his throat, slapped the side of the van, and began, "I think that the bear are avoiding us. I think that they expect their hunters to be macho, or at least manly. This means that even if we eat beans out of the can the whole trip, play stud poker at night, cut our chaw from a plug with a well-honed knife, and carry a powerful, well-oiled firearm, still the bear will not let us kill them if we arrive on the scene in a Ford minivan. No self-respecting black bear wants his hide carried home in a minivan. The bear, I believe, prefer pickup trucks or a suitable derivative thereof."

"That being the case," declared Frank, "we're screwed. I'm not renting a truck. Now let's go get some bear."

Again they climbed into the van and drove into the mountains.

They never saw a black bear.

The locals at the diner told the three hunters that the they were about two weeks too early to hunt black bear. "They're still denned up," one gentleman informed them. "Come back at the end of May, you'll have more luck."

"Kind of a wasted trip," another fellow added.

"No, not really," Frank said. "I just figure that the bears forfeited, most likely out of fear. We win, all the way around. Besides, we'll be back again."

45

The trip back east was fast and fairly routine. They slept in shifts, drove in silence, smoked until their fingers yellowed, and drank coffee until their bladders bellowed. About half way to Missoula, Edison remembered that he had left his copy of Great Expectations on top of the wardrobe. For all he knew, and for all he cared, it would stay there forever.

They stopped again in Sioux City, spent the night with Mrs. Fester and Charolais, and headed out at the crack of dawn.

When Frank was sound asleep in the backseat, Skeet, who was driving, turned to Edison. "Man, I hate to sound like a pansy, but I think I love her. I'm sick of saying good-bye to her. She's so far away. On our way out it wasn't that bad to say 'bye' because I knew we'd be back in a handful of days, but now? When will I ever see her again? Will I ever see her again?"

Edison turned to face Skeet and assured him, "You'll see her again. Go to college out there."

"Yeah, lucky for you and me, we don't really give a crap about academics. Some of those people in our class have worked so hard for all these years just to get into a particular school," Skeet said. "You and I, we'll go to any school that takes us, and base our decision more on convenience than anything else."

"Yep," Edison agreed. "College is just four more years of this and that."

"I know," Skeet continued, "that we always figured we'd go to the same school. You don't feel like I'm bailing on you, do you?"

"Look man, Charolais is something special. You can't let her go."

"Yeah," Skeet agreed, "she is, and I can't. Besides, you're not irreplaceable or anything. There's peckerweeds everywhere."

"What are you going to do if Charolais transfers to Harvard, or Duke, or Stanford?"

"I don't know. Then she might transfer to someplace else. She got into Harvard, but didn't tell her mom. She said she'll stick around South Dakota until her mom has everything ironed out. So, she'll be in Brookings for at least a year. Her mom is gonna be pissed if she ever finds Charolais could have gone to Harvard straight off, full scholarship."

"Geez. Harvard?" Edison marveled. "What will you do if she transfers? I guess you could study, work real hard, get good grades, and transfer wherever she does," Edison offered, as seriously as he could.

"Or," Skeet countered, "I could continue to be a slacker, and then get accepted to some community college near whatever college she gets into next."

"Well, that's a good plan, too."

"What are you going to do?"

"Dad said I could go anywhere I wanted, as long as it's West Virginia Wesleyan. He gets half-off tuition since he's a Methodist pastor."

"Where's Lynn going?"

Edison exhaled slowly. "Uh, somewhere with a swim team, I guess. WVU maybe, hopefully. She also mentioned Texas and Stanford. She wants to be a teacher. And an Olympic swimmer."

"Well, Wesleyan's only about an hour from WVU," Skeet calculated. "You can do that easy, a couple of times a week. Gray Jesus will take you there, my son."

"Whole lot easier than you trying to get from Morgantown to South Dakota every weekend," Edison laughed.

"Yeah. I was sorta thinking about that. I reckon Dad might actually let me go to school out here 'cause he knows, as soon as I'm on my own, I'll be coming out here anyway."

They rode silently for a few miles.

"What do you want to be?" Skeeter asked.

"Same thing you want to be. As near as possible to the only girl who ever really paid attention to me, besides my mother."

"I meant professionally."

"Don't know," Edison shrugged. "Biology? Work for the Department of Natural Resources? EPA? Forest Service? You?"

"No idea. History, maybe. Looks easy. But what do you do

with that? I think Charolais is serious about being a doctor or a veterinarian. That means grad school. So, with a history degree, I guess I could go to grad school, too."

"I'll pretend I did not just hear you volunteer for more school," Edison exclaimed with mock disgust.

"Right. I'd like to have my last statement deleted from the record."

"So noted."

Skeet cleared his throat and lit a cigarette. "As long we are striking things from the record as soon as we say them, I'd like to say something to you that you might find odd."

Edison lit a cigar, looked at Skeet with some interest, and ordered, "Shoot."

"Now, hear me out here, and don't get pissed. I know it's weird, but sometimes I," Skeet paused, took a deep breath, "sometimes I get irrationally jealous of Lynn. I mean, I love her, I wish you and her no ill will whatsoever, but part of my brain keeps telling me that if you weren't with her, well, you wouldn't think twice about coming to South Dakota with me. Is that weird? For me to be jealous of Lynn? For me to be jealous that you have a girlfriend?"

Edison laughed so hard he woke Frank.

46

They rolled into Skeeter's driveway at 3:30 in the morning.

"We'll unpack tomorrow afternoon," Frank said.

Edison was glad to hear it. He stumbled across the lawn to his own house, let himself in the kitchen door, and went to his parents' room. He knocked once on the door, stuck his head into the room and announced, "We're home."

His mom said, "Oh, good. I was getting worried."

Dad asked, "Did you get any bear?"

Edison answered, "No. I love you both," and went to bed.

He woke up at noon in a sweat, with the sun beating down on him through the window. He rolled over, glad to be in his own bed. He threw back the covers, got up, dressed, and went to the kitchen.

"Lynn called," his mother said.

Edison rubbed his eyes as he searched the refrigerator, seeking milk and juice. "I'll eat a bowl of cereal and then call her."

"You don't know enough about women," his mother informed him. "So, I'll tell you. Call her before the cereal."

Edison took the phone off the wall as he walked to the table.

"Did you have fun?" his mom asked.

"Loads."

Mrs. Janzen said, "Sorry there were no bear."

Edison smiled, "It's not your fault, Mom."

"Don't be so sure. The power of prayer, and all that," she replied.

"You prayed we wouldn't kill any bears?" Edison asked, laughing. "How could you do that to us?"

"Well," she explained, "not exactly. I prayed that no one would get hurt. If by 'no one' God understood me to mean the bears as well... Well, who am I to argue with God? Lynn prayed, too."

Edison laughed, and dialed as he ate. "Hey baby," he greeted her when she picked up.

"Edison!" she yelled happily, "when did you get in?"

"About 3:30 this morning."

"Why didn't you call?"

"Because your dad would have driven over here and shot me."

"Oh, that. Are you coming over?"

"Yep, soon as I take a shower. Maybe an hour?"

"Okay," she whispered, and then added, "I love you."

"I love you, too. And I missed you."

His mother made a noise like a sick sheep.

Edison took the first real shower he'd had in two weeks, and he took his own sweet time. He got dressed, kissed his mother goodbye, and was walking out to Gray Jesus when he remembered that he needed to help Frank and Skeet unpack. He turned toward their driveway. The van was nowhere to be seen, so Edison knocked on the Barth's backdoor. Mrs. Barth answered.

"Hi, Edison," she greeted him happily. "Skeeter was just telling me all about your trip. It sounds like you guys had a lot of fun."

Skeet sat at the kitchen table, the information and application for South Dakota State spread before him.

Edison answered Mrs. Barth saying, "Yes, we had a great time. I came over to see about unpacking the van."

Skeet grinned at his friend, "Dad said to tell you not to worry about it. He had to go over to Rainelle for something or other. He said he'd unpack when he got back, and for you to go see Lynn."

"Great! See you later."

Edison didn't quite know how he felt about Skeet leaving, but he knew he wanted to see Lynn. He deliberately didn't think about Skeet as he crossed the yard and got into Gray Jesus. Instead, he wondered if the car would start after sitting idle so long. The car started just fine, and Edison pointed it toward Lynn's house. On the drive over, all he thought about was seeing Lynn, and possibly going down to the river with her. If he could talk her into it.

Lynn was sitting on the front porch when Edison pulled up to her house. She ran down the steps and sidewalk before he could get out of the car. She jumped in the passenger seat, her face flushed and smiling, and commanded, "Drive."

Edison had already turned the car off. "Lynn, I gotta go in and say hello to your folks. It'd be rude not to."

She sighed, "Okay. I know. But kiss me first. Oh- and you're in for a surprise."

Edison leaned over, hugged her tight and then kissed her deep, anticipating the surprise. He could see Lynn's folks standing on the front porch when he opened his eyes. And behind them was the massive form of Sheriff Hasbro. Edison, blushing, said, "Oh. Crap." He released her.

Lynn saw her people on the porch and whispered, "Surprise." Lynn and Edison got out of the car and walked up to the porch.

"How do?" Hasbro asked. "You look s'prised ta see me."

"I almost always am. You have that effect on folks. At least you ain't in uniform," Edison smiled. He felt he could be a little flip since Lynn parents knew him, and liked him. He also suspected they knew the whole story about the heart attack.

"I got my gun though," Hasbro informed him.

"Well. You look great. How's your heart?"

"Fine as frog hair. An' the Doc's got me on a special die-it. It's like ta kill me. I got a gooood rest while you and 'at other moron was off in Montana. Did you see Charolais? An' Helen?"

"Yes, Sir. They're doing great."

They sat on the porch with Lynn's folks for about half an hour as Edison gave a brief description of what had gone on in Montana and Sioux Falls.

"Okay," Lynn finally announced, "we are going down to the falls on the river." She grabbed Edison's hand and jerked him out of the swing. He followed, embarrassed. "Good-bye," he called over his shoulder as he and Lynn walked to the car, bumping shoulders and laughing.

"Telling your parents that we are going to the falls, at least the way you did it, is about the same thing as telling them that we are going to go fool around," Edison grumbled when they were in the car.

"You don't think they know that that is where, and why, we are going, already?" Lynn asked.

"Well, sure they know, but why not just let all of us, me and them anyway, live in our little dream world where we pretend your dad and mom and Uncle Hasbro don't know that I am interested in anything but your conversational skills and joyful companionship?"

It took about ten minutes to get to the falls. The falls were where folks went to swim, drink, walk in the woods, and participate in other activities for which they created socially acceptable euphemisms. Lynn and Edison walked into the woods, found a quiet spot, and remained there for some time, not saying much of anything—but catching up on two weeks apart.

Afterward, they walked to the river. There was no one else around so the couple swam in their underwear until the stars filled the sky. The air was chilly, but the rocks still held the heat of the day, and while Lynn stretched out on the rocks to warm herself, Edison got a fire going. They got out of their wet underwear and, eventually, into their dry outerwear. They sat next to the fire leaning on each other, watching the flames and smoke.

"So?" she asked, "Was it fun."

"It was a blast. We never so much as saw a bear but we, you know, we had fun anyway."

She looked at him, smiling, and asked, "Are you trying to tell me, without saying it, that the three of you did a little bonding?"

"What?" Edison yelled. "Heaven forbid! We just got along well and had a good time with each other."

"Did you learn new things about each other?"

"I guess so."

"Then you bonded," she smiled in her words.

"Couldn't have. Impossible. We men don't bond."

She pinched his thigh. "How's Charolais? Did you see her much?"

"I didn't," Edison said. "But she and Skeet saw, I would bet, all of each other."

"You still jealous of her?"

"Geez," he complained, "what are you, the trip psychologist? No, I'm not jealous of her. Ironically, it turns out Skeet is jealous of you. But, I think he is going to go college out there in South Dakota. Charolais got a full scholarship to a school near her house. And, as it turns out, to Harvard. But she didn't tell her mom."

"I know," Lynn said quietly. "And I figured Skeet was a little jealous of me."

Edison raised an eyebrow. "Why do even to bother asking me questions?"

"It makes you feel important, necessary."

"Hmmph," Edison grumbled. "Anyway, Frank, Skeet, and I went to visit Charolais' college. Skeet took a tour and picked up an application. He was filling it out this morning."

"Well," Lynn said, nestling in a little closer, "I guess that's how life is." She paused, pulled his head towards hers, kissed him and said, "I'm going to apply to Wesleyan."

Edison was overcome. "Really? That's great. Dad really wants me to go there because he gets such a break on tuition, him being a preacher and all. But I thought you wanted to go somewhere with a better swim team."

"I got scholarship offers to eight schools—academic and swimming. I can go anywhere I want. Here's the deal, Edison Janzen. I got a scholarship to Wesleyan for swimming. In one year I am transferring to a larger school, with one of the best swimming programs in the country. I promised my parents. Then I'm going to the Olympics. So, if you want to stay with the hottest girl in the world, the future Olympic Gold Medalist from Faybour County, West Virginia, than you have one year to work your ass off at school. Get straight A's, and get an academic scholarship to the school I want to go to. I talked to your dad. He told me that you and Skeet scored so high on the SAT that everybody thought you'd cheated. So they made you take it over again."

"Twice," Edison replied, "but it's not nice to brag."

"Anyway, I talked to your dad. He said he'd cover the difference to any school you want to go to if you get even a partial academic scholarship. I know you can do it. You could be in Harvard. But I know you won't do it for the sake of education, and I'm not asking you to do it for me. I'm just telling you that I'm giving you a year to catch up, if you want to stay with the world's prettiest girl."

"And gold medalist."

"Yes. And that."

Edison stared at the sky. He exhaled dramatically. "Hardly seems worth it. Getting a top notch education just to be with the world's fastest girl and prettiest swimmer."

She punched him hard, but lovingly, in the rib cage.

"Oh. Got that backwards. Prettiest girl and fastest swimmer. It'll be the first time in my life that I've had an honest academic incentive."

Edison and Lynn sat whispering on the rocks until the fire was mostly gray ash, and then he drove her home.

47

Skeet had missed the deadline to apply for the fall semester at the South Dakota State, and his grade point average fell just below the minimum requirements. Nevertheless, he received a letter of acceptance late in July.

Skeet, Frank, and Edison sat on the Barths' front porch.

"I'll be derned," Frank remarked after reading the letter. "They must have some sort of quota to fill. They must need a student from West Virginia."

"They'd accept me because of that?"

"Yep. Colleges like to have people from all over. It makes them look good," Frank answered. "Does that hurt your feelings?"

"Hurt my feelings?" Skeet laughed. "How would it hurt my feelings?"

"I don't know, make you feel like they are not accepting you for who you are, but for where you're from."

"Dad," Skeet explained, "if anything, it makes me wonder about the school. They must really need some good-looking numbers if they accepted me just to say they have a student from West Virginia. I don't care why they accepted me. I'm just glad. Besides, I'm proud to be a West Virginian. If that's the reason they took me, that's good enough for me. I'm going to call Charolais."

"Son," Frank cautioned, "when I was your age I had a girlfriend who lived about thirty miles away from us. That was a long way, back then. My dad told me that I should find a similar model, closer to home. I'm not going to give you that advice. I think you and Charolais are too young to be this serious, but I like her, and I like Helen. And you have been together forever.

"I am going to tell you that it is going to cost me a bundle to send you all the way out there to school. It'll cost gas money and plane tickets, along with out-of-state tuition and everything else. What I am saying is, I love you, and I want you to be happy, but if you go out there and screw-up, fail a class, anything like that, you're coming home. Fast. You got that? And you ain't gettin' married until you graduate. And if you get that girl pregnant, I'll whip you good. And if you get any other girl pregnant, well, I reckon Charolais will rip your Willard right off of you and feed it to a vulture. You got all of that?"

Skeet nodded solemnly and said, "Yes, Sir. Thanks Dad." Then he chuckled, "Willard? I've not heard that before."

Edison laughed, too. And then Sheriff Hasbro pulled up in front of the Barths' house and labored out of his car. Edison and Skeet hadn't done anything wrong, or at least illegal, for a long time. Still and all, they both flinched.

Frank exclaimed, "Good Lord, what'd you two do now?"

"Howdy," Sheriff Hasbro called. "Don't run. I'm jist stoppin' by ta chat."

"It could be a trap," Edison muttered to Skeet.

"We ain't done nothin' wrong."

"You ain't datin' his niece."

Sheriff Hasbro came up from the road puffing on a cigarette. Frank lit one himself as Hasbro made his way up the porch steps.

"I thought you were supposed to quit those things," Edison said.

"I am," Hasbro replied. "An' I'm sp'osed ta lose weight, too. But I cain't do both. When I smoke I can die-it, when I put the cigarettes down, I eat like a hawg. Mind yer own bee's wax, anyhow."

Frank asked, "If these two knuckleheads haven't broken any laws, or at least aren't suspects in any particular crime, then to what do we owe the honor of this visit?"

"Oh, guess I was jist wonderin' how Charolais and Hele, er, Mrs., er, the ex-Mrs. Fester are doin'?"

"I talked to Charolais this morning," Skeet reported. "She said she and her mom're fine. Charolais starts college in September, South Dakota State University. Mrs. Fester is finishin' her own degree. Then she might move up to Brookings, where the college is."

"So I hear, so I hear," the sheriff said.

"Skeet's just gotten accepted to the same college as Charolais. He's headed out there this fall. Brookings, South Dakota. Hell of a long drive." Frank announced proudly. "You want a beer, Sheriff?"

"On the clock. Cain't have nobody see me sippin' from a can, or a bottle."

Frank nodded and turned to Skeet. "Go get two beers in coffee cups. Well, we'll celebrate. Get four."

Skeet went into the house.

"How long it take y'all ta drive clear ta Sioux Falls?" Hasbro asked, lighting a new cigarette.

"Well," Frank said, "hold on. I'll get my log." Frank went into the house as Skeeter came out and passed mugs of beer to Hasbro and Edison. All three were self-conscious. Without Frank to act as an exemptor, the boys were just two underage kids drinking beer, and Sheriff Hasbro was a cop drinking on the job.

Frank returned holding his log from their trip out West. He took his beer from Skeet, and everybody took a cold, relaxing drink. "Let's see, we left here at 4:17 in the afternoon, and got to the parking lot where we met the ladies, in Sioux Falls, at 12:14 p.m., central time. So that's about nineteen driving hours, with the time change factored in. My first calculations said we could do it in about seventeen, but we got stuck here and there, and we were taking our time. On the other hand, there were three of us, so we could drive straight through. I figure a guy doing it alone would have to stop and sleep for a while."

Sheriff Hasbro nodded his head thoughtfully.

Skeet asked, "Why do you ask, Sheriff?" He wanted to call Hasbro by his first name, Gaylord, so badly that he could taste it. But he didn't know what Gaylord might do to him. Could be a dungeon under the courthouse reserved for folks who used the sheriff's given name without authorization. Plus, Skeet knew Hasbro didn't like the name, and Frank would get on him about being disrespectful.

"Hmm, oh, well," Hasbro stammered. "You might not believe this, but I ain't never been outside Wes' Virginia, 'cept back when I was in the service fer a while. I was thinkin' of takin' some time-off, maybe take a l'il trip to Sioux Falls. Might do my heart some good." And then Sherriff Hasbro winked at the boys.

48

It was hot the day Skeet left for Brookings. The sun was setting fast, like a red coaster falling behind a table, when Skeet threw a duffle bag on top of all the other stuff in the back of his truck, and Edison helped him pull a tarp tight over it all.

"You'd better hope it doesn't rain for the next few thousand miles," Edison said.

"Yep," Skeet agreed. "Well, I guess I'm gonna roll out."

The two friends looked down at the driveway, shuffled feet, cleared throats, and wiped eyes on the sly.

"Right," Edison began, looking up, "well, listen, um, I'll miss you."

"Me too," Skeet said. He knocked on the fender of his truck, looked away. "I'll miss you too. I'll be back for deer season, or Christmas, anyway."

"It's been to nice knowing ya'. Glad you moved in next door." Edison squeezed his nose.

Skeet cleared his throat. "Listen, um, I never thanked you for, for, well, sticking with me when the Festers jumped me."

"You mean…? Back when we were seven?" Edison asked, his mouth twisting into a disbelieving smile.

"Yeah. So, thanks. Sorry I made fun of your busted rib."

"Oh," Edison chuckled. "Forget about it. Apology accepted. Hardly even feel it anymore." Edison tapped his ribcage. "Sorry I punched you when you shot my bear."

Skeet grinned.

They stared at each other for a second or two, chuckled at their embarrassment, then hugged. "You and me," Skeet whispered.

"You and me," Edison agreed.

The rest of the Barths came out of their kitchen door. Edison stepped back and watched them say goodbye. Then Skeet got in the truck, turned the key, and pulled out of the drive.

Edison stood in the driveway, watching Skeet's truck through the dust in the air. Skeet turned toward the highway, and the truck dropped out of sight. Edison knew the route—north to Charleston, I-64 through Huntington, Ashland, and then on to Sioux City. Sioux City, of all the God-forsaken places. When would he ever see his pal again? It wasn't as if Charolais and Mrs. Fester were coming back for Christmas to visit the rest of their clan, so Skeet wouldn't be coming back either, not for a while anyway.

Edison hadn't seen Skeet come into town. Edison had simply arrived home from the grocery to find Skeeter in Mrs. Crankberry's backyard, but Edison had sure watched him go.

He turned and started toward the house, intending to go through the kitchen, but that was no good. His mom might want to talk about it. He didn't want to talk. Instead, he went back across the driveway and got into Gray Jesus. He started it up and drove south, thinking that it was one of the few times in their lives when Skeet and he had deliberately gone in opposite directions. He drove lightly over the back roads, watching Skitter Creek turn and deepen, turn and quicken, turn and dry out. Driving by the flowing waters, all alone in Gray Jesus, Edison hurt. He followed the creek for hours, until the only place to go was Lynn's. It was a nice thought. A good place to be. They could be alone now. So could Skeet and Charolais. Finally.

Edison parked across from Lynn's, walked up the path, and knocked on the door.

"Sorry, honey," her mom said, "she's over to Beckley. Didn't she tell you?"

"Yeah," he answered, "I just thought she might be home by now."

"No, not yet. You want to wait? It'll be a while still."

"No thanks. Just please tell her I stopped by."

"I will."

He started back down the steps.

"Edison," Lynn's mother called. He turned. "She really likes you."

He grinned. "Thanks. That's good to know. I really like her, too."

Lynn's mom smiled.

Edison got back into Gray Jesus, drove down the highway a bit, took the Meadow Bridge exit and went up Lockbridge Holler. After the usual negotiations, he bought a six-pack from Rex. Then drove home.

It was dark, nearing eleven, and the crickets were in full strum as he sat behind the garage and sipped his third beer. He heard a car turn into the drive, the crunch of gravel. The car stopped, a door opened, and the crickets hushed. The car door closed. Edison got up and went around the garage. Lynn walked toward the back of the house, breaking left toward Edison's window. He watched her walk, trying to be quiet. She was beautiful. And she had come to see him.

"Hey," Edison called softly, trying not to frighten her.

She jumped anyway. "Dang Edison. You scared me."

Edison apologized as she walked toward him. She didn't say another word. She put her arms around him, and Edison rested his head on her shoulder. She smelled of perfume.

"My mom said you came by."

"Yeah, I wanted to see you."

"Mom told me you said you liked me."

"I do like you."

"Mom said you meant it when you said it."

"I did. I do."

"What are you doing out here?"

"Drinking beer. You want one?"

"Sure."

Edison and Lynn held hands as they walked behind the garage. They sat down next to each other and Edison opened a beer for her.

"Edison," she said quietly, "it's okay to be sad he's gone. He's your pal. He's likely out there on the road somewhere feeling a little bad, too. Even if he is going to see his Charolais."

"You like her a lot, don't you?"

"I sure do," Lynn agreed. "And I like Skeet. And if he is willing to go all the way out to South Dakota to go to college, just to live near her, I'm sure she's worth going for. Romantic as it gets." She sighed and then added, "The four of us made a heck of a set." She leaned over to kiss Edison.

Edison was three beers in, and glad to see Lynn, but he had to pee. "Hold on," he whispered, getting up.

"Where you goin'?"

"I gotta pee."
"Well don't waste any time. I'm a lonely girl tonight."
"Right," Edison answered over his shoulder, "I'll hurry."

49

Edison went around the corner of the garage and unzipped his fly. He was looking into Skeet's yard. He got ready to pee on the wall of the garage, but then he had an idea. He smiled, laughed out loud. Edison waddled across Skeeter's yard, right up to the old oak tree he had claimed for his own so long ago.

Edison inhaled deeply through his nose, smelling the night, the beer, Lynn's perfume. He smiled. Then he dropped his pants and peed on the big, old oak tree. Ms. Crankberry's yard was his again—at last.

Nice to know.

Acknowledgements

Thanks Paula, Noah and Ellie — for the time to get this done, for the support, and for the love.
Thanks Mom and Dad.
Thanks Paulette and Glynn.

Thanks Ken Sullivan.
Thanks Buck-dog. Thanks Deacon. Thanks all dogs.
Thanks Justin.
Thanks Scott and Jenny.
Thanks Frank and Judy.
Thanks Jan and Dave.
Thanks Emily Jean, BJ, Pat, and Sarah.
Thanks Jeff and Donna.
Thanks Gary and Juanita.
Thanks Tijah.
Thanks all of Meadow Bridge.
Thanks all of Philippi.
Thanks Steven and Paul. Thanks Mike and Sean.
Thanks Ted. Thanks Liz. For taking the first chance.
Thanks Bill, and Tammy, and QP.
Thanks Jimmy, Susan, Becky, and the rest of the folks at the International Storytelling Center.
Thanks to all the festivals that have hired me. I want to name you all, but if I leave out just one, I've done a disservice. There's no room to name you all.
Thanks Kim, and Harry, and the West Virginia State Parks.
Thanks Edward Patrick S. (AKA P-Eddie-P) You got this all going.
Thanks to all the tellers who have influenced me.
Thanks to everyone who has come and listened to me tell a story.
Thanks to everyone who has bought a book, tape, or cd.
This all your fault.

About the Author

Bil Lepp is a nationally acclaimed storyteller and humorist. He performs regularly at festivals, schools, and corporate events all around the country. Bil has published three books of short stories and eight audio recordings. His books and cds have won several Storytelling World Awards, one American Library Association "Notable Book" citation, and a Parents' Choice Approved award. *HALFDOLLAR* is his first novel.

You can find out more about Bil at www.buck-dog.com.